Lawrence Tibbett

Lawrence Tibbett. Photo: David Berns studio. From the Editor's collection.

Lawrence Tibbett
SINGING ACTOR

Edited by
Andrew Farkas

With an Introduction and Discography by
William R. Moran

AMADEUS PRESS
Reinhard G. Pauly, General Editor
Portland, Oregon

ISBN 0-931340-17-9

Printed in Hong Kong

Amadeus Press
9999 S.W. Wilshire
Portland, Oregon 97225

Library of Congress Cataloging-in-Publication Data

Lawrence Tibbett, singing actor.

Includes index.
1. Tibbett, Lawrence, 1896–1960.   2. Singers
—United States—Biography.   I. Farkas, Andrew.
ML420.T52L4   1988   782.1′092′4   88-26272
ISBN 0-931340-17-9

CONTENTS

Introduction

by

William R. Moran

Being born at the right time helps, as long as one is mentally and physically equipped to take advantage of the opportunities that happen to be available at any given period. So it was with Lawrence Tibbett. The article in the 12 January 1925 issue of *Time,* which carried the story of Tibbett's "discovery" at the Metropolitan Opera, also carried on the music page an item which *Time* editors evidently considered newsworthy:

> In a formal drawing room, softly rugged—the studio of Station WEAF, Manhattan—sat a score of notables in evening garb. In the broadcasting room stood John McCormack. In front of him was a microphone. He sang *Adeste Fideles* with quartet and orchestra, the *Berceuse* from *Jocelyn.* Then Miss Lucrezia Bori rendered *La Paloma,* airs from *La Traviata;* then the two of them sang a duet from the same opera. Before Mr. McCormack sang his crowning ballad, *Mother Machree,* telegrams began to arrive from far states congratulating the singers. At the concert's end, the selected notables in the reception room rose and beat their palms together.

> Results: Mr. McCormack was advertised; Miss Bori was advertised; the Victor Talking Machine Co. was advertised; millions of radio fans heard two great singers pipe their sweetest; tremors shook the frames of Broadway producers, managers. During that evening, many plush playhouse seats had been left gaping by folk who had stayed home to hear Miss Bori, Mr. McCormack.

> Said Arthur Hammerstein, producer: "Broadway lost over $100,000 because of that concert."

Said William A. Brady, producer: "I enjoyed over the radio free of charge a program which I can only describe as gorgeous. The plain truth is that we of the theater are headed straight for ruin.

The Victor Talking Machine Co. had inaugurated a new series of radio concert broadcasts featuring exclusive Victor Red Seal artists, and it was no chance that the selections they sang were already available on Victor Records, or soon to be recorded. The "host" for the show, as they would say today, was Victor Red Seal A&R man, Calvin G. Child. A photograph in the Victor house organ, *The Voice of the Victor,* shows Messers. Child and McCormack in tails and Mme. Bori in concert dress as they stand not before a television camera, but an old fashioned carbon microphone, suspended on springs. Many of the radio listeners who heard that program listened with earphones attached to a home-made crystal set. Some, of course, heard the broadcast through a loudspeaker that looked like a question mark over a puzzled Krazy Kat. Some had vacuum tube receivers, run on "A" and "B" batteries; one had to be careful to tune all three of those dials to the same station on the table model Atwater Kent. A very, very few possibly had the new-fangled "battery eliminators" which only the rich could afford to buy from the Philadelphia Storage Battery Company, later to be known as Philco.

"Talking Pictures" were still two years in the future; the Western Electric Company was cutting experimental "electrical recordings" at Victor's Camden, N.J. laboratories, but in the strictest secrecy. They would not be announced to the public for another year and a half. Lawrence Tibbett's first "trial" recordings for Victor, made on 18 March 1925, were undoubtedly sung into the old fashioned recording horn; a second trial on the 13th of April, would have been with a microphone very like that used in the Bori-McCormack broadcast; his first real recording session took place on 3 March 1926.

A classical vocal radio concert was considered "news" in January of 1925, and Victor was, as they had been for many years, the real bellweather of the advertising industry. Before long there would be other regular programs, reaching out to wider and wider audiences as network broadcasting developed; Atwater Kent wanted to advertise its radios, and did so with the "Atwater Kent Hour". There was the American Radiator Company with the "ARCO Hour"; the General Motors Concerts (with a young Milton Cross as announcer) featured the New York Philharmonic, with vocal soloists. There was the Chesterfield Hour, and a little later The Ford Sunday Evening Hour from Detroit, The Voice of Firestone, and The Telephone Hour. Initially, all these programs had more or less the same format: a symphony orchestra would open the concert, followed by one or two major arias and a group of songs, usually interspersed with short orchestral numbers, or a speaker with a "message from the sponsor". Sometimes the guest would be an aging Frances Alda, Geraldine Farrar, Frieda Hempel, or even Fritzi Scheff. More often the guest would be from the current Metropolitan roster: Swarthout, Bonelli, Crooks, Talley, Mary Lewis or Lawrence Tibbett. It was seven years after the news-making Victor broadcast that regular broadcasts were started from the Metropolitan Opera, on Christmas day, 1931. It was a new way of life for the opera and concert singer! In addition to greatly improved recordings, given new life by the electrical process, a singer's name and personality could become well known throughout the country, to those in small towns and on farms who had never before had access to concerts, let alone opera.

Frances Alda had her own weekly broadcast from her apartment in the Waldorf Astoria; "Mother" Ernestine Schumann-Heink sang and talked for fifteen minutes each week for Gerber Baby Foods; Mario Chamlee was kept busy adding new Italian songs to his repertory for his part as "Tony" in the "Tony and Gus" show, one of the original "soap operas" with a thin thread of drama to connect the weekly episodes.

It was indeed a new deal for the opera and concert singer! The extra income from radio not only helped fill the financial gaps, but created demand for "in person" concerts. Opera singers were becoming personalities whom people wanted to see as well as hear. Those, like Tibbett, who had the real dramatic flair, took to the new media and were much in demand. He had become almost an American hero and was proclaimed by the press as the first fully American trained artist to break into the foreign-dominated Metropolitan, which of course was not true: conveniently forgotten were Althouse, Case, Chamlee, Murphy, Ponselle, Werrenrath, and many others.

Soon Hollywood began to beckon: sound films had added the dimension that was needed to make some opera singers stars of the silver screen. And again, there was Lawrence Tibbett, a singer who had begun his career as an actor: young, good-looking, somewhat flamboyant, it was just what Hollywood needed. Victor set up recording studios on the West Coast, first in Oakland, then in Hollywood. After seeing a film by Gloria Swanson, or Dolores del Rio, or Lawrence Tibbett, one could stop by the local record shop and obtain recordings for the home phonograph of selections heard in the theater. Some movie houses even sold these records in the lobby to catch the public as it left the theater.

Yes, Lawrence Tibbett, through no fault of his own, had chosen the right time to start a career. He was in at the beginning of a thrilling new and profitable era, but one which saw many accompanying problems. The orchestras with which he sang had long been subject to some form of labor union control; Hollywood had its share of labor unions, and the rights of recording companies and the use of recordings on radio were being questioned. But the performing artists had no one to look after their interests. What better place to look for help than in their own ranks. Someone had to take the lead, and what better person than one who was involved in opera, concerts, radio and motion pictures. Most artists shun the area of business, leaving such mundane matters as contracts to their managers, but this was a new and complicated era. Lawrence Tibbett is credited with the original organization of the American Guild of Musical Artists, Inc. (AGMA), a national labor union, founded in 1936 and chartered in 1937. He was its first president, an office he held until June, 1953, when he was succeeded by John Brownlee. Other early officers were Jascha Heifetz, Richard Bonelli, Alma Gluck, Queena Mario and Frank LaForge. The Board of Governors included such names as Crooks, Elman, Gauthier, Hackett, Iturbi, Jagel, Melchior, Melton, Pinza, Whiteman and Zimbalist, while an Advisory Board included Damrosch, Ganz, Hanson, Koussevitzky, Lotte Lehmann, McCormack, Martinelli, Moore, Pons, Rodzinski, Spalding and Swarthout. A major move was made by AGMA in 1938 when preliminary meetings were held between AGMA officials and representatives of Columbia Artists Management, Inc. and the National Concert and Artists Corporation. The establishment by collective bargaining of the respective rights between artists and managers was one of the dominating reasons for the formation of AGMA as envisioned by Tibbett and the other founding fathers, who all con-

9

tributed their time and effort to this organization which was designed to help the little fellow in the music business far more than themselves.

Whenever Tibbett is remembered, the question of his vocal decline comes up for discussion. In an interview published in *The Etude* in 1935 (which is included in this collection) the singer mentions certain danger signals "of the utmost importance and [which] must not be ignored if the voice is to be saved". He goes on to suggest an infallible test: the ability to repeat a phrase in the lightest *pianissimo* without change in technique. "A voice that can sing only in full voice is not being correctly produced; and, unless this tension or muscular interference is eliminated, it is actually dangerous . . . to continue practicing." If Tibbett believed his own test, he must have been well aware of his own vocal problems. These are tragically documented in recordings. Perhaps Tibbett never saw another interview in the same magazine, in the January 1914 issue, when Nellie Melba, then in her fifty-third year, offered what she said was one of her most important secrets: *Never give the public all you have.* "The singer who sings to the utmost every time is like the athlete who exhausts himself to the state of collapse . . . I have never strained, I have never continued roles that proved unsuited to me, I have never sung when I have not been in good voice . . .". Tibbett could have profited from that advice!

I recall a Tibbett concert in the War Memorial Opera House in San Francisco on 19 April 1937: he opened the concert with an aria from Cesti's opera *Il Pomo d'Oro*, which he followed by "I Am a Roamer Bold" from Mendelssohn's *Son and Stranger*. Next we had a group of four songs by Schubert, Wolf, Rachmaninoff and Moussorgsky. These were followed by an encore: "A Song for Lovers" by Deems Taylor. Next came "Nemico della patria" from *Andrea Chénier,* after which he gave us as encores "Di Provenza" from *Traviata,* and the "Evening Star" from *Tannhäuser.* Returning from an intermission, we had a group of four songs and two encores: "Shortnin' Bread" and "Old Mother Hubbard". The last group consisted of Vaughan Williams' "The Water Mill" and a Shakespeare setting by Buzzi-Peccia. As final encores we had "I Got Plenty o' Nothin' " from *Porgy and Bess,* the "Prologue" from *Pagliacci,* "De Glory Road", "Drink to Me Only" and finally, "Long Ago in Alcala". Sixteen programmed items, and a total of ten encores! And this was not exceptional: Tibbett never spared himself, and his public got full measure.

Nor did Tibbett ever hold back or save himself when singing theatrical material. He had an actor's flair for the dramatic, and was very fond of doing emotional songs like some of the works of Carl Loewe. He would make high drama out of songs like "De Glory Road" with explosive declamation of the kind not at all soothing to the vocal chords. Vitality and vehemence are two words found most often in his reviews. In 1933, he created the role of Brutus Jones in Gruenberg's *Emperor Jones* at the Metropolitan, a role which Pitts Sanborn characterized as "one of pitiless exactions". It consists of an unmerciful mixture of spoken and sung declamation culminating in the throat-tearing "Standin' in the Need of Prayer", which Tibbett recorded commercially. The first Metropolitan performance was broadcast, but doesn't seem to have survived; a "Packard Hour" radio adaptation, with Tibbett, from 16 October 1934, has found its way onto long-playing discs. Listening to this available evidence today, one wonders how human vocal cords could survive such treatment. The real wonder is, with such abuse, how the voice lasted another seven years before the deterioration became really evident.

Vocal problems, of course, can stem from many things, and often a combination of many things. The honest biographer cannot ignore the persistent reports of Tibbett's problems with alcohol, especially when they come from those who were his close friends. One colleague, who was present at the affair, blamed the start of Tibbett's problem with an unfortunate accident which took place during one of the rehearsals for the American premier of Richard Hageman's *Caponsacchi,* which had its first Metropolitan performance on 4 February 1937. Tibbett, playing the role of the villainous Guido, lashed out with a knife and gave one of the choristers a glancing blow on the arm. The man sustained a severe gash, and died a few hours later. The coroner's verdict was that death was due to a coronary arrest, and Tibbett was not held responsible. However, the matter was a very grave shock to the singer who blamed himself for the unfortunate event.

A word should be said about Tibbett's recorded legacy, for it is by the sound of his voice which has been preserved on records that he will be remembered in the years to come. That legacy is extremely rich, but it is indeed unfortunate that the period which it covers lasted too long. Tibbett's recording activities with Victor began in May, 1926 and ended with a session in January, 1940. Some records were made in each of the intervening years, except 1937 and 1938. The repertory is a varied one, from standard operatic arias, classical songs, songs from his films, and selections he performed in concerts. Fortunately, this is nicely expanded by material which has been rescued (sometimes in poor quality recordings) from Tibbett's many radio programs and Metropolitan Opera broadcasts. The year 1939 was especially active, and while there is a suggestion that the voice is not as fresh and free as in earlier years, it is still magnificent, as witnessed by the two recordings made that year from *Simon Boccanegra.* For the most part the recording of the Victors is excellent, with the notable exception of the selections from *Otello,* which were made in a sonically dead studio. Most of the Lp transfers of this set are superior in sound to the original 78s.

Especially fine examples of Tibbett's early work are found in his recordings of "Believe Me, If All Those Endearing Young Charms" and "Drink To Me Only With Thine Eyes", and "The White Dove" and "When I'm Looking at You" from *The Rogue Song.* Outstanding are his recordings of "Eri tu" from *Un Ballo in maschera,* the "Largo al factotum" from *Il Barbiere di Siviglia* and the "Toreador song" from *Carmen,* the more so when the competition is so intense from the numerous recordings made by other singers of these popular arias. The recording of "Wotan's farewell" from *Die Walküre,* with the Philadelphia Orchestra under Stokowsky is distinguished, although the microphone placement was such that the voice sounds somewhat distant.

In September 1940, it was reported that Tibbett had a serious illness, the exact nature of which was never disclosed, but it apparently affected his throat. He should have closed his recording career at that time. Some of the material he left for various odd-labels in the mid-fifties can only be described as tragic. This is especially unfortunate, as much of this material seems to be considered "in the public domain" and Lp re-issues of the same poor recordings continue to appear on different labels, and are often the only Tibbett recordings available in music shops today. These late recordings should be avoided; they are a travesty on the art of a very great singer and do his memory an injustice.

Tibbett was greatly admired and respected by his colleagues, as an artist and as a man. A number of years ago, during a long conversation with the American soprano

Dusolina Giannini, I asked the singer if she could recall any one performance in which she had taken part which was especially outstanding. Without hesitation she replied, that one of the greatest thrills she ever experienced on the stage was during a performance of *Aida* at the Metropolitan Opera on 12 February 1936. Tibbett was the Amonasro. During the Nile Scene, she said, something absolutely magical took place during the duet which begins "Ciel! Mio padre!". Everything was "right" as their voices blended; she felt inspired as never before, and sang as she never had before. Tibbett, too, was enmeshed in this same emotional experience as his voice poured out with unbelievable beauty. The feelings of the two singers were somehow transmitted to the orchestra, the conductor (Panizza), and the audience. After the performance, the two singers tried to understand what had happened, but neither could explain it. They both felt it was one of those inexplicable things which occur perhaps once in a lifetime. But certainly the ingredients were all there, with these two very great singers. On two different occasions, people who were in the audience at that performance have recalled it as their most memorable experience in the opera house, but they were at a loss to explain what had happened. "It was as though an electric shock had passed through the audience", one of them told me. "It was visible: people sat forward in their chairs."

A personal story tells a great deal about Lawrence Tibbett, the man. It was the summer of 1939 (August 15, to be exact). I had completed my freshman year at Stanford University, during which I had done volunteer work in the office of the student-managed concert series and I had been awarded the position of Assistant Manager for the following season. Part of my job had been to help select the slate of artists for the 1939–40 series. It was a delicate matter to set seat prices for season and individual concerts, and to select artists whose fees would not overrun our budget, as we had to at least break even. There were three of us in on the battle, and I won two of my nominees, Lawrence Tibbett and Bidù Sayão (the other two events were the Don Cossack Choir and the San Francisco Symphony Orchestra under the direction of Pierre Monteux, and featuring the maestro's 19-year old protege, Isaac Stern). I must admit that winning my colleagues' consent for Tibbett was easy. He had sung at Stanford before, the last time being 17 February 1930, before the advent of our new Memorial Hall, when the baritone gave his concert in the basketball pavilion. Besides, everyone knew who he was. Sayão was different. No one could pronounce her name, she had never sung on the West Coast before; but I had fallen in love with her from her Metropolitan Opera broadcasts and some of her early Brazilian records which I had managed to obtain. I remember bringing a phonograph to the office and giving a concert of recordings to prove to the others that she was all I said she was. But that's another story . . .

To get back to 15 August 1939. Tibbett was announced for a concert in The Hollywood Bowl, with the Philharmonic Orchestra of Los Angeles, conducted by Werner Janssen. Of course I was there. Tibbett's part of the program, accompanied by the orchestra, consisted of "Vision fugitive" from *Herodiade*, "Largo al factotum" from *Il Barbiere di Siviglia,* and "Wotan's farewell" from *Die Walküre*. The program closed with four songs with orchestra: "The Wanderer" (Schubert); "If Love Hath Entered Thy Heart" (Marx); "None But the Lonely Heart" (Tchaikovsky) and Moussorgsky's "Song of the Flea." As an encore, Tibbett sang "O du mein holder Abendstern," followed by "The Volga Boatman." The audience demanded more but apparently no other selections had been prepared with the orchestra, so a piano was rolled out and, miraculously, famed pianist Emanuel Bay just happened to be on hand (he was not listed on the program, and Tibbett introduced him to the audience) to accompany the singer in "Water Boy" and "De Glory Road." I think there were other encores, but I do not recall what they were.

After the concert, I went back stage to the Bowl Green Room and stood in line with the rest of the fans. When my turn came to speak to Mr. Tibbett, I told him of my exalted position with the Associated Students of Stanford University Concert Series, and informed him that we had signed a contract with his managers for him to sing at the University during the coming season. "I hope," Mr. Tibbett responded, "that you no longer hold your concerts in that awful basketball pavilion!" I explained that we had a beautiful new concert hall with excellent equipment and acoustics, which the singer was pleased to hear. "And what do you want me to sing?" said he. With the strains of Wotan's wonderful music still in my mind, I asked: "Have you ever sung 'Wotan's farewell' in concert with piano?" "No," he replied, but turning to Bay who was standing nearby, he asked, "How do you think the fire music would sound on a piano?". Bay immediately turned to a piano which was in the room, flipped up the keyboard cover, and began to play Loge's music. "I think we can do it!" he said, whereupon Tibbett turned to me and said, "Well, it won't sound like the Phil-harmonic, and we may have to cook up a special piano transcription, but why not? What else?" I hadn't expected anything like this, and was not really prepared, but I thought while I had things going my way, I might as well be bold about it. "What about the 'Cortigiani, vil razza dannata' scene from *Rigoletto?* have you ever done that in concert?" "You must be a real opera fan", Tibbett replied, "but why not? What else?" "Well," I replied, "as long as we are making an operatic night out of it, could you do 'Eri tu'? Your recording has always been the standard to which all others are compared." "I don't know about that," the singer replied "but we'll do it."

By this time the rest of Mr. Tibbett's fans were getting a little impatient, so I decided I had better quit while I was ahead. "Thank you, Mr. Tibbett," I managed to get out, "we'll be looking forward to hearing you at Stanford." "I'll look forward to it too, Bill", said Mr. Tibbett offering his hand.

A slightly dazed college boy somehow found his way out and home. I remember thinking to myself, "Well, this was great fun, but there's a fat chance that he will remember any of it."

But remember it he did. Several months later, the typed program was received at Stanford from the Evans and Salter office in New York. In the first group was "Eri tu." The second group concluded with "Wotan's farewell"; the fourth group con-sisted solely of the long scene from *Rigoletto.* What fun I had writing the program notes! And what a thrill I had during the concert itself. I was back stage, of course, and during the *Walküre* music, I was flipping through a little pile of sheet music Mr. Wille had left on a convenient shelf. Tibbett was roundly applauded by the largely student audience. When he came off after acknowledging the applause, he spotted me with some of his music in my hand. "Did you find something you'd like for an encore?" he asked. Without a word, I handed him the music for Erich Wolff's "Du bist so jung". Tibbett glanced at it and handed the music to Wille, and they returned to the stage.

The *Rigoletto scena* was a triumph! Tibbett was magnificent in his portrayal of first the unconcerned jester, then the enraged and finally the pleading father. The audience loved it and gave him a standing ovation. "I never thought that would go over so well in concert," Tibbett said as he came off after I don't know how many curtain calls. "What will the encore be this time?" "How about the 'Credo' from *Otello*?" I ventured. "The 'Credo' it is," said the singer, and went on stage to announce the selection.

The local press, the next day, remarked on the heavily operatic content of Mr. Tibbett's program. Dorothy Nichols of the *Palo Alto Times* wrote:

> One of the greatest dramatic singers of our time came to Stanford last night in the person of Lawrence Tibbett, and the welcoming audience overflowed into the orchestra pit and onto the stage. . . . This was a thrilling concert, though it was not a song recital; for a time it looked as if the evening was going to be made up of Gems from the opera.
>
> The gems, however, were some of opera's most precious jewels. Tibbett has the rare distinction of being equally capable in expressing the gay ferocity of Verdi, and the broad, rich sweep of Wagner. He had the fiery passion for "Eri tu", for that most moving appeal from *Rigoletto*. . . . The "Credo" was most superbly sung, for Tibbett's dramatic feeling is from within; he used no tricks (up to the encores), and it was all in the music.
>
> ". . . Wotan's Farewell" has an abstract song quality which makes it possible to remove it from the opera. You cannot, however, divorce it from the orchestra . . . [or] reduce the orchestra to piano, especially when the piano is played as accompaniment, and the triumphal song is a monologue, the Magic Fire fades out to a black and white photograph. In the age of radio and recordings there is no need to concertize Wagner. Yet Tibbett's glowing voice, and the special quality of regal compassion, make him so perfect a Wotan that it was almost worth it to hear him read the part.
>
> The evening was not all operatic selection. There was plenty of drama in the bloody ballad, "Edward", a masterpiece Tibbett has made his own. There was Strauss' "Allerseelen", a charming spring song. "Du bist so jung", and Tchaikovsky's "None But the Lonely Heart" which could not have been more perfectly interpreted, a phrase that is meant to include Stewart Wille's accompaniment . . .
>
> In music we like what we know, and the audience was completely happy with "Water Boy" (which was exquisite), "The Flea", ah yes, and "Mandalay" which it cheered. There was also a cowboy song by David Guion, which would make anybody happy. . . .

Orchestra or no orchestra for the Wagner, there was one very happy college boy after that performance. Through the years since that 1940 concert, I have heard and come to know many singers, but I have often wondered how many of them would be so kind and thoughtful to an unknown student. Is it any wonder that his memory is one I cherish?

PART 1
Thomas R. Bullard: Lawrence Tibbett

1. The many faces of Lawrence Tibbett.

2. A very young Tibbett in New York City. From the Editor's collection.

3. Tibbett's first publicity photograph as a member of the Metropolitan Opera House, photographed by the official photographer of the Met, Herman Mishkin. Photo: Mishkin. Courtesy of Peter Bence.

4. Tibbett learned the role of Valentin in *Faust* in three days to step in for a sick colleague at the Metropolitan on 30 November 1923. Photo: Mishkin. Courtesy of Kurt Binar.

5. Another picture of Tibbett in his second role at the Metropolitan, Valentin in *Faust*. Courtesy of Metropolitan Opera Archives.

6. Lawrence Tibbett and soprano Elisabeth Rethberg in the mid-1920s. From the Editor's collection.

7. Tibbett's early Escamillo in *Carmen*. He first appeared in the role on 12 February 1924, and sang it only six times at the Met and twice on tour. Courtesy of Metropolitan Opera Archives.

For
Persis Smith
with the sincere
regard of
Lawrence Tibbett
March – 1925 New York

8. Ford in *Falstaff,* the role that made Tibbett a star overnight. The dedication is dated March 1925, only two months after his debut in the role. Photo: Mishkin. Courtesy of Kurt Binar.

9. Tibbett as Ford in *Falstaff*. Photo: Mishkin. Courtesy of Metropolitan Opera Archives.

10. A very young Tibbett as Ramiro in Ravel's *L'Heure Espagnole*. He first sang the role on 7 November 1925. Photo: Mishkin. Courtesy of Metropolitan Opera Archives.

11. Tibbett first sang Neri on 21 January 1926, a role he alternated with Titta Ruffo, in Giordano's *La Cena delle Beffe (The Jest)*. Photo: Mishkin. Courtesy of Metropolitan Opera Archives.

12. Tibbett as Tonio in *Pagliacci,* singing the famous Prologue. He "graduated" from his original role, Silvio, to Tonio on a Met tour, on 21 April 1926. Photo: Lumiere. Courtesy of Metropolitan Opera Archives.

13. A later version of Tibbett's Prologue, this time costumed as Tonio in the opera proper. Courtesy of Metropolitan Opera Archives.

14. Tibbett singing the *Pagliacci* Prologue in the 20th Century Fox film *Metropolitan.*
Courtesy of Metropolitan Opera Archives.

15. Tibbett in an unidentified role, possibly as St. Francis of Assisi. The photograph is dated October 1931. (See p. 85) Courtesy of Metropolitan Opera Archives.

16. Tibbett as Eadgar in Deems Taylor's *The King's Henchman*, a role he created at the world premiere on 17 February 1927. Photo: Mishkin. From the Editor's collection.

Lawrence Tibbett

by

Dr. Thomas R. Bullard

FROM *THE RECORD COLLECTOR*, VOL. XXIII, NOS. 11–12, PP. 243–272.

On January 2nd, 1925, the Metropolitan Opera revived Verdi's *Falstaff* (absent since 1909) as a tribute to the veteran baritone Antonio Scotti. His interpretation of the title role was expected to dominate the stage action. The second baritone role of Ford was to be sung by Spanish baritone Vincente Ballester, but illness forced him to bow out of the cast. The relatively unknown Lawrence Tibbett replaced him, with unexpected results. During Act II his powerful acting and singing electrified the audience. While the other singers were rewarded with curtain calls following this act, Tibbett was on his way backstage to change his costume for Act III. Realising that the young singer was not being allowed a solo bow, the audience began chanting "Tibbett! Tibbett!". Giulio Gatti-Cassazza, the Met's General Manager, hurriedly called Tibbett back for a lengthy ovation and the result was intense publicity with national headlines telling how an American singer had achieved overnight stardom. In the next few weeks editors frantically scrounged for background information.

This sensational young singer was born in Bakersfield, California on November 16th, 1896, the youngest of four children of William and Frances (Mackenzie) Tibbet. He was named Lawrence Mervil Tibbet (the final "t" was added later). His father was sheriff of Kern County, following in the footsteps of earlier members of this pioneer family, which had resided in the state of California since the 1849 Gold Rush. Young Larry was brought up in a strict Methodist household which regarded the stage as sinful. He took piano lessons from his mother who was a soloist at the local church. In 1903 the six-year old boy made his first appearance, before a local audience. He forgot the words to his song but won applause by singing the "Star Spangled Banner"—the only song he could remember. Since he wanted to become either a cowboy or an actor, he had no musical ambition.

17

Later that year Larry's father was killed in a gun battle with a local outlaw, and the family moved to Long Beach, California. After five years they moved on to Los Angeles, where Mrs. Tibbet ran a boarding house.

Larry delivered newspapers and did neighbourhood chores to earn money. While in the seventh grade he appeared in a brief solo number, convincing some teachers that he had musical talent. While in his four years at Los Angeles' Manual Arts High School (1911–15), where future aviation hero James Doolittle was a classmate, Larry performed in school plays and with the glee club. By the time he graduated in 1915 he had impressed his fellow students as a versatile actor who could perform any kind of role. His principal asked him if he intended to go to New York or stay in Hollywood for a film career. Without really thinking, Larry answered that he hoped to become an opera singer.

He had already begun appearing before Kiwanis Club luncheons and banquets, earning a few dollars for each performance. In 1915 he was one of the singers at the Eisteddfod at the World's Fair in San Francisco. While singing in a local production of Horatio Parker's *Fairyland,* he was heard by Joseph Dupuy, the father of one of his classmates. Dupuy thus became his first voice teacher, and helped Larry increase his local concert appearances. During 1915–16 he frequently appeared with the Orpheus Club in Los Angeles. He was also touring with a Shakespearean troup led by Tyrone Power, Sr., the noted actor, although he achieved little notice. Membership in a local musical-theatrical group gave him the opportunity to sing in works by Victor Herbert, Gilbert & Sullivan and Rudolf Friml. By the end of 1916 he had earned the reputation of a serious and quite versatile young singer.

While trying out for a role in a production of *The Mikado* in 1916, he met Basil Ruysdael, a former Metropolitan basso and the local company's leading star. Ruysdael was impressed by Larry's voice but disliked his "artificial" style of pronunciation (he sang wind as "wye-end", for example). Ruysdael became Larry's second teacher, and he sternly forced the young singer to follow natural speech patterns while singing. He also used a program of physical exercises which allowed him to sing while doing push-ups, or while rolling on the floor. In later years Tibbett would consider Ruysdael the most important influence upon his career, especially for his determination to train his pupils in the proper singing of English.

Following some concerts in early 1917 the budding artist enlisted in the U.S. Navy, hoping for combat. During the World War I period he was assigned to the S.S. *Iris* as a shipboard instructor, teaching young sailors how to tie knots. In 1918 he was stationed in Baltimore, but left for San Francisco as soon as the war ended. Before he could return home he was sent to Siberia aboard the transport *Cadaretta,* as part of the Allied intervention in the Russian revolutionary warfare. After being discharged in 1919 he stopped off in Nagasaki on his way home. A local musician heard him sing and admired his voice. She assumed Larry was a member of an opera troupe that had just given a series of performances in Nagasaki. He was impressed by her opinion and began to wonder if he might not have an operatic career.

On May 19th, 1919 he married Grace Mackay Smith, and struggled to find work in Los Angeles. In 1920 twin sons (Richard Mackay and Lawrence Iwan) were born, increasing the economic pressure on the young singer. One-night guest appearances, at five dollars each, comprised Larry's lot during much of 1920 and 1921. For fifteen weeks he earned $50 per week by singing at Sid Grauman's theater, being featured as the soloist in the interludes between films. He would later say he got the job because Grauman thought Larry resembled Charles Ray, a popular silent movie star of the early 1920's. After he failed to sing *Eili, eili* with sufficient pathos, Grauman cancelled his contract. By this time Larry was winning local attention by his work with the Los Angeles Civic Repertory Company, performing plays by Shakespeare, Synge, Masefield and Ibsen. On February 20th and 21st, 1920 he played Iago in two performances of *Othello,* winning critical acclaim. He had studied the role with the company's star, Reginald Pole, leading to a life-long interest in the part. His friends did not believe the reviews were his, since he had used the stage name of Lawrence Mervil.

At a 1921 concert he performed two songs by the prominent local raconteur, musician and poet Rupert Hughes. Impressed by Larry's handling of the English-language text, Hughes became the singer's sponsor and promoter. Hughes was convinced that Los Angeles was no place for a major career, and sought a way to raise funds to send Tibbett (as the name was by now spelled on local concert programs) to Europe. James G. Warren, a local business leader, organiser of the Orpheus Club and benefactor to local artists, agreed to help. He suggested a $2000 loan to enable Tibbett to study in Vienna, but when he realised this would be spent for transportation costs alone, he agreed to change the plan to a $2500 loan to send Larry to New York. It was decided that he would study with Frank LaForge, a famous teacher and accompanist and the teacher of Warren's daughter Elinor.

In 1922 Tibbett began his New York studies, beginning a flourishing concert career, along with other LaForge pupils. Charles Wagner heard him and was so impressed that he became the young singer's first manager. Wagner had helped organise the Alda-Metropolitan Quartet, initially comprising Frances Alda, Carolina Lazzari, Giovanni Martinelli and Giuseppe De Luca. In 1922 De Luca left and was replaced by Tibbett. For three concert seasons (1922/23 through 1924/25) Tibbett sang with the quartet, earning roughly $250 per appearance (minus a ten percent commission to Wagner). He continued his studies with LaForge, following the latter's special method for learning roles. LaForge had his pupils write out their arias (and the music for other characters in each opera) ten times, improving their memory while sparing their voices. During 1922/23 Tibbett also sang at the North Avenue Presbyterian Church in New Rochelle, along with a young tenor named Richard Crooks. Some of LaForge's friends suggested that Larry call himself Lorenzo Tibetto, but both teacher and pupil rejected this advice. He was born plain Larry Tibbet (now spelled Tibbett), and he would not Italianize his name.

In January, 1923 LaForge decided Larry was ready for a Metropolitan audition, and arranged one for April. Four arias were memorised: Valentin's aria from *Faust,* "Eri tu?" from *Un Ballo in Maschera,* the Prologue to *Pagliacci* and Iago's Credo from *Otello.* While preparing for his audition, Larry appeared on the broadway stage as Edgar in a new production of *King Lear.* Critics were impressed and a producer offered him a full-time contract as an actor, but his operatic hopes won out. La Forge planned to use the *Pagliacci* "Prologo" as the audition number. When he announced this, a sigh came from the darkened auditorium. La Forge immediately launched into "Eri tu?" and all went well until Tibbett's voice cracked, ending the audition. La Forge and his friends appealed to Frances Alda, then married to Gatti, and she persuaded her husband to schedule another audition in May. This time Larry sang the "Credo" from *Otello,* amazing observers with its vocal power. A middle-aged man congratulated Larry and was thanked in return. Not until he talked with La Forge, did Tibbett realise he had been congratulated by Scotti. The result was a contract for $60 per week (Alda claimed she had Gatti raise the price from the traditional $50).

Tibbett returned to Los Angeles and secured a special engagement from the Hollywood Bowl for two concerts, where he would be featured soloist at the famed open-air amphitheater. On August 3rd, 1923 he sang the Prologue to *Pagliacci* before an estimated 10,000 people. He later presented a second program, singing Wotan's "Farewell" from Die *Walküre* impressing critics with his ability to handle the difficult music. On September 20th and 22nd he sang Amonasro in two special performances of *Aida* (with Bianca Saroya, Viola Ellis and Morgan Kingston)—his operatic debut. While in Los Angeles, he also arranged a private audition before Rosa Ponselle, then on a concert tour. She had expected just a young baritone, but after his first aira, she realised he was already a singing actor of great promise. She predicted success but also gave him some advice: be prepared to sing any role, no matter how small, whenever it was scheduled. This would give him experience and enable him to assume a wider variety of roles later in his career. In October he returned to New York for a series of concerts preceding his Met debut, but sudden illness prevented this concert plan.

Tibbett's debut at the Met was as Lovitsky in *Boris Godunov* on November 24th (with Chaliapin and Mardones in the cast). It was such a small role that he merely wore monk's robes over his street clothes and left as soon as he was finished. After two repetitions on tour, he would not sing the role any more in his career. His second role was Valentin on November 30th (with Alda, Martinelli and Chaliapin). Vincente Ballester had been scheduled for the part, but ill health delayed his New York appearances. Gatti asked Tibbett if he could sing the role and Larry said he was ready. Actually, he was terrified and rushed off to Wilfred Pelletier, then an assistant conductor, for some hurried coaching. Still nervous, he got through the performance, aided by Americans in the chorus, who helped prompt him. The critics were impressed, although they felt his voice lacked volume. One exception was the Brooklyn *Eagle,* which compared him favourably to Chaliapin. He would sing the role six more times that season, with continued success (performance numbers include both the house and tour data).

Most of his other roles that first season were minor, including four Marullos in *Rigoletto* (the first on December 1st), two Flevilles in *Andrea Chenier* (the first on December 17th), three Morales in *Carmen* (the first on January 11th), and a single D'Obigny in *Traviata* on January 24th. The first of three Heralds *(Lohengrin),* long considered a basic role for beginning baritones, came on January 8th, winning slight praise for being "adequate". Three Silvios (the first on December 19th, with Rethberg, Fleta and De Luca), although the "second baritone" in *Pagliacci* is a substantial role, were similarly ignored. His most unusual role that season was the High Priest in Riccitelli's *I Compagnacci* (with Rethberg, Gigli and Didur). The first of three performances—the American premiere—was on January 2nd. Met concerts allowed him to sing two major roles, but only for one act each: the High Priest in Act I of *Samson et Dalila* (January 20th) and Escamillo in Act IV of *Carmen* (on February 12th).

An attack of pneumonia threatened Tibbett's second Met season, but he recovered just before the season of 1924/25 opened. On November 6th came the first of five performances as Tchelkalov in *Boris Gudunov* (with Chaliapin, Rothier and Tibbett's long-time friend, Mario Chamlee). On November 12th he sang the first of six Flevilles, a typical comprimario role. On the following evening he performed the first of six Schlemils in *Les Contes d'Hoffmann* (with Bori, Fleta and De Luca). Critics thought he was better than the big names in the cast, especially Lawrence Gilman of the *Tribune,* who called it "the most successful thing we have seen him do at the Metropolitan." Much of the rest of the season was a series of familiar roles: a single Valentin, and five performances as Silvio. At this point Tibbett might have wondered if his career would ever go anywhere, but one role that season would alter these worries.

When Ballester was unable to sing Ford in the *Falstaff* revival, there was a crisis. Gatti doubted that another baritone could learn the role in time for the January 2nd premiere. Tullio Serafin, who would conduct, was convinced that Tibbett would be able to handle the role's demands, and began coaching him in the role. In rehearsals the Italian members of the cast made jokes about Tibbett's diction which he did not understand (although he guessed what was going on). Critics who saw the dress rehearsal were moderately impressed, but still unprepared for the actual performance. Tibbett later said that he just "let himself go" and stunned the critics even more than the wildly applauding audience. The New York *World* praised his "amazing vocal richness, vitality and dramatic resourcefulness." The *Musical Courier* stated "without question his is the best baritone voice of the Metropolitan today, the only one . . . that is still fresh and young, with all its bloom and warmth." The American public expected instant rewards for "their" singer, and were surprised to learn that he won only a raise to $100 per week (plus a bonus for each of six Fords that season). Concert fees could improve Tibbett's position, and his real fame as a concert artist began that season, leading him to end his association with Wagner—he subsequently went to Evans & Salter. Many people probably failed to see the nature of Tibbett's "competition" at the Met. He was forced to sing smaller roles because there were so many major baritones: Scotti, De Luca, Ruffo, Danise, Whitehill, Bohnen and Schorr.

After concertising, Tibbett joined the next season in time for the Met premiere of Ravel's *L'Heure Espagnole* on November 7th, 1925 (with Bori, Errolle and Didur), followed by six later performances. Critics praised his flair for comedy and began to realise his ability to sing off-beat roles. Several familiar roles were performed during the 1925/26 season: seven Silvios, two Tchelkalovs, one Herald, two Flevilles and a single Valentin. On January 25th came a major success: the first of two Neris in Giordano's *La Cena delle Beffe* (with Alda and Gigli). Ruffo had sung the first two performances and critics doubted the younger singer could match him. Their unanimous opinion was that he came close, with tremendous dramatic presence. While on tour in the spring, Tibbett added three new roles: Tonio in *Pagliacci* on April 20th, Wolfram in *Tannhäuser* four days later, and Mercutio in *Romeo et Juliette* on the 29th.

Tibbett's first role in the 1926/27 season was Kothner, on November 3rd. This performance, like the two that followed, drew critical displeasure. Although the New York *Times* found him "very amusing, with some fresh business", others felt his clowning did not fit in with a traditional *Meistersinger*. Gilman, now with the new *Herald-Tribune,* thought his "acting was amateurish, his singing the worst we have heard from him, and his make-up beyond belief. May the ghost of Richard Wagner forgive him." Critics also disliked his Melitone in *La Forza del Destino* (the first of three performances on December 11th, with Ponselle, Martinelli, Danise and Pinza). Ponselle disagreed with this view, and has informed the author that she found his acting and make-up perfect for the role. Most other roles in New York were standards: Valentin, the Herald, Neri, Ford and Silvio. He got to add Manfredo in *L'Amore dei tre Re* (with Bori, Johnson and Ludikar) on January 29th, as well as two Mercutios—both roles winning mild praise. On March 1st came the first of two Dappertuttos in *Hoffmann*—yet another revival of that work which received lukewarm praise. On tour, he added three roles: Germont, Alfio (in *Cavalleria*) and Telramund in *Lohengrin*. The last two of these roles were not his most important. Indeed, he never had the opportunity to sing Telramund in New York, since the Met had enough German baritones on hand.

The high point of the 1926/27 season was the world premiere of Deems Taylor's *The King's Henchman,* with libretto by the celebrated Edna St. Vincent Millay. Gatti had been trying to produce a successful American opera and commissioned Taylor to compose an opera in 1925. He and Miss Millay planned an opera on the story of Snow White, but changed their plans after she discovered the charm of an old Anglo-Saxon story which she had found while studying the origins of the English language. The libretto was difficult, requiring singers with a complete command of the English language. The first of seven performances that season came on February 17th, starring Florence Easton, Edward Johnson and Tibbett as Eadgar. The singers were praised more than the opera, which was seen as too complicated and dull. The entire New York press singled out Tibbett's work for special praise, considering him the supreme English-language artist in the house. His most famous passage, "Nay, Maccus, lay him down," was to have been cut from the score, but after Miss Millay heard the dress rehearsal she refused to allow this to happen, thus preserving a future concert staple.

Tibbett's fame had now reached the point where he could accept offers from other opera companies, and from this point on he would sing longer seasons, starting in other cities before coming back to the Met. Thus the 1927/28 season began in San Francisco on September 20th as Ford (with Peralta, Mario, Bourskaya, Tokatyan and Scotti). Critics were delighted by his performance, and the *Examiner* claimed that "this young fellow has psychology in his art; by subtlety and intuition he has penetrated into the dark places of the soul." On the 29th he sang Neri in a *Cena delle Beffe* (with Peralta and Tokatyan) that was completely sold-out. Critics praised both singing and acting, echoing the praise of the press in New York.

Tibbett followed these San Francisco appearances with a concert tour, and he didn't reach the Met until December 17th, 1927, when he sang the first of four Wolframs with an otherwise German cast for *Tannhäuser* (Jeritza, Kirchhoff and Mayr). Critics admired his lyric singing, yet felt that he was unable to really act in this role. On January 3rd came the first of four Escamillos (with Jeritza and Johnson). He sang the famous Toreador Song from a table top, much to the dislike of the critics. They were forced to admit that it was not really his fault, since he was merely trying to match the overdone acting of Mme. Jeritza. His French diction was considered perfect, and his costumes were praised. The rest of the 1927/28 season was devoted to familiar roles: Silvio, Eadgar, Manfredo, the Herald, Mercutio, with Tonio and Amonasro on tour. In June he received an honorary M.A. in Music from the University of Southern California.

The 1928/29 season began in San Francisco, where Tibbett sang five roles. The first was an Amonasro on September 15th (with Rethberg, Johnson and Pinza). The *Examiner* found him "primitive, virile, heroic," despite the fact that he was a last-minute replacement for Danise. On September 17th he repeated his powerful Neri (with Vettori and Tokatyan). Two days later Tibbett sang his very first Scarpia, opposite Jeritza and Tokatyan. Critics admired his singing, yet felt his acting was too unsubtle. They preferred the style of Scotti—an unfavourable comparison that remained with Tibbett for the remainder of his career. His costumes were also criticised for making him look like a misplaced New England Puritan from the colonial period of American history. On the 24th he sang Manfredo (with Vettori, Johnson and Pinza), winning praise again. He finished the San Francisco series with a Tonio on October 3rd (with Vettori and Johnson). Critics found his interpretation superb, especially admiring his powerful characterisation of the evil clown. Following these appearances he continued with his growing concert career during most of October and November.

Additional concerts delayed Tibbett's return to New York until December 27th, 1928, when he sang the first of two Tonios for that season. On January 11th he sang the first of two Alfios (with Jeritza again stealing the show). It is interesting to observe that these two operas, usually performed together, were frequently done with other works (ballets or other short operas). On February 8th came the first of three Marcellos in *La Boheme* (with Müller, Martinelli, Didur and Pinza), a role rarely done thereafter. Critics paid little attention to these performances but they were quite interested in his next new role—the title character in Krenek's *Jonny Spielt Auf*. Tibbett sang the first of two performances on February 27th (with Manski, Kirchhoff and Schorr). The great Michael Bohnen had sung the earlier performances, making Jonny a rather grotesque giant. Tibbett played him as a sophisticated cabaret singer, quick-witted and light on his feet. As the New York *World* observed, "if all God's chillun got voices like Mr. Tibbett's . . . , and a happy genius for doing the black bottom in the midst of . . . travail, then . . . 'Jonny' would have been translated into Harlem English ere this and exposed to the comradeship of his brothers in Upper Seventh Avenue." The rest of the season comprised familiar roles: Eadgar, Manfredo, Escamillo, Tonio, Mercutio, Valentin, Dappertutto and Germont (but this role only on tour). Despite his obvious importance to the company, Tibbett still sang the *Lohengrin* Herald!

After this season had finished, Tibbett came to Hollywood for a screen test. Mack Sennett, noted for one-reel comedies, conceived the idea of a short film in which Tibbett would play an opera star who returned to his home town to present a recital, accompanied by his childhood music teacher—a nice blend of music, sentiment and "home-town" humor. Sennett offered Tibbett $3500 to play this role, but he turned it down and signed a contract with Metro-Goldwyn-Mayer for *The Rogue Song*. Directed by Lionel Barrymore, it was a strong action musical about a Russian bandit leader who fell in love with one of his female captives. The film also starred Catherine Dale Owen and the team of Laurel and Hardy. The music was by Herbert Stothart (very adapted from Lehár's Zigeunerliebe), with lyrics by Clifford Gray and direction by Lionel Barrymore. When the film opened in New York, on January 28th, 1930, critics were most impressed by Tibbett's voice and screen presence. They were critical of the soundtrack's engineering, which was not surprising—Tibbett later recalled how the impact of his voice caused problems for the engineers. L. B. Mayer immediately offered Tibbett a full-time contract, hinting that he was wasting his time at the Met.

After completing this film, Tibbett came back to New York for the 1929/30 season. His first role was Jack Rance in a revival of Puccini's *La Fanciulla del West,* with the first of seven performances on November 7th (with Jeritza and Martinelli). Tibbett was always amused by his work's odd blend of American and Italian styles. He was most critical of the "kissing cowboys" and the unrealistic dialogue. Using his father's own experiences as a lawman, Tibbett attempted to add realism to his portrayal. He took particular delight in emphasising any English-language words which were in the score. The New York *Times* felt he dominated the stage while the *Herald-Tribune* disliked both make-up and costume (describing him as resembling a slick country preacher). The rest of this season comprised earlier roles: Tonio, Alfio, Wolfram and Dappertutto. On April 19th he had the chance to sing his first N.Y. Germont, winning modest praise for a role that would soon become one of his major successes.

After the close of the season he returned to Hollywood for two more films. The first was *The New Moon,* based on a Broadway musical by Sigmund Romberg and Oscar Hammerstein II, with the location changed from Florida to Czarist Russia. In the film Tibbett played a Russian cavalry officer in love with a beautiful princess (played by Grace Moore) who was engaged to a wealthy admirer (Adolphe Menjou). Sent to the steppes by his jealous rival, the young hero defeated a tribe of nomadic bandits and won his beloved's hand. When the film opened (December 2nd, 1930), it won immediate praise. As *Variety* noted, "with possibly the screen's best pair of pipes involved, it's probably as far as a film can go in a vocal way." Other critics thought the film proof that Tibbett was the leading male singer of the silver screen. For reasons unexplained, Tibbett and Miss Moore were never again co-starred in a film. Tibbett's second film was *The Prodigal* (also released as *The Southerner*), New York premier, June 27th, 1931. With music and lyrics by Bess Meredyth and Wells Root, it was the story of a wealthy young southerner who roamed the countryside with two hoboes (Gilbert Young and Cliff Edwards, better known as "Ukulele Ike"). He subsequently fell in love with his brother's wife and ended the film by going off screen, singing the only "hit" number: "Without a Song." The score did not impress most critics although *Photoplay* thought it was the type of film to "put a song in your heart."

Films and concertising meant Tibbett did not get back to the Met's 1930/31 season until January 21st, when he sang the first of two Amonasros (with Rethberg, Martinelli and Pinza), impressing critics with his virile conception of the role. For the rest of this season he sang only five Germonts, three Scarpias, and one performance each of Dappertutto, Mercutio and Valentin. His most important role was Colonel Ibbetson, in the world première of Deems Taylor's *Peter Ibbetson,* on February 7th (with Bori and Johnson). Constance Collier arranged the libretto (having starred in a stage production with the Barrymores many years before). Despite ten more performances (including some on tour), critics were disappointed by Taylor's second opera, calling it weak. Many joked that since Tibbett's villainous character was so strong the work should have been called *Peter Tibbettson!*

Tibbett returned to Hollywood that summer for his fourth film—*Cuban Love Song.* Bess Meredyth and Gardiner Sullivan produced this story of a trio of Marines sent to

Cuba around 1910 (Tibbett, Ernest Torrence and Jimmy Durante). Tibbett played a dashing young officer who fell in love with a peanut vendor (played by Lupe Velez), leading to one of the film's hit songs: "The Peanut Vendor". The three men went off to World War I, following an affair which produced an illegitimate child (although in the film Tibbett eventually married a childhood sweetheart, in keeping with contemporary Hollywood moral traditions). Tibbett had expected clashes with Miss Velez, long known as a "Latin Spitfire", but soon discovered that once he began praising her voice he could gain her friendship, allowing film work without any friction. When the film opened on December 4th, 1931, critics admired Tibbett's ability to sing, act and handle comedy. They found Miss Velez too coy and Mr. Durante too hammy. Needless to say, the moral implications of the plot also won disfavor. About this same period, Tibbett's private life underwent a major change when his first marriage ended. On January 1st, 1932 he married Jennie Marston Burgard, the daughter of a New York banker, who had met Tibbett at a Los Angeles recital.

The usual mixture of films and concerts delayed Tibbett's arrival at the Met until January 14th, 1932, when he sang the first of two Germonts (with Bori and Tokatyan). Critics were unanimous in praising his subtle acting and singing. Less critical attention was paid to several other roles of that season: three Wolframs, two Amonasros, two Mercutios and four Dappertuttos. On January 11th, while singing the first of seven Ibbetsons, Tibbett was injured. As Peter and his father struggle, the Colonel is supposed to call for help, breaking open a window in the process. On this particular evening, the pieces of glass dropped into Tibbett's boot, gashing his heel. As a result he had to remain off his feet for a while, presenting some problems for the new production: the American première of Verdi's *Simon Boccanegra*. Tibbett was especially interested in the role and may well have requested Gatti to stage the work for him. The first of six performances for that season was on January 28th (with Müller, Martinelli and Pinza), Tibbett having rehearsed while seated on a couch. As in the case of *Falstaff*, Serafin coached him. This serious study paid off, for critics were overwhelmed by his portrayal of the Doge. Henderson, in the *Sun,* compared his overall performance to Chaliapin's Boris, while the *New Yorker* said he "obliterates thoughts of all other baritones." Gilman, in the *Herald-Tribune,* was so impressed that he ignored most of the other members of the cast:

> Mr. Tibbett makes him an engrossing and impressive figure, almost a great one. His denotement of the Doge's magnanimity, his courage, his tenderness, his . . . imperial dignity, his tragic pathos, is quite the finest thing that Mr. Tibbett has accomplished in opera. This is a remarkable embodiment in its truth, its power, its authority, its ease, its fluency and grace.

At the close of the season, Tibbett and his wife left for a four-month honeymoon in Europe (from July through late September). This was Tibbett's first trip to Europe, and he used it as an opportunity to see the great European opera houses at first hand. Upon his return he told interviewers that the Metropolitan was the equal of any overseas company and that American singers were as able as any in Europe. In effect, he believed that young singers could stay in the United States for their training, instead of going overseas, as had been the custom. While travelling through Spain, the Tibbetts met Titta Ruffo, then in retirement. The two baritones sang at a party, and each carefully complimented the other. In Switzerland, Tibbett spent some time with composer Louis Gruenberg, then completing his opera, *Emperor Jones,* which would be given at the Met, with Tibbett in the title role. Tibbett later told reporters that he loved the dramatic power of the work (based almost literally upon the O'Neill play), although he admitted there were no "melodies" in the score.

In many ways, the 1932/33 season was the high point of Tibbett's career. On November 2nd he opened the season in the first of five *Simon Boccanegras* (with Müller, Martinelli and Pinza), one of the American singers to perform on opening night. During the season he also sang a variety of roles: one Mercutio, one Valentin, one Wolfram, three Germonts, and three Amonasros. On January 7th came the world première of *Emperor Jones,* considered Tibbett's most memorable role. Henderson was horrified by the musical crudities and near-*sprechstimme* singing, but admired Tibbett's work, which he called "brutally incarnate and plasticity perfected." Gilman (*Herald-Tribune*) was stunned by Tibbett's "imaginative grasp and embodiment of a cruelly exacting role, his power . . . and his control of climax." Olin Downes of the New York *Times* thought "he has done nothing more effective in his entire career." He sang eight more performances with the Met, plus two each in Los Angeles and Chicago. Critics everywhere admired his role but disliked the opera itself. His two Chicago performances (on May 2nd and 5th) were part of a double bill with *Pagliacci*. One wonders what the strain of two roles per night for two nights (and both difficult parts) did to his voice—local critics were astounded. At least *Pagliacci* was a more logical partner for the Gruenberg than the usual Met choice: *Hansel und Gretel*.

On November 9th, 1933 Tibbett was presented with the gold medal of the American Academy of Arts and Letters—the first singer to receive this honor. The ceremonies noted that he was a leader in the fight for English-language opera in America and a master in the field of diction. Following this award, Tibbett went to San Francisco, for four performances. There were two of *Emperor Jones,* on November 17th and 30th. As usual, local critics praised Tibbett but condemned the opera as unsingable. On November 21st he sang Tonio (with Bori and Martinelli), followed by a Germont on the 24th (with Muzio and Dino Borgioli). Critics praised both performances and noted that they had not heard either sung so well in years.

The Met's 1933/34 season was shortened by the impact of the depression, forcing a delay of roughly one month. Thus, opening night was December 26th, with *Peter Ibbetson,* the first time an American opera had been so honored. This would be a major season for American works and for Tibbett's ability to perform them. There were three Ibbetsons and five Joneses (once on a double bill with *Pagliacci,* with Tibbett singing Tonio). On February 10th he sang Wrestling Bradford in the world stage première of Howard Hanson's *Merry Mount* (with Göta Ljunberg who had difficulty with the English text, Gladys Swarthout and Edward Johnson). The world première had been a 1933 concert performance with John Charles Thomas as Bradford. Tibbett admired the dramatic opportunities, but wondered if the audience would accept a story about a Puritan leader who sold his soul to the devil in order to win the beautiful wife of another leader (who was murdered), and who concluded the opera by burning down the entire village. Gilman thought the opera showed promise, but virtually all the other critics called it too hard on human voices, although Tibbett was praised. Tibbett sang five more performances, then relinquished the role to Richard Bonelli for the last two appearances at the Met. He also sang one Marcello (in *Boheme*), two Valentins, two Germonts and two Tonios to round out the season. In

June he received an honorary D.Mus. degree from New York University, as a tribute to his career as the "foremost American singer" of his era.

The 1934/35 season, Gatti's last, opened on December 22nd, with *Aida* (starring Rethberg, Olszewska, Martinelli, Tibbett and Pinza). In 1908 Gatti opened his first season at the Met with the same work (with Destinn, Homer, Caruso, Scotti and Didur). Most of this season was a series of Tibbett standards: four Amonasros, four Wolframs, three Germonts, two Valentins, two Marcellos, two Bocceanegras and one Tonio. On January 24th came the world première of Horatio Seymour's *In the Pasha's Garden* (with Jepson, Jagel and Tibbett). The three performances that season were all for the weak work, which featured Tibbett as a stern pasha who buries his wife's lover alive in a trunk (in which he had been hiding). Gilman thought Tibbett "walked away with the show, after his habit" and Seymour told Tibbett there would have been no success without his singing. On March 21st he sang his first Scarpia in the Met (with Lehmann and Martinelli), with a second performance on the 28th. Critics admired his voice but considered his acting inferior to that of Scotti.

Tibbett sang two special concerts that spring, each something different than what had gone before. On March 31st came the gala farewell for Gatti, with an incredible array of scenes and operatic satires. Tibbett sang a song called "Der Wurm Turns", making Fafner a hero, uttering such lines as "The fates I'd even pardon for a part in Pasha's garden." A sketch entitled "Putting the Rah into Opera" featured a condensed *Pagliacci* played in a football stadium, with Tibbett (playing Silvio!) tackling Charles Hackett (as Canio). On April 12th a special gala was given, celebrating the fiftieth anniversary of Walter Damrosch's first New York concert, and in its honor a complete third act of *Die Meistersinger* was staged. The performance was in English, with Tibbett as Sachs, Helen Jepson as Eva and other American singers in the cast. Critics praised Tibbett's voice, acting, nobility, bearing and superb diction. It was believed that he would soon sing the role at the Met.

Tibbett then went to Hollywood for a new film. Musical movies had not done well in 1932/33 and Tibbett had abandoned films after *Cuban Love Song*. The success of a series of films with Jeanette MacDonald and Nelson Eddy reversed this trend and singing actors were back at work. Tibbett's film, his only one for Twentieth Century Fox, was *Metropolitan,* produced by Darryl F. Zanuck. Tibbett played a popular American singer "trapped" in small roles by the Met's overwhelming European bias. An eccentric woman (played by Alice Brady) organised an all-American company, starring Tibbett, a soprano (played by Virginia Bruce) and a young tenor (Cesar Romero). The company began a tour, then was abandoned when the wealthy patroness lost interest, forcing the singers to improvise a "season". Tibbett was allowed five musical numbers, including two of his concert favorites: "De Glory Road" and "The Road to Mandalay". He also sang three arias, but only the *Pagliacci* "Prologue" was performed in the traditional style. The Toreador Song from *Carmen* was presented in a glossy Hollywoodish style (presenting more of the scene than was usual for films), and the "Largo al factotum" from the *Barber of Seville* was done in work clothes, against a set resembling a street corner. Critics at the October 17th premiere called it the best musical of 1935, citing Tibbett as the chief reason for its success. *Variety* considered the film proof that Tibbett was an idol of the silver screen.

The 1935/36 season opened on December 16th with *Traviata* (with Bori, Jagel and Tibbett). This was mainly an Italian season for Tibbett, with three Germonts, four

27

Amonasros, and one Marcello. A single Scarpia on January 30th (with Lehmann and Crooks) again received criticism for his lack of true evil. Two Wolframs were praised for lyric warmth—critics felt they had not heard the role sung so well for many years. Two new roles were added that season, starting with the first of six Rigolettos on December 28th (with Pons and Jagel). His voice was powerful, but critics found his acting overdone (in one scene he was so carried away that he forgot that he was supposed to be wearing a hump on his back). Henderson thought he would become a superior Rigoletto, once he grew accustomed to the role. Criticism greeted his other new role: Gianni Schicchi. The first of three performances was on January 27th (with Hilda Burke and Giuseppe Bentonelli—formerly Joseph Benton of Oklahoma). Tibbett's acting and make-up were described as overdone and the use of an English translation was unpopular for requiring the singers to emphasise diction over singing.

In the summer of 1936 Tibbett made his final film, back at MGM. In *Under Your Spell* he played an overworked opera star who sought peace and quiet by disappearing into the wilderness, pursued by a wealthy heiress (Wendy Barrie) who eventually married the hero. There were two arias, both done in costume as big production numbers: "Largo al factotum" and "Le Veau d'or" from *Faust*—allowing audiences a rare chance to see Tibbett perform a role he never sang on stage. At the New York premiere (November 6th) the film was shown on a double bill with *Give Me Your Heart* (with Kay Francis and George Brent), and critics were shocked to see that movie given top billing. The music for *Under Your Spell* was by Arthur Schwartz, lyrics by Howard Dietz, direction by the young Otto Preminger. The latter worked well with Tibbett, although he had expected difficulties in directing a singer.

In late 1936 Tibbett sang with local companies in both Chicago and San Francisco. On November 6th came a San Francisco *Rigoletto* (with Josephine Tuminia, Kullman and Pinza), winning considerable praise for singing and acting. On the 11th came a special double bill—*Pagliacci* (with Vanna and Martinelli) and an English-language *Gianni Schicchi* (with Tuminia and Kullman). As in New York, critics were displeased with the Puccini work, but his Tonio was praised for its raw power. On November 18th he sang Scarpia (with Lehmann and Kullman)—perhaps the first time this role won him real praise from any critics. On November 20th he sang his first Iago (with Rethberg and Martinelli). The *Chronicle* reported he seemed "a kind of slender baritone Mephistopheles, complete with swishing cape and feathered cap." On November 27th he sang another Iago in Chicago (with Edith Mason and Martinelli). Critics complained he was too "Hollywoodish" but the audience cheered his portrayal. On December 5th he sang Rigoletto (with Antoine and Bentonelli). Critics were delighted with his fully-rounded portrayal, offering a full look at all the character's moods.

Much of the 1936/37 Met season offered Tibbett in Italian roles, including three Germonts, six Tonios (now sporting a bright red wig), four Rigolettos, and one Amonasro. On January 14th came a revival of *Contes d'Hoffmann* especially for Tibbett, who sang four roles: Lindorf, Miracle, Coppelius and Dappertutto (with Andreva, Burke, Halstead and Rayner). In one of the three later performances Vina Bovy sang four soprano roles. Critics apparently hoped his interpretations would surpass those of the last baritone to successfully attempt all four roles—Maurice Renaud. Unfortunately, they were disappointed. Lindorf and Coppelius were praised for their remarkable psychological insights and brilliant costumes. His Dappertutto, with a bright red coat, was too garish, while his Miracle (complete with death's head mask) was too sensational. He later revealed that he had not planned these costumes, and blamed an unnamed member of the Met's costume department. On February 4th came the first of two appearances of Richard Hagemann's *Caponsacchi* (with Jepson and Chamlee) in its American premiere. Tibbett played Guido, a ruthless Italian nobleman who had his wife executed on a false charge of adultery. Tibbett's acting was praised, but critics rejected the opera as too coarse. As the season came to a close Tibbett was busy in his work organising the American Guild of Musical Artists, becoming it's first president. AGMA was created in an effort to protect the right of musicians in the United States, and marked a major step in Tibbett's efforts to create a career outside the opera house.

As early as January, 1937 there were reports that Tibbett would tour Europe in the summer. In February it was revealed that he would be absent from the United States for seven months (May through November). On May 14th he made his Covent Garden debut as Scarpia (with Cigna and Martinelli). The *Times* found him "powerful in voice and gesture", while the *Daily Telegraph* and the *Daily Herald* thought his virile acting better than his singing. The *Musical Times* (in its June issue) criticised his voice as well, suggesting that he might damage his upper register with the role. The *Spectator* followed the American critical view by attacking his lack of subtlety, longing for Scotti's "refined mental sadism". After both this performance and the repeat on June 3rd the audiences cheered him and there were long lines outside the door backstage. On June 11th came a single Amonasro (with Cigna, Stignani, Martinelli) hailed for vocal power and virile stage presence. On June 24th he created the title role in the world premiere of Eugene Goossens' *Don Juan de Mañara,* with a second performance four days later. The composer had demanded that the company hire Tibbett for the role and his singing and acting won high praise, while the opera did not. The music was described as too orchestral, while Arnold Bennett's libretto was attacked for its unnecessary violence (seven murders onstage). On June 26th Tibbett sang his last London role—Iago (with Norena and Martinelli). Critics preferred his singing to his unsubtle acting, but audiences were quite enthusiastic. In between these performances Tibbett gave recitals, notably one on May 21st, including songs and arias in several languages. Ernest Newman, writing in the *Times,* thought Tibbett was actually a bass with muffled tone. He did admire Tibbett's ability to sustain long phrases and his mezza-voce.

Tibbett then went to Scandinavia for concerts and opera. A concert in Copenhagen on September 15th won praise for its variety and dazzling style. On the 21st he gave a concert in Oslo to similar praise. The *Nationen* described him as "a great artist with a rich fantasy, a virile human being with his soul and heart in the right place, a joyful and exuberant man." On the 24th he sang Rigoletto at the Royal Opera in Stockholm (with Hjördis Schymberg and Jussi Björling). The *Aftonbladet* praised his skill in creating "a living, pathetic figure." On the 26th he sang Scarpia opposite the husband-wife team of Irma Björck and Einar Beiron. The *Svenska Dagbladet* considered his performance a real blend of acting and singing. He was the guest at a special banquet, being toasted by the Swedish Company, with special musical tributes from Björling and Carl Martin Öhmann. As a climax to his Swedish visit, Tibbett was presented the *Liberis et Artibus* medal by King Gustav V—one of the few foreigners to be so honored.

On October 5th Tibbett made his Paris debut as Iago (with Eidé Norena and Martinelli). The *Excelsior* said he "belonged to the race of the great lyric tragedians . . . One admires the wide variety of his resource, from the fierce . . . Credo to the whispered venom into Otello's ear." *Le Temps* praised his ability to "direct all the drama" on the stage, plus his "generous voice." He returned to Paris for a *Rigoletto* on the 21st (with Norena and Aldo Sinnone) to equal praise. In between these performances had come a *Rigoletto* in Prague on October 7th (with M. Kocovà and B. Chorovic), winning a standing ovation. The *Prager Tageblatt* called it "an achievement bearing the hallmark of genius." On October 11th Tibbett sang another Rigoletto in Budapest (with Mária Gyurkovics and Imre Grodin). The *Pester Lloyd* was amazed by his voice "which could do simply everything." He became one of the few foreigners to win an audience demand for an encore (for "Cortigiani"). He won even greater praise for a Budapest recital on the 15th which included songs in English, arias in several languages and Lieder in German.

Perhaps his most critical reception came in Vienna, beginning with a special banquet on October 8th. The following evening he sang Iago (with Maria Reining and Joachim Saettler) in Italian, with the rest of the cast singing in German. Without proper time for rehearsals the performance received mixed reviews, with critics blaming the management. The *Neues Wiener Tagblatt* said he was "neither a vocal Croesus nor a fascinating bel cantist . . . His baritone is approximately good middle class." The *Neue Freie Presse* thought he lacked what it termed "star quality", and expressed a preference for Alfred Jerger (often called the "Viennese Tibbett"). *Der Morgen* considered him "typically American . . . a kind of socially polished Mephistopheles." His October 14th concert was more successful, with critics hailing his skill in singing Lieder in German. The *Neue Freie Presse* was astonished by this "quite unexpected" triumph. The *Anbruch* (in its November issue) recorded that he received a "stormy ovation", while *The Echo* claimed "there does not exist an interpretative style which he does not master thoroughly." On the 17th he sang Rigoletto (with Maria Gerhart and Imre—now Emmerich—Grodin). Critics again criticised the company's directors for failing to provide an adequate supporting cast for such a distinguished guest. They hoped conditions would improve for Tibbett's next visit, in October 1939 (which he "promised").

From late October through November Tibbett returned for concerts throughout the British Isles, from Glasgow to London and major points in between. On October 24th he gave a lengthy recital in Queen's Hall in London. The *Times* admitted that he was indeed a great singer, but criticised his "operatic mannerisms", which spoiled his singing. The reviewer (possibly Newman?) also objected to his use of English translations for Lieder and his efforts to emphasize the drama within the various selections. A recital on November 4th in Glasgow was received with more praise, the *Herald* stressing his fine diction and "his ability to negotiate long phrases."

As soon as he returned to the United States, Tibbett went to Chicago for an *Otello* on November 29th (with Mason and Martinelli), receiving mixed reviews. The *Tribune* thought it modernistic while the *Daily News* admired his work. On December 8th he sang Rigoletto (with Björling), hailed as the best seen in Chicago since Ruffo. Following these performances Tibbett began a short 1937/38 Met season, including one Amonasro, two Wolframs, one Schicchi (still thought hammy), two Germonts and a Rigoletto. His most important new role, Iago, was sung eight times (mainly with Rethberg and Martinelli). It was said that Met had revived the opera following favorable reviews from San Francisco, London and Paris. Now critics preferred his singing to his acting. As Oscar Thompson noted in the *Sun:*

> Subtler Iagos than that of Lawrence Tibbett undoubtedly have walked the same boards. But one may question whether parts of the music, particularly the narrative of Cassio's dream, "Era la notte", have been more beautifully sung. The Credo was delivered with sting and power. And there was no evasion of the upwards curve to high A natural, commonly indicated rather than sung. . . .

Pitts Sanborn, in the *World-Telegram,* called his interpretation "Mephistophelean in half-tints." Objections were raised regarding his costumes (too much like Robin Hood) and a slight hamminess.

The spring and summer of 1938 were spent on tour in Australia and New Zealand, with appearances in Hawaii at the beginning and end of the seven-month period. He made 55 appearances including 11 in Melbourne, 15 in Sydney (the last two being extra concerts to meet public demand), and the remainder throughout the country. The journey covered 32,000 miles and must have been exhausting, since most of these recitals were long. Throughout the trip he was besieged by hopeful parents who brought in their youngsters for "auditions", hoping for a miracle. Tibbett usually advised them to either study or to forget their dreams—they lacked real voices. During this trip Tibbett spent his spare time reading two Shakespeare plays—*Henry IV* and *The Merry Wives of Windsor,* preparing for a Met revival of Falstaff. On the way back to New York came three Chicago performances, starting with an opening night *Otello* (with Jepson and Martinelli) on October 29th, followed by *Rigoletto* on November 4th (with Hilde Reggiani and Tokatyan). On the 7th he treated Chicagoans to his three villains in *Hoffmann* (with Antoine and Elen Dosia in two soprano roles). His singing was praised but his acting was considered hammy.

The 1938/39 Met season was exclusively Italian as far as Tibbett was concerned, beginning with an *Otello* on opening night—November 25th (with Caniglia and Martinelli). The *Herald-Tribune* found him more Shakespearean, "more fluent and plastic and subtle, a puissant and terrible instrument of evil . . ." Similar improvements were noticed in his four Scarpias that season. There were also two Amonasros and one Rigoletto. On January 13th *Simon Boccanegra* was revived (with Caniglia, Martinelli, Warren and Pinza). For both Boccanegras that season, Tibbett won his customary praise. More controversial was his Falstaff, introduced to the public on December 16th (with Morel, Petina, Castagna, Caniglia and Kullman). The New York *Times* thought he was "a delight for humor and adroitness, extravagance that kept within the bounds of genius, comedy and admirable singing." Most other papers thought his singing was crude and his padded costume grotesque. Leonard Warren was scheduled for Ford but was replaced by John Brownlee. There were rumors that Tibbett insisted upon the change, remembering how he had stolen the show from Scotti in 1925.

The summer of 1939 was devoted to concerts in the United States, since the diplomatic situation prevented a planned European tour. On September 23rd and 29th he sang Rigoletto in San Francisco (with Pons and Jagel), as well as a single Otello on the 27th (with Rethberg and Martinelli). A *Traviata* on the 30th replaced a planned

Tosca, cancelled by Caniglia's detention in Italy. On November 27th the Met opened the 1939/40 season with *Simon Boccanegra* (with Rethberg, Martinelli, Tibbett, Warren and Pinza). Tibbett sang two Boccanegras, three Rigolettos, one Amonasro, two Scarpias and three Germonts that season, each winning favorable reviews. On December 1st he sang Wolfram (with Lawrence, Manski, Melchior and List) with poor reviews. He had restudied the role, changing the costumes and make-up (including a new putty nose). He also adopted a more open way of singing, with unfortunate results.

During the summer Tibbett had to fight a bitter battle with James C. Petrillo whose American Federation of Musicians clashed with AGMA over jurisdiction. The final victory was won in court by the AFM in 1941. Tibbett did not tour that summer, staying instead at his farm (Honey Hill) in Connecticut. On September 17th it was announced that he had been stricken with a mysterious throat ailment, forcing a cancellation of all engagements through the rest of 1940. This medical disaster over-shadowed Tibbett's remaining decade at the Met and has never been explained. Many popular writers said he had lived too hard a life (and hinted at alcoholism). Virgil Thomson has suggested to the author that it was the penalty for singing a series of concerts through a heavy cold in the spring. Several writers have suggested that this was merely the price for too many heavy roles, especially Emperor Jones and Scarpia. Finally, a doctor was quoted in *Newsweek* (January 24th, 1949), insisting that Tibbett was suffering from a severe case of "spasticity of the larynx muscle". As Tibbett's career in opera declined he would compensate by additional concert and benefit activity. During the war he would tour for the U.S.O., singing for soldiers through-out the country. He also became involved in organisations working for American-French ties and French war relief (as related to the author by Martial Singher).

The 1940/41 season at the Met meant only 12 performances for Tibbett (including the tour). He sang Rigoletto on January 3rd (with Pons and Kullman), noted for superior acting and cautious singing. His Tonio on January 9th (with Greco and Martinelli) began well, but he tired during the second act. An Iago on the 11th (with Stella Roman and Martinelli) was better—a private recording suggests that his voice had almost recovered. Each role was repeated once, with three Rigolettos, two Tonios and one Iago on tour.

Tibbett apparently decided to resume a full schedule for 1941/42, starting with three performances in San Francisco. On September 19th he sang Rigoletto (with Pons and Peerce), praised for dramatic conviction and generally good singing. On the 22nd he sang his first and only Figaro (in the Rossini opera—with Sayão, Pinza and Baccaloni). Both papers praised his humor and costumes, but felt he was too power-ful for the role, and hoped he would improve with practice. On November 1st he sang the title role in the San Francisco premiere of *Simon Boccanegra* (with Roman, Jagel and Pinza), considered his best work that season. On November 12th he sang one Iago (with Della Chiesa and Martinelli) in Chicago, praised for rapidly improving acting. On November 29th he sang the first of three Met *Traviatas* (with Novotna and Peerce). Critics cautiously suggested his voice was recovering. An Iago on December 4th (with Roman and Martinelli) was considered too mannered. As Robert Lawrence of the *Herald-Tribune* suggested, "it needs more voice and less stage business", as well as costumes which did not make him look so much like a "Venetian Clifton Webb". On December 18th he sang a Scarpia (with Moore and Kullman), noted for its new sense

17. Tibbett as Eadgar in Deems Taylor's *The King's Henchman*. Photo: Mishkin. Courtesy of Metropolitan Opera Archives.

18. Tibbett in his first major Wagnerian role, as Telramund in *Lohengrin*. He first assumed the role on 29 April 1927 and sang it only twice more, all three times on tour. Photo: Mishkin. Courtesy of Peter Bence.

19. Tibbett preparing for a Carnegie Hall recital on 13 November 1927. Photo: Lumiere. From the Editor's collection.

20. Tibbett on the occasion of receiving an honorary Master of Music degree from the University of Southern California, at the June 1928 Commencement exercises. He also sang the title role in Mendelssohn's *Elijah* at the Shrine Auditorium on June 5 given as part of the university's semi-centennial program. Photo: U.S.C. News Bureau. From the Editor's collection.

21. Tibbett as Amonasro in Verdi's *Aida.* He added the role to his growing Metropolitan repertory on 30 April 1928. Courtesy of Metropolitan Opera Archives.

22. Tibbett being made up for the role of Giorgio Germont in *La Traviata*. Photo: Wide World Photos, Inc. From the Editor's collection.

23. A very young elder Germont in *La Traviata*. Courtesy of Metropolitan Opera
Archives.

24. A more mature Giorgio Germont in *La Traviata*. From the Editor's collection.

25. A scene from the Metropolitan's *La Traviata*. Tibbett is shown with soprano Nadine Conner in the title role. From the Editor's collection.

To
— My good friend Clifford
— remembering always the most
delightful of relationships
sincerely
Lawrence Tibbett

26. Lawrence Tibbett, the established artist of the Metropolitan. Courtesy of William R. Moran.

27. Lawrence Tibbett at the piano. Note the first appearance of the mustache. Photo: Russell Ball. From the Editor's collection.

28. Tibbett as Jonny in Krenek's *Jonny spielt auf* at the Metropolitan. He took over the role from Michael Bohnen on 27 February 1929. Photo: Carlo Edwards. Courtesy of Metropolitan Opera Archives.

29. Tibbett as Jack Rance in Puccini's *The Girl of the Golden West.* The Met revival took place on 2 November 1929. Photo: Carlo Edwards. Courtesy of Metropolitan Opera Archives.

30. Another portrait of Tibbett as Jack Rance. Photo: Carlo Edwards. Courtesy of Metropolitan Opera Archives.

31. Lawrence Tibbett—movie star. From the Editor's collection.

MGMP-21014

32. Publicity shot for Tibbett's first motion picture, *The Rogue Song,* made by MGM and first shown in New York on 28 January 1930. The actress in his arms is Catherine Dale Owen. From the Editor's collection.

33. Tibbett as Yegor in *The Rogue Song.* From the Editor's collection.

of refinement. Later that month an attack of appendicitis prevented him from appearing for the rest of the season (weakening a revival of the *Barber of Seville*).

Following concerts in the summer of 1942, Tibbett opened the Chicago opera season in *Aida* on November 7th (with Milanov, Martinelli and Kipnis). He sang Germont on the 16th (with Novotna and Melton), beginning quite badly but recovering in time for a show-stopping "Di Provenza il mar". On the 28th an Iago (with Roman and Martinelli) was praised for subtle insights lacking the previous year. A December 12th *Rigoletto* was considered superb. The Met season had already opened, and Tibbett sang the first of five Germonts on December 5th. There would also be three Scarpias, two Wolframs and two Amonasros. He also added a new role: Don Carlos in *La Forza del Destino,* sung four times that season. After the first, on January 9th (with Milanov, Baum, Pinza and Baccaloni), critics suggested that it was embarrassing to hear an obviously unwell artist tackle such a role too late in his career.

In the summer of 1943 Tibbett made his debut with the Cincinnati Summer Opera Company (popularly called the "Opera in the Zoo", since that was its unusual location for many seasons). His first role was Scarpia on the opening night, June 27th (with Roman and Kullman)—with two repeats. The Cincinnati *Enquirer* found him "an eminently commanding personality", revealing all of the role's complex facets. On July 2nd he sang the first of three Rigolettos (with Antoine and Eugene Conley). The *Enquirer* described this performance as "sensational", both in terms of singing and acting. There was no indication of serious vocal problems.

Back at the Met, on November 27th, 1943 Tibbett sang the first of two *Forzas,* again criticised as too demanding for his weakened voice. The first of five Rigolettos (with Pons and Peerce) on December 3rd won praise for acting but his voice was described as wooden and forced. Three Germonts, one Scarpia and one Tonio were better and there was more optimism that he was defeating his vocal ills. The first of two English-language *Falstaffs* was on January 14th (with Steber, Harshaw, Kullman, Brownlee, conducted by Beecham). His diction was praised while his costumes were again attacked as over-padded. The *Musical Courier,* however, felt "his portrayal of the fat knight was a perfect piece of characterisation, unctious, rollicking and cowardly" by turns. On January 20th he added yet another role: Golaud in the first of two performances of *Pelléas et Melisande* (with Sayão, Harshaw, Singher and Kipnis). Critics thought he was too powerful and uncouth, yet Sayão (according to Robert Lawrence's letter to the author) thought he was perfect.

For 1944/45, Tibbett began the season in Chicago with the first of two Iagos on October 28th (with ex-mezzo Rose Bampton and Martinelli), now praised for superb acting. His two Golauds (with Sayão, Singher and Moscona) were criticised by the *Daily News* while praised by Claudia Cassidy of the *Tribune*. She admired his "dark, almost sombre voice, that unerring focus, that feeling for costume that underscores drama . . ." Between November 30th and February 14th he sang seven times at the Met: one Amonasro, two Golauds, two Rigolettos, and two Germonts (plus one Golaud and one Amonasro on tour). Critics now felt that his voice had deteriorated to the point where he was beyond any hope of recovery. It was believed that Tibbett's days as a major singer were long past—yet he would continue to sing new roles with the Met!

In the summer of 1945 Tibbett returned to Cincinnati for four performances. The first of two Iagos was June 26th, praised for acting and singing. One Rigoletto, on July

3rd (with Doris Martinelli and John B. McCormick) was seen as Tibbett's show. A single Scarpia on the 5th was seen as perfect. After a short break, Tibbett made another debut—with the Philadelphia-La Scala Company, then on tour around the country. He sang three Rigolettos with that group, each in a different city. On September 28th he appeared in Buffalo, being praised by the *Evening News* for his powerful acting and "bold full-bodied resonance for the climactic moments". On October 3rd he appeared in Detroit and the *Free Press* thought his performance of Act III "recalled his days of greatest glory". On November 22nd came a performance in Washington, D.C., with attention devoted to Agata Borgi, making her debut as Gilda—Tibbett was virtually ignored. These performances were squeezed in between appearances in Chicago. His two Rigolettos, on October 10th and 15th were compared by the *Daily News* with Macbeth or Richard III. Two Golauds, on October 31st and November 5th produced divided opinions. The *Daily News* thought he was boorish, while the *Tribune* compared him to Chaliapin's Boris.

At the Met he sang only eight performances and three roles between December 5th and February 9th. A single Germont on January 23rd and five Scarpias won praise—now critics felt he had mastered the subtleties of the latter role. There was even new optimism that his voice had stopped its deteriorations. On January 5th he sang the first of two Micheles in *Il Tabarro* (with Albanese and Jagel)—yet another new role. Critics thought he tired easily, yet a recording from one broadcast suggests that he was not that worn. On February 23rd he sang one *Traviata* (with Albanese and Landi) in San Antonio, as part of that city's Festival of Opera. The San Antonio *Express* praised his singing and especially his superb "Di Provenza il mar", while *Musical America* thought the entire cast sounded tired. It was hinted that he should take the summer off and relax, but this advice was not taken.

In the spring of 1946 Tibbett made a lengthy European tour, presenting recitals for American soldiers and German civilians in Stuttgart, Wiesbaden, and other cities, with his recitals often including at least twenty songs and/or arias. He then went to Italy, presenting a pair of very long recitals, including a special benefit in Florence to raise money for repairs on the bomb-damaged opera house (the Teatro Communale). In Rome he also presented a special concert of arias, songs and excerpts from *Porgy and Bess,* with Robert Lawrence—the conductor for the tour—introducing the audience to works by Copland and Thomson. Rome was also the scene of two Rigolettos, on May 27th and 29th. The first resulted in a riot when the audience demanded an encore for Giacomo Lauri-Volpi's "La donna è mobile". Lawrence tried to continue the opera, but the tumult increased until the encore was allowed. Backstage the tenor and conductor engaged in a shouting match, threatening the second performance. Tibbett was not involved—it was merely a clash of wills.

Upon his return from Europe, Tibbett returned to Cincinnati for two performances. The first was an August 1st *Rigoletto* (with Antoine and Franco Perullo), described by the *Enquirer* as the best ever heard in that city. On August 4th Tibbett sang Germont to good reviews, although it was noted that his voice sounded tired, and he was forced to take "Di Provenza" so slowly that it fell apart. After a short rest, Tibbett went to Chicago for two performances of *Emperor Jones* on October 4th and 14th, winning audience applause, although critics still disliked the score. There was a single San Francisco *Rigoletto* (with Pons and Peerce) on October 19th. On November 1st and 9th he sang *Traviata* in Chicago (with Micheau and Tokatyan). Perhaps because of his long European tour, his voice was tired. At the Met Tibbett sang only five times in 1946/47: two Rigolettos, one Amonasro, one Germont and one Iago— only the last of these (on January 9th) won any praise, and critics were surprised to notice its vigor and vocal ease, reminding many of his pre-1940 years.

Early in 1947 there had been rumors of a foreign tour, possibly to Sweden, or even to the U.S.S.R. In reality Tibbett went to London for a short period, being featured with the N.B.C. Symphony (conducted by Adrian Boult) on June 9th. Critics said little about this performance, but it was felt that his voice had aged terribly. He then went on to a successful concert tour in South Africa from mid-June through the middle of July. Included were three appearances as Rigoletto in Johannesburg on the 23rd, 25th and 29th of June (with Albina Bini and Francis Russell). All local papers, both English and Afrikaans, agreed that he was the greatest singer-actor to appear in the Union. His concerts, often quite lengthy (an average recital included over one dozen scheduled songs), won equal praise, although at least one member of the audience complained that his encores were worthless trivia.

For Tibbett, the 1947/48 season was the shortest of his career. In October came four appearances in San Francisco. His Iago of October 7th (with Albanese and Svanholm) was rated good, although nothing like the 1930's. A Golaud on the 10th (with Sayão, Singher and Alvary) also won praise, although his acting was considered too powerful. A Rigoletto on the 12th (with Pons and Peerce) was described as nearly as effective as his prewar work. His last local season's appearance was on the 17th, as Germont (with Conner and Kullman), described as "average". He was scheduled for three Scarpias at the Met but illness cancelled two of them. Thus, his only appearance for the entire season was on November 20th (with Dosia and Peerce).

During the 1948/49 season Tibbett sang only two roles at the Met, including three Rigolettos. He added yet another role, singing Balstrode in three performances of *Peter Grimes*. This role won him critical favor, especially for his superb English diction. After the first of the three performances, on January 21st, Tibbett was honored by a special celebration on the Met's stage, marking 25 years with the company. He was presented with a silver bowl, inscribed "To Larry", and a set of book-ends. There were over 300 singers and staff members present, and the local press gave the event considerable coverage.

Tibbett was scheduled to sing in Cincinnati in the summer of 1949 but illness forced him to miss the season. He would have sung his first Gerard in a new production of *Andrea Chenier*. On September 20th he sang the first of three Scarpias in San Francisco (with Barbato and Björling), but critics felt his voice had declined too far for him to continue singing. Two performances of *Hoffmann* (as both Miracle and Dappertutto) on October 14th and 20th marked the end of his San Francisco career. On November 10th and 12th he sang two performances of *Salome* in New Orleans (with Varnay and Jagel), his Jochanaan being hailed as "stalwart" and "worthy". It was his only role in a Strauss opera and his only role with the New Orleans company.

Tibbett's 1949/50 season was his last at the Met, and comprised only two roles: Scarpia and Prince Ivan in the first American production of *Khovanchina*, with two and four appearances in these roles, respectively. At his second *Tosca*, on February 28th, Tibbett received some unexpected action. This was a gala honoring Edward Johnson's last season as General Manager, and Paul Schöffler had been scheduled as Scarpia. At the last minute he was forced to bow out, having unexpectedly sung Sachs the evening before. Angered by the substitution, Ljuba Welitsch directed her frustration on Tibbett, who was subjected to kicks, scratches and punches. His Prince Ivan suffered no such indignity, and critics praised his subtlety in this, his last new role. Unfortunately, they disliked the score itself (sung in English and heavily cut). On March 18th Tibbett sang a single Rigoletto in Providence, Rhode Island, at the opening of the new auditorium (with Laura Castellano, Thomas Hayward and the veteran Virgilio Lazzari). Six days later he sang his final Ivan—his last appearance at the Met and in any opera.

Although there were rumors that he might succeed Johnson as the Met's manager, the post went to Rudolf Bing and Tibbett settled down to what might be called a busy retirement. On November 2nd, 1950 he appeared on Broadway in the first performance of *The Mulatto,* a play by Langston Hughes, with music by Jan Meyerowitz. Critics admired his portrayal of a conscience-stricken southerner, but the play itself did not survive long. In the summer of 1951 he travelled for a while with a touring production of the play *Rain*—a non-singing role. In November he began a tour with a travelling production of the musical *Peter Pan,* as Captain Hook. While his impersonation of the colorful pirate was admired, Veronica Lake's Peter was considered too formal and the tour ended early in Chicago. During 1950–52 Tibbett worked with a local television group, attempting to broadcast televised opera, in condensed form, to fit within a one-hour format. *Carmen* and *Traviata* (the latter starring Tibbett), were broadcast but the experiment did not last very long. In 1956 he appeared in *Fanny* on Broadway, replacing Ezio Pinza. His last public appearance of note was on March 2nd, 1960, when he led the applause for Leonard Warren at a revival of *Simon Boccanegra.* Within a few months both baritones would be dead (Warren dying onstage during *La Forza del Destino* on March 4th). On June 27th Tibbett underwent surgery following an auto accident which aggravated a head injury received in 1938. He lapsed into a coma and died on July 15th.

TIBBETT THE ARTIST

Tibbett's career was based on certain basic principles which were derived from his outlook on music and life in general. He considered music "good" or "bad" on the basis of its ability to arouse emotional responses within listeners. As he explained in "Along the Glory Road" (*American Magazine,* August 1933):

> All classical music is not good and all popular music is not bad, and the only way to judge singers and songs is to decide whether they do well the job they set out to perform.
>
> I like Rudy Vallee's singing. I think he is the best of the crooners. I admire Al Jolson. . . .
>
> There are singers of classical songs who have no little prestige but who leave their audiences utterly cold. Some of the patrons of the Metropolitan Opera Company would consider it sacrilege to mention Jolson and Vallee in the same breath with these inadequate operatic performers, but to me Jolson singing "Sonny Boy" is more truly a real artist than these near-greats ever have been or ever will be. . . .
>
> I like all kinds of good music and I sing all kinds. I do not try to force any particular brand upon the public. . . .

To Tibbett music had to be entertaining and musicians had to break their old image of being boring. If the artists could convince audiences that they enjoyed performing, then the American public would be more likely to enjoy more music. As he told Rupert Hughes (quoted in the *American Magazine* for May 1930), " 'Singing . . . is just about the best fun that the human animal can have. It is a gorgeous sensation, simply because a tune is the most perfect expression of emotions . . .' " This sense of enjoyment was one of the keys to Tibbett's style.

Tibbett's concert tours were a logical extension of this desire to enjoy singing good music. At his peak period he travelled up to 25,000 miles per year, with a concert repertoire of some 500 songs and arias. His concerts represented a blend of styles and languages. As he explained in the August 1933 *American Magazine,* an artist had to appeal to all members of his audience.

> In my concerts I always sing one or two operatic numbers, because in the smaller cities the people do not get opera and they have a genuine love for the best operatic music. I do not . . . sing operatic numbers that are strange to the ears of an audience. . . .
>
> I sing a few songs in French and German and Italian, because, in addition to the handful who really enjoy them, there are always a number of people in an audience who feel they have been classically cheated unless they have been given something they do not understand. . . .

This blend of classical and popular music was not so successful outside the United States. London critics disliked his use of English-language Lieder, while one member of the audience in Cape Town was shocked by his non-classical items, having expected only "art". The *Cape Times* carried a letter from Mrs. M. Versveld on July 10th, 1947, which objected to "all of the encores, which were . . . of cheap music-hall standard. In his 'Texas Cowboy Song' Tibbett whistled—and so did I!" Five days later, the same paper carried a rejoinder from a columnist named "Plebs" who insisted that variety was necessary in a vocal recital, in order to prevent monotony. "A vocal artist . . . cannot please all the people all the time; and when it comes to a toss-up between the tastes of Mrs. Versveld and that of the masses, the latter must prevail."

Tibbett's recital career began nearly a decade before his Met debut with limited contributions to Los Angeles programs. By the end of the 1920's he was a star— singing lengthy recitals lasting up to three hours each, featuring a blend of songs and arias. J. A. Hamilton was in the audience at a recital in Edmonton, Alberta (Canada) in 1938 and recalls Tibbett performing numerous encores, following suggestions from the audience.

It is interesting to look through notes on Tibbett's recitals and to see what he actually performed. At a February 17, 1930 recital at Stanford University he sang fifteen programmed selections: "Where'er You Walk" (from Handel's *Semele*); "Già il sole del Gange" (Scarlatti); "The Bailiff's Daughter" (old English); "Le Petit Mâitre" (Ponchon); "Le Thè" (Koechlin); "Verrat" and "O liebliche Wangen" (Brahms); Credo from Verdi's *Otello;* "Tell Me Your Dream" (Romelli); "Travelin' to the Grave" (arr. Reddick); "Bricklayer Love" and "The Roustabout" (Rupert Hughes); "Things" (George Bagby); "Jazz-Boys" (John Alden Carpenter) and "Captain Stratton's Fancy" (Deems Taylor). There were eight encores: "Old Man Ned" (arr. Somervell); "Retreat" (Frank La Forge); Song to the Evening Star from

Wagner's *Tannhäuser;* "The Cloths of Heaven" (Dunhill); Prologue from Leoncavallo's *Pagliacci;* "A Kingdom by the Sea" (Somervell); "Old Man River" (Kern); and "Song of the Flea" (Mussorgsky). This was at a period when his voice was at its peak, and he seemed able to sing anything without strain.

In the summer of 1947, while touring South Africa, Tibbett gave three lengthy recitals, plus a solo appearance with the local symphony orchestra. The last of these three programs was the longest, comprising the following: "Would that I were a Tender Apple Blossom" (Londonderry air), "There is a Lady" (Bury), "The Bailiff's Daughter" (old English), "Sapphic Ode" (Brahms), "Treachery" (Brahms), "Serenade" (Schubert), "The Lord's Prayer" (Malotte), the Toreador aria from *Carmen,* "Song of the Volga Boatmen", "In the Silence of the Night" (Rachmaninov), "Captain Stratton's Family" (Taylor), "Through the Years" (Youmans), "Sigh no More, Ladies" (Aiken), "When I have sung my Songs" (Charles), "Song of the Shirt" (from *The Rogue Song*), "Largo al factotum" (*Barber of Seville*), "Old Man River" (Kern), "Without a Song", Road to Mandalay", "One Alone", "The White Dove" plus unnamed encores. This long mixture of arias, songs, film music and Lieder was delivered on a hot July 20th, 1947, when Tibbett's voice was no longer young, yet critics reported he was in excellent condition and the audience was clearly enjoying this program—in contrast to two earlier programs which Tibbett had begun with oratorio selections. Then the audience had expressed its boredom by coughing (48 times in one song—according to a local critic), and smoking cigarettes. Despite vocal problems, Tibbett clearly had no intention of slowing down, and he was continuing to give everything he had.

Tibbett considered films and radio as extensions of the concert platform or opera stage and hoped full-length films could be made of operas, allowing audiences to understand the plot by use of close-up shots, special effects and complete translations. For many years he used radio to bring a wide range of musical styles to the American public. In 1922 he broadcast over station *KHJ* in Los Angeles, one of the first singers on the air. He then starred on the Atwater Kent Radio Hour (1922–31), the Voice of Firestone (1932–33), The Packard Hour (1934–36), Chesterfield Presents (1937–38), The Circle (presented by Kellogg's, 1939), and the Ford Sunday Evening Hour (1939–40). In 1945 he replaced Frank Sinatra for 26 weeks as host of "Your Hit Parade". After 1950 he hoped to see television bring opera into the homes of Americans, but broadcasting's commercial requirements defeated his efforts (1950–52).

Tibbett's efforts to increase his fellow American's appreciation of music went beyond the use of new media. The formation of AGMA was an attempt to protect American performers so that they could gain financial security. He was AGMA's first president from 1936 until 1953, when he was made honorary president. He helped organise the American Federation of Radio Artists (now the American Federation of Television and Radio Artists), serving as its vice-president in 1937–39 and president in 1940–45. In the spring of 1935 he actively tried to persuade Congress to pass legislation creating a cabinet-level Department of Science, Art and Literature. He believed such a move would allow every city to have its own symphony and over 50 opera houses could be operated in the United States. Suggested in the midst of a depression, this plan was buried in a congressional committee and never revived.

All of this activity helped keep Tibbett's name in the news and increase his overall popularity. He was so well known as a symbol of opera that a radio comic could produce a strange noise and claim it was Tibbett singing a "high Q sharp"—the highest note ever used! While many critics called him a prototypical American singer, Giacomo Lauri-Volpi, writing in his book *Voci Parallele,* went to almost an extreme, calling Tibbett the "voice of America" and a "bold baritone of the far west". Most reviews of his concerts were described by local critics in such words as masculine, virile, rich, powerful, brilliant, sonorous, etc. Observers like Elinor Warren, Robert Lawrence, Blanche Witherspoon and Ruth Chamlee all agree that his voice was a unique blend of power and beauty, a voice which could fill the largest hall and then scale down to a whisper. Rosa Ponselle has compared it to the voices of Ruffo, Caruso or Chaliapin—unforgettable and completely unique. At the time, however, relatively few observers attempted to write down any overall description of his voice.

One of the few critics who accomplished this task was Amy Freeman Lee, a critic in San Antonio, Texas, who heard Tibbett give a recital there around 1939 or 1940. In her book, *A Critic's Notebook,* occurs the following:

> His voice is generally described as rich, powerful, and marvelously expressive and his stage presentations as splendidly vivid and human. The most distinctive thing about his voice is that is a cultivated rather than a natural one. . . .
>
> It is in reality more complimentary than disparaging to say that Tibbett by learning and applying the technical means of his art was successful in producing excellent effects with his voice. . . . With his almost faultless technique, he compensates for any deficiencies that his voice lacks in natural tone and quality.
>
> If this were his only accomplishment, he would be merely a craftsman, though a superb one, but he is also an exceedingly fine stylist. The variety and richness of his imaginal impressions and his ability to project them into an objective medium is best seen in his operatic roles.

Claudia Cassidy, recalling Tibbett's career in the *Chicago Tribune* on November 18th, 1951, observed:

> Once he really got in stride, his world was a baritone's oyster. He had a quicksilver brilliance onstage, a big beautiful voice glinting with highlights and rich with shadows.

Tibbett's basic style was the result of methods learned from Frank LaForge. A letter to LaForge, claiming continued application of his teacher's methods has been preserved in the library at Lincoln Center (written in 1940). Tibbett carefully memorized his roles and examined them for dramatic meanings. According to a letter to the author from Vincent Sheean, Tibbett learned his roles phonetically, since he could not speak any foreign languages. He vocalised with the sound "ay", a favorite LaForge method. His working days began at 8:30, with 30 minutes of exercising, a cold shower then an hour of vocalising. Another hour was spent studying roles, often with the help of his long-time accompanist, Stewart Wille. By 11:30 he was ready for rehearsal, lasting until at least 3:30. Afterwards Tibbett walked back to his apartment for exercise. Although he would listen to other singers' records, he never copied anyone. Tibbett also did not hesitate to sing "ugly" notes if called for by the role.

During his lifetime Tibbett sang 52 roles and 644 performances, of which 48 roles were sung at the Met—his major operatic home for 27 years. These roles are listed in the following table:

Date 1st perf	Role (opera)	Met	Met tour	Other U.S.	Other	Total
20/9/23	Amonasro (Aida)	18	11	*4	1	34
24/11/23	Lovitsky (Boris Godunov)	*1	2	—	—	3
30/11/23	Valentin (Faust)	*14	6	—	—	20
1/12/23	Marullo (Rigoletto)	*2	2	—	—	4
12/12/23	Tchelkalov (Boris Godunov)	*8	3	—	—	11
17/12/23	Fleville (Andrea Chenier)	*9	1	—	—	10
19/12/23	Silvio (Pagliacci)	*18	3	—	—	21
2/1/24	Herald (I Compagnacci)	*3	—	—	—	3
8/1/24	Herald (Lohengrin)	10	*3	—	—	13
11/1/24	Morales (Carmen)	*7	1	—	—	8
24/1/24	D'Obigny (Traviata)	*2	—	—	—	2
12/2/24	Escamillo (Carmen)	*6	2	—	—	8
13/11/24	Schlemil (Contes d'Hoffmann)	*6	4	—	—	10
2/1/25	Ford (Falstaff)	*16	6	1	—	23
31/3/25	Kothner (Meistersinger)	3	*1	—	—	4
7/11/25	Ramiro (L'Heure Espagnol)	*5	2	—	—	7
21/1/26	Neri (La Cena delle Beffe)	*4	2	2	—	8
21/4/26	Tonio (Pagliacci)	13	*10	5	—	28
24/4/26	Wolfram (Tannhäuser)	13	*9	—	—	22
29/4/26	Mercutio (Romeo et Juliette)	7	*4	—	—	11
11/12/26	Melitone (La Forza del Destino)	*3	—	—	—	3
25/1/27	Manfredo (L'Amore dei Tre Re)	4	*6	1	—	11
17/2/27	Eadgar (The King's Henchman)	*14	3	—	—	17
1/3/27	Dappertutto (Les Contes d'Hoffmann)	*9	5	3	—	17
21/4/27	Alfio (Cavalleria Rusticana)	4	*4	—	—	8
25/4/27	Germont (Traviata)	31	*17	8	—	56
29/4/27	Telramund (Lohengrin)	—	*3	—	—	3
19/9/28	Scarpia (Tosca)	19	8	*9	3	39
8/2/28	Marcello (La Boheme)	*3	5	—	—	8
27/2/29	Jonny (Jonny Spielf Auf)	*2	—	—	—	2
2/11/29	Jack Rance (La Fanciulla del West)	*6	2	—	—	8
7/2/31	Col. Ibbetson (Peter Ibbetson)	*16	6	—	—	22
28/1/32	Simon Boccanegra (Simon Boccanegra)	*18	2	1	—	21
7/1/33	Brutus Jones (The Emperor Jones)	*10	5	6	—	21
10/2/34	Wrestling Bradford (Merry Mount)	*4	3	—	—	7
24/1/35	Pasha (In the Pasha's Garden)	*3	—	—	—	3

*denotes where the first performance occurred

Date 1st perf	Role (opera)	Met	Met tour	Other U.S.	Other	Total
28/12/35	Rigoletto (*Rigoletto*)	*22	10	22	10	64
27/1/36	Gianni Schicchi (*Gianni Schicchi*)	*4	—	1	—	5
20/11/36	Iago (*Otello*)	14	5	*12	3	34
14/1/37	Lindorf (*Les Contes d'Hoffmann*)	*3	1	—	—	4
same	Coppelius (*same*)	*3	1	1	—	5
same	Miracle (*same*)	*3	1	3	—	7
4/2/37	Guido (*Caponsacchi*)	*2	—	—	—	2
24/6/37	Don Juan (*Don Juan de Mañara*)	—	—	—	*2	2
16/12/38	Falstaff (*Falstaff*)	*6	1	—	—	7
22/9/41	Figaro (*Il Barbiere di Siviglia*)	—	—	*1	—	1
9/1/43	Don Carlos (*La Forza del Destino*)	*4	2	—	—	6
26/1/44	Golaud (*Pelléas et Melisande*)	*6	1	5	—	12
5/1/46	Michele (*Il Tabarro*)	*2	—	—	—	2
21/1/49	Captain Balstrode (*Peter Grimes*)	*3	—	—	—	3
10/11/49	Jochanaan (*Salome*)	—	—	*2	—	2
16/2/50	Prince Ivan (*Khovanchina*)	*4	—	—	—	4
TOTAL	52 roles	384	163	87	19	643

Tibbett was best-remembered by many for his English-speaking roles, for his European repertoire was somewhat selective. Thus, in the field of Russian opera, he sang two small roles in *Boris Godunov* and a larger one in *Khovanchina*—none in Russian. In an interview in the intermission of the Metropolitan broadcast of January 1st, 1935 (conducted by Geraldine Farrar—a typed script has been preserved in Lincoln Center's Music Library), he indicated a desire to sing Boris.

> That is a role that I want very much to do. And I would like to do it in English. . . .
> It is the type of opera that should be translated. It's dramatic rather than lyric and I really believe it would translate better into English than it has been into Italian which is a much less dramatic . . . language than either Russian or English. . . .

He hoped that any such translation would follow the original scoring and not the Rimsky-Korsakov revision.

In German opera, Tibbett sang a smattering of roles, although there was little choice. Wagner was popular at the Met, but he would not have been able to sing the Dutchman or Wotan, and he realised this from the beginning of his career. He also would have faced the competition of a large number of Germanic baritones present at the Met. One role he hoped to sing was Sachs, as *Die Meistersinger* was his favorite opera and Sachs was his "dream role". As he noted in *Music on the Air* (ed. by Hazel G. Kinscella):

> Consider its purity, mellowness, and . . . supreme beauty. Consider Hans Sachs . . . one of the finest creations in all opera, a man old enough to look on life with mellow understanding, and young enough to respond to youth and nature with warmth and affection. Here was a man with the height of tenderness and self-comprehension.

Aside from the 1935 Act III Tibbett never realised this ambition.

French opera provided Tibbett with interesting roles in a wide range of works—Gounod, Ravel, Offenbach, Bizet and Debussy. Critics seemed to feel that his best roles were those which allowed a change for characterisation—as with Schlemil. In many cases he would be tempted to overdo certain roles. Thus, in an effort to match Jeritza. His portrayal of the villains in *Hoffmann* was another example. Critics blamed Hollywood for developing a melodramatic style they felt inappropriate for French opera—as they also blamed it for his powerful Golaud. Yet his colleague Frederick Jagel thought his multiple *Hoffmann* stint was one of the greatest things he had ever seen. In an interview with a New York *Times* correspondent, printed on April 3rd, 1932, he indicated a desire to sing one role which he never attempted: Pelléas. Although it was high for his voice, he believed he could handle the tessitura.

Tibbett's most numerous roles were from Italian opera, although he never sang some roles that might have been expected: Di Luna, Barnaba, Renato *(Ballo)* since the works were given at the Met. Aside from a single Figaro, he never sang any Rossini, Bellini or Donizetti. Verdi and Puccini provided most of his staple roles, including four with a common feature—they all were fathers: Amonasro, Rigoletto, Boccanegra and Germont. This feature determined his acting, while their various ages determined his costumes. Boccanegra was his favorite of the lot and the most popular with critics. Germont was his most popular with audiences. Rigoletto was a difficult role, and most critics could not decide whether they liked it or not. According to Frederick Jagel, who frequently sang the Duke opposite Tibbett's Rigoletto, it was the best part for his voice. His Amonasro was a powerful role and Rosa Ponselle has told the author of one performance which resulted in Tibbett throwing her across the stage with such force that she was shaken up.

Iago was one of his greatest roles, and one of the most controversial. As early as 1932 he was trying to talk Gatti into letting him sing it. He had been familiar with the role since 1920. Various critics felt he was too fussy—both in acting and in costuming, yet singers were fully impressed. Alexander Kipnis has written the author that he never forgot the incredible impression he received when he first saw the blend of voice and acting that was Tibbett's speciality. Ruth and Mario Chamlee also admired his ability to chill the blood with his portrayal of evil. Claudia Cassidy (in the Chicago *Tribune* for November 18th, 1951), thought Tibbett "was a catlike Iago, part Puck, part Mephisto, and his voice was velvet, deep crushed in shadows, pulled sheer from the darkness of innuendo to even more insinuating light. Catlike, but no house cat, more a panther on the prowl." Tibbett himself saw Iago as a young man of 25 or 30, an insider jealous of his position and social rank. As he explained in *Opera News* (December 20th, 1937), "Iago is in a sense the Greek chorus of the spoken drama. . . . In his soliloquies he takes the audience into his confidence. The strings are all in his hands."

Falstaff was worlds away from the evils of Iago, yet critics also were unable to admire all aspects of Tibbett's performance. He carefully read through the plays used by Boito but preferred to spend equal time on the libretto itself. As indicated in an interview in *Musical America* (issue of February 10th, 1944), he refused to listen to Maurel's recording of "Quand' ero paggio" because he did not want to absorb bad mannerisms. Tibbett tried to combine the different Shakespearean scenes used by the composer and librettist and this may be one reason for his troubles with the critics.

"One point above all others I found it necessary to make clear—that Falstaff, for all the adventures and preposterous situations in which he finds himself, is the one *gentleman* in the piece. . . . In the end, he is the strongest, most enduring type of the lot." He is a clown, therefore, but not just a buffoon.

In the field of veristic opera, Tibbett's roles were fairly numerous, from Fleville to Neri. His most important role in this type of opera was clearly Scarpia, which he sang for many years with a wide range of sopranos. He attempted to show the dual nature of the man by wearing one type (and color) of costume for Act I and another for Act II—perhaps symbolising day versus night. Throughout his career he was saddled with comparisons with Scotti, the "definitive" Scarpia for all critics who had been attending the Met since about 1920. They complained he lacked his predecessor's subtlety and overemphasised Scarpia's cruelty. Robert Lawrence has suggested that one reason for this attitude was Tibbett's psychological and modern approach to the role. He emphasised movement and contrasts of mood, and if this style clashed with the old-fashioned approach of some prima donnas there would be unintentioned humor—but not mere "Hollywood mannerisms". Ruth Chamlee recalled one night when she was in the audience and saw Tibbett and Jeritza clash violently over stage positions, with much clawing and kicking. Jeritza was the "star", but Tibbett was the actor.

ACKNOWLEDGMENTS

This article would have been impossible without the encouragement, advice and help provided by the following, and I am indebted to them for the information provided about all aspects of Tibbett's life and career: Mary Ellis Peltz and the staff of the Metropolitan Archives; Mrs. Susan R. Waddington (Head, Art and Music Department, Providence Public Library); R. Jayne Craven (Head, Art and Music Department, Public Library of Cincinnati and Hamilton County); Harriet Ranney (Music Librarian, Free Public Library of Philadelphia); the staff of the Music Department of the Performing Arts (in Lincoln Center, New York City); Alfred V. Frankenstein; Robert Lawrence; Winthrop Sargeant; the late Vincent Sheean: Virgil Thomson; Elinor Remick Warren; Ruth Chamlee; Frederick Jagel: Alexander Kipnis; the late Lotte Lehmann; Rosa Ponselle; Martial Singher; Blanche Witherspoon; J. A. Hamilton; W. R. Moran; Richard M. Tibbett; Francis Robinson; and James Dennis and Charles Baldwin of *The Record Collector*.

PART 2
Lawrence Tibbett: The Glory Road

The Glory Road

by

Lawrence Tibbett

PRIVATELY PRINTED, 1933. COPYRIGHT BY THE CROWELL PUBLISHING COMPANY. PUBLISHED BY PERMISSION AMERICAN MAGAZINE. PRINTED BY E. L. HILDRETH & COMPANY, INCORPORATED BRATTLEBORO, VERMONT.

I

ALONG THE GLORY ROAD

It seems to me that I have been unusually fortunate in having in my short but turbulent and hilarious and hysterical life a great number of moments that gave me real cause for rejoicing.

There was the night at the Metropolitan Opera House in New York when I sang Ford to Scotti's Falstaff, and the next morning awoke to find, for the first time, reporters and photographers and news-reel men at my door. There was the recent première of *The Emperor Jones* and there was the first night of *The Rogue Song,* a motion picture which the forecasters had predicted would be a very sour can of colored film and which I guessed would be worse—but which proved to be pretty good, after all.

But none of those moments compare in importance to one in Los Angeles when I was twenty-five years old. This was the turning point in my life.

I was just another hammy singer and didn't know it. In five minutes Basil Ruysdael, huge, hearty, blunt, with a torrid vocabulary, changed my entire point of view toward music. He made an honest baritone out of me.

He taught me to pronounce "wind"—the wind that blows.

Ruysdael, now a radio announcer, had been a successful basso at the Metropolitan Opera House and had come to Los Angeles to teach singing. He was engaged by the California Opera Company to play the bass lead in a production of *The Mikado,* and I went to the theater where he was appearing to find out if I couldn't get a job in the show.

I had been singing in movie theaters and in churches and thought I was something very high-class. In choir lofts when I sang solo I threw back my head and sang with eyes half closed and fixed upon my music, which I held parallel to the floor, at shoulder height, with arms extended. I was oozing Culture, Elegance, and Art.

Ruysdael, I knew, was a fine artist. I was determined to show him that even in Los Angeles there was at least one singer who had a true appreciation of the classics.

For my tryout I sang a love song, in my most elegant manner. It was about the wafting of the south wind, the frisking lambs, and God's own out-of-doors. I expected that it would knock Ruysdael over, but when I finished and turned to look at him he was still in a perpendicular position. He stepped up to me, put his fists on his hips, fixed a cold eye upon me, and said, "Listen, fellow, what is this south 'wined' that seems to be blowing out here in California?"

"Why, why—" I was flabbergasted. "Wined? Why, you know—wind."

"Uh, huh. What kind of language is this you're talking? What's this 'ahn-da' and 'lahm' and 'lo-va' and 'kees' and 'Gawd'?"

"Well, er," I tried to explain. "You know how it is—when you sing you pronounce a little differently."

"Why?" he demanded bluntly.

"Well, if you don't know, Mr. Ruysdael," I said hopelessly, "a big Metropolitan star like you—if you don't know, I can't explain. It's just that in high-class singing you say 'ahn-da' instead of 'and,' and 'lahm' instead of 'lamb.' I never heard a singer say 'win-d.' It's always 'wined.' "

I shall not attempt to record here the volcanic comment that my statement inspired. Women fled from the theater, one hand over one ear. Men trembled. My knees were shaking.

Finally Ruysdael calmed down and almost crushed my shoulder in his huge hand.

"Look here, fellow," he said. "Singing is just speaking words to music. Try that song again. Sing it as you would tell me about it if we were sitting together at lunch— just speak the words on the tune."

It was the best singing advice I ever had. It had never occurred to me that the best singing is the most natural singing.

I tried again, and for the first time in my life sang "win-d" instead of "wined," and pronounced naturally "love" and "God" and "kiss." When I finished I felt as stimulated as though I had taken a cold shower. The sham and the strut that I had believed to be a necessary part of Cultured music were wiped right out of my technique. It was a tremendous relief to find out that it was all right for a singer to be himself.

"That's better," Ruysdael said, when I had finished. "You ought to be able to do Pish Tush. You have a very fine voice and I'd like to help you. But listen," he warned me, "if you ever go arty on me, I'll break your neck."

As far as I know, from that time until this, I have never gone arty. I have had a few bad moments, however, with music committees in one or two churches. It seems that it is more reverent when you mispronounce words.

I am indebted to many teachers and conductors and coaches, but Ruysdael's instruction was the most important of all because he caught me in the formative

48

34. Tibbett as Yegor and Florence Lake as Nadja in the film *The Rogue Song*. From the Editor's collection.

35. Tibbett warming up in his dressing room before a concert. From the Editor's collection.

LAWRENCE TIBBETT—Metro Goldwyn-Mayer

36. An early publicity photo for Metro-Goldwyn-Mayer. From the Editor's collection.

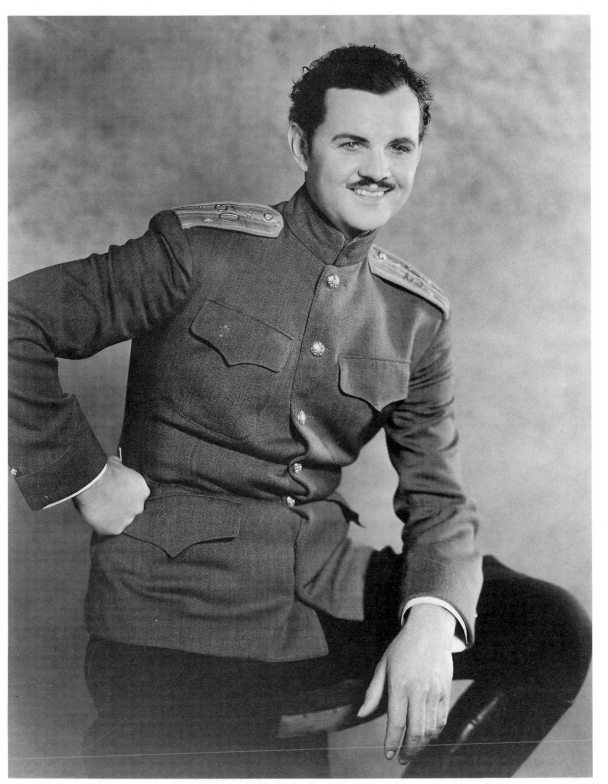

37. **Tibbett as Lt. Michael Petroff in the MGM film** *New Moon.* **It was first shown in New York on 23 December 1930. From the Editor's collection.**

38. NBC photo of a debonair Tibbett in his third consecutive season on *The Voice of Firestone* nationwide radio broadcast of the NBC-WEAF network. Tibbett alternated with his colleague from the Metropolitan, Richard Crooks, on the Monday night recitals. From the Editor's collection.

39. Tibbett as Scarpia in *Tosca*.
From the Editor's collection.

40. Tibbett in his
apartment at The
Carlton in Washington
while on tour with the
Metropolitan. The
photograph is dated 17
April 1931. Photo:
Underwood & Under-
wood. From the
Editor's collection.

41. Tibbett and Jimmy Durante perform an impromptu duet during rehearsals for his new picture *The Cuban Love Song*, in September 1931. From the Editor's collection

42. Lawrence Tibbett in 1931. Photo: Acme Newspictures, Inc. From the Editor's collection.

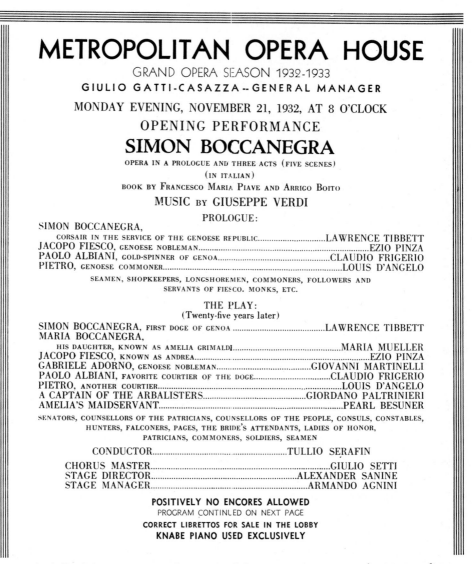

METROPOLITAN OPERA HOUSE

GRAND OPERA SEASON 1932-1933

GIULIO GATTI-CASAZZA -- GENERAL MANAGER

MONDAY EVENING, NOVEMBER 21, 1932, AT 8 O'CLOCK

OPENING PERFORMANCE

SIMON BOCCANEGRA

OPERA IN A PROLOGUE AND THREE ACTS (FIVE SCENES)

(IN ITALIAN)

BOOK BY FRANCESCO MARIA PIAVE AND ARRIGO BOITO

MUSIC BY GIUSEPPE VERDI

PROLOGUE:

SIMON BOCCANEGRA,
CORSAIR IN THE SERVICE OF THE GENOESE REPUBLIC............................LAWRENCE TIBBETT
JACOPO FIESCO, GENOESE NOBLEMAN...EZIO PINZA
PAOLO ALBIANI, GOLD-SPINNER OF GENOA...CLAUDIO FRIGERIO
PIETRO, GENOESE COMMONER...LOUIS D'ANGELO

SEAMEN, SHOPKEEPERS, LONGSHOREMEN, COMMONERS, FOLLOWERS AND
SERVANTS OF FIESCO. MONKS, ETC.

THE PLAY:
(Twenty-five years later)

SIMON BOCCANEGRA, FIRST DOGE OF GENOA ....LAWRENCE TIBBETT
MARIA BOCCANEGRA,
HIS DAUGHTER, KNOWN AS AMELIA GRIMALDI..MARIA MUELLER
JACOPO FIESCO, KNOWN AS ANDREA..EZIO PINZA
GABRIELE ADORNO, GENOESE NOBLEMAN..GIOVANNI MARTINELLI
PAOLO ALBIANI, FAVORITE COURTIER OF THE DOGE................................CLAUDIO FRIGERIO
PIETRO, ANOTHER COURTIER...LOUIS D'ANGELO
A CAPTAIN OF THE ARBALISTERS...GIORDANO PALTRINIERI
AMELIA'S MAIDSERVANT...PEARL BESUNER

SENATORS, COUNSELLORS OF THE PATRICIANS, COUNSELLORS OF THE PEOPLE, CONSULS, CONSTABLES,
HUNTERS, FALCONERS, PAGES, THE BRIDE'S ATTENDANTS, LADIES OF HONOR,
PATRICIANS, COMMONERS, SOLDIERS, SEAMEN

CONDUCTOR...TULLIO SERAFIN

CHORUS MASTER...GIULIO SETTI
STAGE DIRECTOR..ALEXANDER SANINE
STAGE MANAGER..ARMANDO AGNINI

POSITIVELY NO ENCORES ALLOWED

PROGRAM CONTINUED ON NEXT PAGE

CORRECT LIBRETTOS FOR SALE IN THE LOBBY
KNABE PIANO USED EXCLUSIVELY

43. Playbill of the opening performance of the 1931–32 season at the Metropolitan Opera House.

44. Tibbett as the young Boccanegra in the Prologue of Verdi's *Simon Boccanegra*. Photo: Carlo Edwards. Courtesy of Metropolitan Opera Archives.

45. Tibbett in the title role of *Simon Boccanegra,* a role he first sang on 28 January 1932. Photo: Carlo Edwards. Courtesy of Metropolitan Opera Archives.

46. Tibbett as Boccanegra in the Council Chamber scene of *Simon Boccanegra* at the Metropolitan. Courtesy of Metropolitan Opera Archives.

47. Tibbett in the third act of *Simon Boccanegra*. Courtesy of Kurt Binar.

48. Another role and another world première: Brutus Jones in Gruenberg's *Emperor Jones*, first performed on 7 January 1933. From the Editor's collection.

49. Tibbett as Brutus Jones in the *Emperor Jones*. Photo: Carlo Edwards. From the Editor's collection.

50. Curtain call after the world première performance of *Merry Mount* by Howard Hanson, 10 February 1934. L. to r.: chorus director Giulio Setti; librettist Richard L. Stokes, composer Howard Hanson, stage director Wilhelm von Wymetal, conductor Tullio Serafin; Lawrence Tibbett as Wrestling Bradford; soprano Göta Ljunberg, dancer Rita De Leporte, ballet director Rosina Galli (the second Mrs. Giulio Gatti-Casazza), tenor Edward Johnson. Photo: Wide World Photos. From the Editor's collection.

51. Lawrence Tibbett, 1 September 1934. Photo: The New York Times Studio. From the Editor's collection.

period when I was about to build pompous-singer habits that might have lasted the remainder of my life. Later, Frank La Forge was to give me the push that put me into the Metropolitan Opera Company. He sent me from third base to home. But Basil Ruysdael put me on first.

After *The Mikado,* I sang in *The Fortune Teller* with him, and in another operetta, the name of which just now escapes me—the one with the "Sympathy" waltz in it.

Ruysdael charged $10 an hour for lessons, but when he found I had no money he taught me for nothing. He was a rough teacher. One of his stunts was to steal up, when I was singing, and yell, "Loosen up!" and give me a clout on the back that would almost knock me to my knees. I'd have to keep on singing no matter what he did to me. He would grab my jaw and shake it from side to side and abuse me roundly if, under such manhandling, I missed a note. As I sang *On the Road to Mandalay* he would make me lie face down on the floor, roll over, get up, and climb on a chair and jump down—and all the time he would be jabbing me in the ribs with his fist and shouting, "Relax! Relax!"

Many years later, at the Bohemian Grove, near San Francisco, I sang a rôle that called for a dramatic baritone solo as I trudged up a steep hill in the redwoods, and the newspapers said it was a remarkable feat. In *Emperor Jones* I sing as I roll on the ground, which acrobatic performance has called forth high praise. If the critics think *that* is good, they should have seen me in Ruysdael's studio lying on my back with my arms outstretched and my feet in the air, singing *I Love You Truly* and getting a touch of Ruysdael's boot every time I tightened up!

I had believed that I had a small voice, but he opened it, giving me power through relaxation. As a golf player gets a longer drive with a relaxed swing, so did I obtain more volume when I didn't try so hard.

The late Joseph Dupuy, one of the best tenors in southern California, had been my first teacher and was of inestimable service and encouragement to me. He was the first musician to tell me that some day I would be a fine singer. That I didn't get even more out of Dupuy was probably my own fault. He was too kind to me and I was lazy. I didn't like to sing those nerve-racking exercises—staccatos, legatos, scales, and cadenzas—that drive honest citizens wild on a summer night when they have a young singer in their neighborhood. I'll work night and day on a tune that means something, but I loaf on the exercises.

I am thirty-six years old, and as I look back it seems that whatever success has come to me has been a result of good luck and generous and patient friends. I was lucky in being born with a good voice, but that alone wasn't enough to carry me through. Added to the voice, thank God, was a passionate love of music, and my enthusiasm, instead of waning with accomplishment, increased year by year. I would rather sing than do anything else on earth.

In this good world are many gracious persons who believe that a good voice is a thing to be cultivated and nourished and who, with sympathy almost unbelievable, over and over again put new strength into my backbone and by lending me money and giving me their services cleared away the jungle that so often blocked my path.

It would be a silly affectation for me to pretend that I let Nature and my friends do all the work. At times I crawled on bloody hands and knees toward my goal; I slaved, I sacrificed, I fought, and died a hundred deaths. But for that I deserve not one cheer. Hundreds of thousands of men have struggled harder than I to achieve an ambition and every one of them has suffered more than I—for I did not suffer at all. I had a magnificent time.

It was a sporting adventure, and I think I am the most fortunate man I ever heard of, because I am making a living by *singing*! Just *singing*!

I am still astonished at my good fortune, for the ghosts of my conservative ancestors tell me that people achieve happiness only through hard work and that hard work is something which nobody likes to do. I feel a little as though I were a shopgirl who had been given a job paying a great deal of money, and her only duties were to go to the movies and chew gum. There must be a trick somewhere.

I do not pretend to understand the psychology that causes people to be so very kind to youngsters who seem to be qualified to become good singers. Potentially great actors, artists, scientists, doctors, architects, writers, statesmen do not receive nearly as much practical encouragement as is given to a young singer. It is quite unfair. But, for singers, it is very pleasant.

The first time I was helped out of a tight place was at a Methodist Church social in Bakersfield, Calif. I was six years old and on the program to sing a soprano solo—*Jesus Wants Me for a Sunbeam.* I was to sing without accompaniment, for in those days when I sang I just went ahead and sang, disregarding pitch and tempo, and no pianist living could transpose fast enough to get his notes into step with mine.

I faced the vast audience of 35 or 40 people and instantly forgot the words and music.

My mother was sitting in the front row, only a few feet away. She leaned over and whispered a cue, but I was too frightened to understand. She tried again. I shook my head helplessly and tears came to my eyes. The audience began to snicker.

A bit angry and disgusted with her stupid son my mother leaned forward and said, hopelessly, "Well, try *The Star-Spangled Banner.*"

With new lift I burst out with "Oh-oh say, can you see-ee!" The audience rose, joined in the singing, and, when we all finished, applauded with the gusto that people seem to believe should reward even the worst singer of a patriotic song. My début was a great success, thanks to my mother and the Grand Old Flag.

Many times since then I have wished that I were back in the Bakersfield Methodist Church, where I could extricate myself from an embarrassing situation by a device as simple as the singing of *The Star-Spangled Banner.*

For instance, there was my first appearance in *The Jest** at the Metropolitan Opera House in the spring of 1926, my third season there. The first three performances had been sung by Madame Frances Alda, Titta Ruffo, and Beniamino Gigli. Gigli sang the part that John Barrymore created on the stage and Ruffo sang Lionel Barrymore's.

Ruffo went to South America and I was given his rôle. It was my first leading part at the Metropolitan and of enormous importance to me. My only success up to that time had been as Ford in *Falstaff,* and the feeling was getting around the Met that I was a one-part singer—the most damning tag that can be put on a man. Once the powers-that-be get that idea into their heads, you're through.

This was a great acting rôle as well as a singing rôle—a ruthless, powerful, murdering, brutal, jealous lover was Neri—and I decided that here was my opportunity to deliver the dramatic goods.

Madame Alda was the wife of Gatti-Casazza (behind his back we call him "The

*Title in Italian: *La Cena delle Beffe.*

50

General''), the Master of the Metropolitan. Madame Alda was a power, too, a very great power, indeed. She helped me tremendously when I was trying to get into the Metropolitan, but now we were no longer friends because I had decided to try concert work alone, instead of going on tour with her quartet.

I was just an American youngster thrown into a cast with great artists—one of them the wife of the great Gatti-Casazza—and according to all rules and regulations I should have been content just to go along for the ride and not to attempt any driving on my own part.

But I was young and headstrong and ambitious. My Neri tore furiously through back-stage tradition. The author had written me rough, and, believe me, I was rough—in spite of Alda's angry protests, hissed between arias.

She was playing the part of my faithless mistress and, according to the story, I was supposed to fly at her in a jealous rage. Momentarily living the part, I lost my head. I struggled with her and threw her from me—and, *kerplunk,* flat on her back in the middle of the stage, feet flying, lay the outraged form of Madame Gatti-Casazza! My boss's wife!

"Oof!" she said. That was all she said then, but what she said at the end of the act was plenty!

I apologized profusely. I was terrified. Perhaps this might mean the finish of everything for me!

That wasn't the end of my troubles. In the last act I was supposed to push her violently off-stage, through a door. In my nervousness I pushed her too soon, and a man who was standing off-stage, waiting to catch her, missed Madame Alda completely and down she went again!

After that all went black. I must have gone satisfactorily through the motions for the remainder of the opera, for the newspapers the next day were very kind. But after Madame Alda took her second sprawling fall I remembered nothing until a friend came into my dressing-room and found me staring blankly into the mirror.

"What do you think this is, Fourth of July?" he asked.

I had been singing *The Star-Spangled Banner.*

I was desolate. The betting was 10 to 1 that Madame Alda would have me thrown out of the Metropolitan Opera House in revenge for her outraged dignity and bruised upholstery. It didn't help a bit when I heard someone—I think it was Gigli—go past my dressing-room humming Chopin's *Funeral March.*

But, except for the fact that Madame Alda refused to speak to me, business continued as usual. Ordinary business, that is. The special acrobatic stage business that my too-realistic portrayal had injected into the production was omitted from then on.

A few months later the opera company was in Atlanta, Ga., and after a performance of *The Jest* a party was given for us. It was a gay party, toasts were drunk, and finally some Atlanta Sir Walter Raleigh proposed that in order to prove our tremendous admiration for Madame Alda, we men should all file past her and each reward her with a kiss. I found myself in line, not knowing just what would happen when it came my turn to kiss a lady who loathed me.

"Well," I said when I reached her, "this is just as embarrassing for me as it is for you. Shall we make up?"

"Of course," she laughed, and I kissed her.

I am a loyal native of southern California, but I must admit that the climate of

Atlanta has its moments. If it could so warm and soften Alda's heart toward me, probably Al Capone will emerge from the Atlanta penitentiary a benign, tender, and forgiving citizen!

In Cleveland a few years later Maria Jeritza and I had a battle on the stage, somewhat similar to the one I had in *The Jest* with Alda—only this was no accident. We were giving *Tosca,* and I was singing Scarpia.

Jeritza had a trick of changing stage business to suit herself. In the last scene Scarpia attacks Tosca and she falls to the floor. From that position she sings her aria. That was the way we had rehearsed it. But this time Jeritza wanted to sing from the far side of the stage, where she would be alone in the spotlight.

As I held her, she whispered, "Let me go! Let me go!"

I hung on, at first not understanding. Before the act began she had said to me, "This is our last performance. Let's make it a good one. Let's go after each other!" So now when she pounded and pushed me I thought she was acting.

When I realized what she wanted to do, I stubbornly decided that there would be a dead Tibbett on the stage before she took over the entire scene for herself.

We fought like wildcats. Following the stage directions, I tried to kiss her on her shoulders. She lunged at me, and the sequins on her dress made deep cuts in my chin. I pulled her hair and she pulled mine. She just wouldn't fall. I wore a heavy brass chain around my neck and she yanked it and broke it, cutting the flesh as the links parted. Neither of us could sing. We just muttered and gasped. Both of us had lost our heads. Jeritza was determined that she would get to the other side of the stage. I made up my mind that she would sing at my feet. I managed to get a hold that was a mixture of hammer lock and half nelson, and I threw her on a couch. She gasped, rolled to the floor—and sang! I had won the wrestling match!

When the act ended we looked like a couple of stray cats. The applause was tremendous. We took our bows and I got ready to weather a volley of invective.

The audience was still applauding when we started toward our dressing-rooms. She looked at me, smoothed her hair, and smiled.

"Well," she said, "we gave them their money's worth."

You never can tell which way opera temperament is going to jump.

I think it was a subconscious spirit of revolt against any surrender to special privilege or knee-bending to monarchs that made me behave not at all like a polite, self-effacing gentleman in the scenes with Alda and Jeritza.

When I was a kid in Manual Arts High School in Los Angeles, I discovered Karl Marx and Robert Ingersoll and Emma Goldman and Tolstoy, and tried to follow them all at one and the same time. Later my radicalism became diluted with common sense, but I am still a nonconformist.

I lost my first great crusade—because my high-school principal was a true diplomat.

I organized a revolt against neckties on hot days, and a dozen of us appeared in school with shirts open almost to our waists. The principal sent us home and told us not to come back until we were fully dressed. I stayed out for two days, determined to give up an education before I would surrender to convention. Then the principal sent for me. The other boys had dressed up and returned to school.

If the principal had used honest argument, if he had threatened dire consequences, I would have resisted until the end—or at least, until my mother took a militant hand in the proceedings. But he played a dirty trick on me. He just said, "With your scrawny neck, Tibbett, and your funny face, you look like a giraffe. Why don't you cover up that Adam's apple and try to look halfway like a human being?"

Humiliated, I went home and put on a tie.

Nothing, however, has been able to temper my radical ideas about music, for no one has ever convinced me that they are radical at all—they're just common sense. From the day I learned to pronounce "wind" and to sing "have" instead of "haw-vuh" I have fought against the hokum that surrounds my profession.

To me, art is good art when it produces a worthy emotion, and if you are charmed by Rudy Vallee's rendition of *I'm Just a Vagabond Lover,* I shall not quarrel with you. The only person I want exterminated are those who don't like any music of any kind.

All classical music is not good and all popular music is not bad, and the only way to judge singers and songs is to decide whether they do well the job they set out to perform.

I like Rudy Vallee's singing. I think he is the best of the crooners. I admire Al Jolson. The expert Harmony of the Duncan Sisters, singing *Remembering* in *Topsy and Eva,* moved me tremendously, and certainly was a more important contribution to art than the efforts of a mediocre pair of opera singers whom I heard a few nights later doing their best with the love duet in *Tristan und Isolde.*

There are singers of classical songs who have no little prestige but who leave their audiences utterly cold. Some of the patrons of the Metropolitan Opera Company would consider it sacrilege to mention Jolson and Vallee in the same breath with these inadequate operatic performers, but to me Jolson singing *Sonny Boy* is more truly a real artist than these near-greats ever have been or ever will be.

At the peak of all music I place the best operatic artists and the best classical music. But in my home, mixed with my most highly prized phonograph recordings of operatic masterpieces sung by Caruso and Amato, I have Paul Whiteman's orchestra, playing *When Day is Done* and *The Rhapsody in Blue;* Duke Ellington's *The Indigo Blues,* and Don Azpiazu's stirring reproduction of *The Peanut Vendor.*

When I was making *The Rogue Song* in Hollywood, every chance I got I dragged Clif Edwards (Ukulele Ike) into my dressing-room and made him play *St. Louis Blues.* Edwards has an amazing natural sense of rhythm, almost equaling that possessed by Bill Robinson, the syncopating Negro tap dancer, whose instinctive sense of rhythm is not surpassed even by that of Toscanini, the great operatic conductor.

I like all kinds of good music and I sing all kinds. I do not try to force any particular brand upon the public. If you get more pleasurable emotion when I sing Oley Speaks' *Sylvia* than when I sing Lully's somber aria, *Bois Épais,* I feel that it is no reflection on your intelligence. In fact, in many cases it is a real sign of superior mentality, because a lot of people who say they like *Bois Épais* are not intelligent at all—they're just *poseurs* and liars.

Frequently I sing *The Song of the Flea,* and every now and then, after a concert, well-meaning old ladies protest that it is quite vulgar. When I point out that the words are by Goethe and the music by Moussorgsky, they say, "Oh, that's different," and, all flustered, apologize. There's intellectual snobbery for you!

In my concerts I always sing one or two operatic numbers, because in the smaller cities the people do not get opera and they have a genuine love for the best operatic music. I do not, however, sing operatic numbers that are strange to the ears of the audience. In spite of the protests from some of my colleagues who say I am lowering myself, I sing usually either the prologue from *Pagliacci* or the toreador's song from *Carmen,* because—although I must admit I am a bit tired of them, myself—those are the two operatic numbers that are best liked by the great majority of non-professional music lovers.

I sing a few songs in French and German and Italian, because, in addition to the handful who really enjoy them, there are always a number of people in an audience who feel they have been classically cheated unless they have been given something they do not understand. They are the folks who believe that sulphur and molasses must be very good for you because it tastes so bad. So, when they hear music that gives them no sensation of pleasure whatsoever, they think it must be something of unusual merit and that, unless they applaud loudly, people will class them as ignoramuses. I like people who, when certain selections give them a pain in the neck, have the frankness to say so.

It is tradition around the Metropolitan Opera House that Caruso said people applauded his name and not his voice, and he proved it. In *Pagliacci* the Harlequin's serenade is sung off-stage by Beppe, a minor character. It brings no more than perfunctory applause. Unbeknown to the audience at the Metropolitan, at many a performance Caruso, as a joke, sang that off-stage aria, and not even the critics ever noticed that the serenade was sung in anything more than an adequate manner.

In Hollywood, at a party one evening at Charley Farrell's, we were sitting in the back yard (*patio* in Hollywood) and I was asked to sing. I stood up and improvised for five minutes, singing in an imitation of Russian—of which language I know not even one word. I sobbed, I laughed, I waved my arms, making up music and words as I went along. Finally I stopped, exhausted by my emotions.

They cheered and applauded like mad—Farrell, Virginia Valli, Paul Bern, Janet Gaynor, Robert Montgomery, Mr. and Mrs. Leslie Howard, and a dozen others.

"What is that?" they asked. "It's magnificent!"

"An operatic number by the Russian composer, Kovlikoffoskowsky," I said, inventing a name.

"Beautiful!" they said.

It was not good music, because I am not a composer. And the words, of course, meant nothing.

An exotic movie actress, reputed to have been a member of the Russian nobility, grasped both my hands.

"Eet ees tremen-*dous*!" she cried. "My fav-rit aria!"

I nodded, "My Russian pronunciation isn't very good, though," I said.

"You are too mo-*dest*," she insisted. "I understood av-ry word!"

I let it go at that.

Perhaps the most popular tune ever written is Carrie Jacobs Bond's *A Perfect Day.* The fact that you may be sick and tired of it makes it no less a great song. I think the words are maudlin, but the music has real merit. Had it been trash, it would not have lived.

I had a long argument about it with Paul Gallico, a concert pianist and father of Paul Gallico, a New York sports writer. He had told me that my artistic standards were low because I sang Ethelbert Nevin's *Oh, That We Two Were Maying.* I knew it was a good song because it always made me weep—which is all I need to know about a song. When I told him what I thought about *A Perfect Day* he had a fit.

A year later I heard him play a Schumann sonata. This sonata begins with a strain that is definitely like the first phrases of *A Perfect Day*. If one was the work of genius, so was the other.

I pointed out to Gallico the parallel and sang the two tunes to him.

"The trouble with you," I said, "is that you've read books in an effort to learn what you ought to like, instead of letting your own emotions and common sense do the judging."

He stuttered, scratched his head, and walked away.

As far as I can remember that's the only argument I ever won from a classical musician about *A Perfect Day*. But I'm still trying.

There is no reason why we should be apologetic about our American music.

Take *The Glory Road,* a Negro spiritual written by Jacques Wolfe, a music teacher in the public schools of Brooklyn, N.Y., who is no more a Southerner than was General Grant. I believe *The Glory Road* is just as fine a musical composition as Leoncavallo's prelude to *Pagliacci*. We have a number of popular patter songs that are as good as *La donna è mobile* from *Rigoletto*—Vincent Youmans' *Hallelujah,* for example.

We are leading the world in popular compositions. Jerome Kern's *Ol' Man River,* Youmans' *Without a Song,* and George Gershwin's *Rhapsody in Blue* equal anything ever written by the Viennese composers of operettas past and present, and surpass in real emotional musical quality half of the arias of standard operatic composers whose works are the backbone of every Metropolitan season.

Of course, we are producing a lot of rot. Tunes are being stolen and imitated. Generally our lyrics are gosh-awful. But the amount of good stuff is astounding.

The history of great music in all nations is that good popular music preceded good classical music. We are building a sound foundation, and one of these days Americans will be turning out operas that will live just as long as *Carmen* or *Tosca* or *Faust* or *Tristan und Isolde*.

We probably would be doing it now, were it not for the fact that composers and librettists have to eat, and the only real financial encouragement they receive comes from musical comedy and from the movies. The system of payment for the work of American operatic composers is murderous to genius. For instance, I doubt that Edna St. Vincent Millay and Deems Taylor in a lifetime will make as much money out of their splendid opera, *The King's Henchman,* as the authors of *Yes, We Have No Bananas* made during the first month the song was on sale.

Victor Herbert wrote *Natoma,* a fairly good grand opera, and could have turned out, I am sure, an operatic score of high rank and lasting quality if he had been willing for a year or two to give up the theater—which he loved and which made him rich and famous—and slave for the opera, which looked upon his genius with neither sympathy nor understanding.

If the millions of persons in America who are interested in better music could only be square with themselves they would encourage honest thinking and expression throughout the world of music. Impresarios, conductors, singers, musicians, composers, and librettists generally cannot express themselves naturally because, the moment they do, influential patrons inhibited by their confounded hokum complexes, unable to relax and to be on the level, will shake their heads and say, "Well, yes. I think I like it. But is it art?"

What nonsense!

The greatest music is that which thrills you most, and no one was ever really thrilled by sham and bombast and pretense.

I have heard magnificent symphony orchestras that left me weak in my chair, famous singers who raised my blood pressure almost to the point of apoplexy, mighty choruses that intoxicated me more than my first bottle of champagne, but I have never been so shaken emotionally as I was a few months ago by 1,500 Negro children singing in a high school auditorium in Birmingham, Ala.

They sang *Standin' in the Need of Prayer* and other spirituals, under the direction of an untrained Negro who knew none of the tricks, none of the "methods," who just believed that the way to sing was to throw yourself naturally into it and sing!

I was wrecked for the remainder of the day, and that night I gave one of the best concerts of my career because, from beginning to end, through classical selections and popular ones, I was inspired by the freedom and simplicity of those children.

They sang parts perfectly, with harmony as sure as that of a great pipe organ. I never heard such precision of attack, never such sheer vitality of tone. You could understand every word uttered by those 1,500 voices. Often at the Metropolitan Opera House, with only four persons singing at the same time, you can't catch a single phrase.

Those children sang for the joy of singing—just opened their throats and let go.

I was tingling all over. Shots of electricity went up and down my spine. My voice choked so that I couldn't speak. Tears ran down my cheeks.

Seldom at the Metropolitan, or at Carnegie Hall, have I found musical perfection, but certainly I found it in the auditorium of a Negro high school in Birmingham, where girls and boys sang superbly because they sang honestly.

If one of the patrons of the Metropolitan Opera had been standing there beside me and at the end had said, "Well, yes, I think I like it. But is it art?" I swear by all the gods that be, I would have killed him.

II

THEN ALONG CAME TWINS

I got my first important job as a singer, not particularly on account of my voice, but because I looked more like Charles Ray, the movie star, than did any of the eight other applicants.

It was at Grauman's Million Dollar movie theater in Los Angeles, which had just opened, and the show for the second week was a Charles Ray picture, the name of which I have forgotten. It was something about a blacksmith. Sid Grauman reproduced in a prologue a scene from the picture, and I was made up as a blacksmith and, accompanied by clanging anvils, sang a song in which I announced that shoeing horses was a very enviable life indeed.

I did so well that Grauman kept me for fifteen weeks, at $50 a week. The spick-and-span theater was equipped with all the latest gimcracks, including a huge orchestra platform that emerged from the pit on an elevator—the first one in the world, Sid said.

After the theater had been open two weeks, Grauman conceived a revolutionary idea in stagecraft. I rose out of the cellar with the orchestra, with the spotlight on me, singing *At Dawning*. I was supposed to be the sun, I believe, and in the darkened theater the house lights in rainbow colors crept up until they blazed forth in an effect that Sid said was just like the aurora borealis, only better. Larks sang and roosters crowed, and it certainly was something swell.

Sid said history was being made and that I should be very proud because I was the first singer in the world to be lifted out of an orchestra pit on an elevator. I *was* proud, too, although I still don't understand why he thought I looked like the sun. I wore a dress suit that had been given me by a high-school friend. It had belonged to his father, who had bought a new one after he discovered that the tailor had made a little mistake and had sold him a coat and trousers of two different kinds of broadcloth. No one ever seemed to notice the difference in material and I got by with that dress suit for years—until after my first year at the Metropolitan.

I lost my job when Grauman booked *The Golem*, a picture with Jewish atmosphere, and I failed utterly in my attempt to sing *Eili, Eili*, the Jewish lament. I never had heard it sung and delivered it rather coldly, not knowing much what the Hebrew words were about. Sid said I was terrible and hired a Jewish song plugger who put a moan into it and, he told me later, laid the audience sobbing in the aisles.

I was a struggling young husband, and that $50 a week had helped the Tibbett family get along rather well, although the birth of twins and resultant doctor's bills cut deep into the family fortune. The expenses would have been greater had it not been for the inspirational logic of my wife.

She had a woman doctor who had agreed on a price for the delivery. When twins came, the doctor sent a bill for double the amount, but my wife insisted that it was all one job and should be performed for one price, and I never did pay the added assessment.

Our first home was a cottage on the side of a hill in a vineyard at La Crescenta, fifteen miles from Los Angeles. The rent was $12.50 a month, and the landlord allowed us to eat all the grapes we wanted. There were times when we lived on grapes, and, strangely enough, I still like them. Our landlord also let me gather firewood from his property—you may have heard from the Los Angeles Chamber of Commerce that the nights are always cold—and once when I was $75 behind in my rent he let me pay out by working in the vineyard.

We thought our home was a mansion, but perhaps we were not good judges of mansions. I rented a piano for $5 a month, and when the men brought it I told them to put it in the living-room, which was on stilts, extending out over the side of the hill. They took one look at the stilts and said they wouldn't risk their piano on such insecure footing. They were afraid it would fall through the floor and roll down the hill. So we put it in the bedroom, which rested on solid ground.

Since I never had known anything about luxury, I was well content to struggle along in what, as I look back, seems to have been at times very close to real poverty.

The earliest days of my life were spent in Bakersfield, Calif., which then was a tiny, raw, tough town in the center of a farming community. Later, with the arrival of the oil boom, it was destined to become a prosperous city, but unfortunately the Tibbett family had no share in that prosperity, for, by the time Bakersfield's oil was flowing freely, we had moved away.

57

Had we remained we might have become rich, like many of our neighbors, and it would not have been necessary for me, later, to borrow nearly $8,000, which, added to the money I was able to earn with my voice, plus contributions of generous patrons, was the cost of turning me into a self-supporting singer.

We lived in a frame cottage at 716 K Street, on the edge of Bakersfield—my parents, my two brothers, my sister, and myself. I was the youngest.

My parents and my uncles and aunts—with the exception of Uncle Ed—were strict Methodists. I was taught to believe that dancing, smoking, drinking, card playing, and the theater were instruments of the devil. I don't remember how the family justified Uncle Ed, who kept Bakersfield's leading saloon. As far as I can remember nobody looked upon him with disapproval. He was a gay, witty fellow and always welcome to the family councils.

I am sure that, had my father lived, he would have opposed my ambition to get into the theater. Some time after he died my mother confessed apprehensively that she really thought the theater was a delightful place to go. My mother wanted me to become a physician, but when she found I was interested only in the stage, with the enthusiastic cooperation of my sister, Betty Lee, she helped me have my own way.

My mother sang in the Methodist church choir in Bakersfield and it was she who first taught me to sing. We were all interested in music. My sister played the piano, my brother Jesse played the mandolin, and my brother Ernest sang very well.

My father was a God-fearing man with a large blond mustache, who believed in strict law and order. It was a family of law enforcers. Even Uncle Ed now and then stepped from behind his bar and joined a posse in pursuit of an outlaw. My Uncle George at one time was sheriff of Kern County, in which Bakersfield is situated, and Uncle Bert—now a detective in Bakersfield—was a deputy sheriff. My father, in his early life a farmer, was later deputy sheriff, then sheriff, and for several years a range rider for the Kern County Land Company, guarding fences and chasing rustlers. He was a dead shot, a splendid horseman, and had killed two cattle thieves.

We had horses and chickens and cows, a setter dog named "Mart" and a blood-hound named "Rod." The bloodhound was a highly bred man-hunter which lived in canine luxury and was ready at any moment to start on the trail of a fugitive. We kids were never allowed to play with him for fear it might soften his reputedly brutal nature. Whenever my father took him out, Rod would sniff the scent, dig all four feet into the ground, tug eagerly at the leash, and bay furiously, with eyes afire.

My father, dragged behind, would wave an arm and shout ominously, "Rod's got him this time!"

But invariably Rod would lead the heavily armed posse to the feet of some innocent-eyed cow or to a coyote den under a pile of brush. That bloodhound promised more and delivered less than any animal I ever saw. He would have made an ideal bond salesman, I'm sure.

Of course my father was my hero, and when we kids played "sheriff and rustlers" in the back yard, I was always the sheriff. I gained the honor without contest for the other boys wanted to be Jim McKinney, an outlaw whose name was a more dreadful phrase in Bakersfield than Billy the Kid's in New Mexico and Arizona. Jim McKinney had killed four men in cold blood.

One day, when I was seven years old, our gang was playing in the back yard, camping out—roasting potatoes and getting ready for a battle.

I saw a man drive up in a buggy. He entered the house, and a moment later hurried out with my mother and they drove rapidly toward town. I gave it little thought for I had important work to do—there were "rustlers" hiding back of the barn and "Sheriff" Lawrence Tibbett had to shine up his wooden gun.

Suddenly an older boy came running up the dusty road, leaped the fence, and yelled at me, "Hey, Larry, Jim McKinney just killed your father!"

At first I thought it was a joke, part of a game.

"Honest!" the boy insisted, all out of breath. "Cross my heart and hope to die! In the Chinese joss house! Your father went after Jim, and Jim got him! They carried him to Baer's drug store! I seen him!"

The emotions of boys are unfathomable. I cannot explain the apparent lack of grief with which I met the announcement. I never have been able to understand why I was not at once crushed. But I did not feel at all like crying. I was only very, very proud. Perhaps a psychoanalyst can explain my pride. I cannot. It was not until that evening that I realized my loss.

McKinney had been ordered out of Bakersfield a few days before, and my father had enforced the order. He got the drop on McKinney, and the bandit, humiliated, galloped away with bullets from my father's six-shooter kicking up the dust behind him.

To show contempt, McKinney promptly robbed a stage near Bakersfield, and my father headed a posse sent out to get him. They chased him through the mountains and found that McKinney had circled back to Bakersfield to see his sweetheart.

Father led the posse into the Chinese joss house where McKinney was hiding. Father was too brave and too reluctant to kill. Instead of shooting on sight, he ordered McKinney to come out. McKinney killed my father with a shotgun and killed Jeff Packard, the sheriff, who came to my father's rescue. But my Uncle Bert got Jim McKinney, with a shot right between the eyes.

A few years ago I was cast to sing Jack Rance, the sheriff, in a revival of *The Girl of the Golden West* at the Metropolitan Opera House in New York. This was the part sung by Amato when the opera was first produced in 1910. Caruso and Emmy Destinn were in the original cast.

In the revival Martinelli sang the tenor rôle and Jeritza sang Minnie.

Puccini's opera is beautifully done, but, after all, it is an Italian's conception of the Wild West, and the music is by no means Western in manner or feeling. A German director was staging the revival at the Metropolitan and the cowboys didn't act like any cowboys I had ever seen—either around Bakersfield or on my uncle's ranch in the Tejon Mountains, where, as a youngster, I had done some cow-punching myself. For instance, in the celebration at the end of the opera the director had these supposedly tough cow hands throw their arms around one another and express their jubilation by kissing each other on the cheek in the best Latin manner.

In the scene where the sheriff enters the cabin, searching for Johnson, the bandit, the director told me to come in crouching, with my six-shooter held at arm's length in front of me. I obeyed, and felt more like Annette Kellerman doing the Australian crawl than I did like a sheriff.

"This will never do," I said. "The sheriff would enter standing erect, on the alert, with the gun held at his hip so he can swing it quickly to any part of the room."

"Poof!" the director said. "What does an opera singer know about sheriffs?"

I told him what I knew about sheriffs.

"Oh," he said apologetically, and shrank away from me. "Oh. Then we shall do it your way."

Upon my advice he eliminated the cowboy osculation in the last act, too, and forever after seemed to be a bit afraid of me. I believe he did not entirely understand my English. He thought I was the one who had done all the killing I had told him about, and he guessed he had better be good to me or I'd run amuck and shoot up the Metropolitan Opera House.

My father had $10,000 in life insurance, and my mother took us to Long Beach, Calif., where she tried to support the family by running a small hotel. Five years later she sold the hotel at a loss and we moved to Los Angeles. Curiously enough, like Bakersfield, Long Beach became a great oil town—after, alas, my mother had sold her property.

I was twelve years old when we left Long Beach. Kindly but inaccurate biographers have said that I helped to support the family by working as a bell boy in my mother's hotel and by selling papers. I did both, but we were not so poor that my efforts were any help. The most I ever made in one day by selling papers was 15 cents, and I was so proud of myself that I went immediately to a drug store and spent it all on a banana split.

While we were at Long Beach I was caught smoking corn silk, and my deeply religious aunts and uncles, who were visiting us, raised as much fuss as though I had kidnapped Marlene Dietrich's baby. I was so frightened that, with very few exceptions, I have never smoked from that day to this. As I grew older my mother would reinforce my principles by telling me that if I smoked I would never be a good singer; but a great many singers smoke, and their voices do not seem to suffer. Caruso and Scotti smoked constantly. Martinelli never smokes, nor do any of the women who sing at the Metropolitan.

About once a year I smoke one cigar, and get great satisfaction out of the feeling that I am doing something terribly wrong and that the devil is patting me on the back. Now and then I have sung parts in which the character had to smoke.

Jeritza and Rosa Ponselle are almost the only singers at the Metropolitan who are terribly afraid that smoke will harm their voices. In *The Girl of the Golden West* the sheriff is supposed to smoke a big cigar. Before the first performance Jeritza asked me not to smoke while she was on the stage, but I did not realize that she meant that I wasn't to smoke at all. Previous to her first entrance I had taken a few dramatic and satisfying puffs. The smoke had vanished, but she smelled it. She sniffed, glared at me, and then began coughing violently, missing her music cue, so that the orchestra had to stop. After that, I just chewed my cigar. I know when to take a hint.

My mother bought a big house at Twelfth and Figueroa Streets in Los Angeles and took in roomers. Whenever she had time to spare she went out as a practical nurse. My brothers married when they were quite young, and Betty Lee and I were the only children at home. Betty Lee taught me how to play the piano a little, taught me songs, and, when, at thirteen, I began taking piano lessons from a professional teacher she joined her threats of violence with my mother's and forced me to practice.

I learned to sing, among other things, *I Love You Truly, Just a-Wearyin' for You,* and *Sing Me to Sleep,* and at the age of fourteen I was able to stand up in the parlor and knock callers cold with my own conception of *The Rosary.*

Although I loved to sing, in my high-school days at Manual Arts in Los Angeles, my ambition was to become an actor. The movies were just beginning to get a toe hold in Hollywood, but at that time I scorned what seemed to be a trivial and transitory toy and I was not interested in lending the support of a Tibbett to those one-reel dramas that were being shown in nickelodeons. It was late in my high-school days when D. W. Griffith gave in Los Angeles the world première of *The Clansman*—later known as *The Birth of a Nation*—which sent all of us kids flocking to the studios in a futile effort to get in on the ground floor in this newly discovered art.

I was taught to take great pride in the family name. My ancestors had come to California in the gold rush of '49 and the name had never been sullied.

All my relatives spell it "Tibbet"—with one "t." A careless or disinterested proof-reader turned it into "Tibbett." That was the way it appeared on the program of the Metropolitan Opera House the night I first sang a real part—Valentine in *Faust*.

Frank La Forge, my teacher, noticed the mistake in spelling, after the performance, and said, "It looks better that way. You should keep that spelling."

I let it stand, and ever since have been "Tibbett" instead of "Tibbet."

My family protested furiously. It was sacrilege! Wasn't the name that was good enough for my forefathers good enough for me?

I shudder when I think what they would have said had I followed the advice of some of my friends, who told me in all seriousness that I could never get anywhere at the Metropolitan with an American name, and that I should change it to Lorenzo Tibbetto. Frank La Forge and Rupert Hughes, who were my ever-present friends in trouble, both reinforced my belief that if I was to succeed it should be as an American and that I should not be swayed by people who were servile to the flap-doodle of so-called European prestige.

Since I successfully snubbed that suggestion, I think I should be allowed to feed my vanity when it hungers for just one extra "t."

In 1920 in Los Angeles, I played Iago in a local production of *Othello,* and had myself listed on the program as Lawrence Mervil. Since Mervil is my middle name, my mother and sister didn't protest very much. They just thought it was silly.

I believed that "Lawrence Mervil" was something very hot—a really distinguished name for an actor. The critics praised Lawrence Mervil, and I went around with clippings in my hands pointing out that Lawrence Mervil in reality was none other than myself. People read the clippings, looked at my long neck and my thin body and my childlike face, and said "You? Iago?" and didn't believe me. So I went back to my real name.

Since I have been at the Metropolitan, I have crusaded militantly against the warped fanatics who worship all that is European in opera and who are ashamed of all that is American. I have been fortunate in that I have been able to give whatever talent I may possess in furthering the success of such fine American operas as *The King's Henchman, Peter Ibbetson,* and *The Emperor Jones.*

On the other hand I have been a party to the criminal acts of performing *in German* a story of an American Negro jazz singer, *Jonny Spielt Auf,* and, *in Italian, The Girl of the Golden West!* In the latter opera I always took secret pleasure in the fact that there were two American words that could not be translated into Italian—"whisky" and "Wells Fargo"—and when I came to one of those words I would roar it out, maliciously, double forte, till the rafters of the Metropolitan rang and the diamond necklaces in the

61

boxes shook with terror as though—I hoped—their owners had heard the bugle call of the revolution.

I was the first American male singer to rise to leading rôles at the Metropolitan without European training, and I hope I have blazed a trail that soon will become a broad highway.

Many American singers are cursed with this feeling of shame when they sing in English. I can roar out "I *love* you!" with all the passion of a Don Juan whose lady love is confined on a desert at the top of a high tower. But many American singers cannot become emotional in English. They will put their very souls into *Io t'amo, Ich liebe dich,* and *Je t'aime,* but on "I love you" they stammer like a schoolboy with his first sweetheart.

Members of our best Puritan families, with librettos in their hands, so that they cannot in any way pretend they do not understand the ribald goings on, will applaud scenes and lines, done in a foreign language, that if performed in English would bring the patrol wagon clanging to the stage door. I maintain that if an opera is vulgar in English it is vulgar in Italian, but even in Los Angeles, one of the strongholds of Puritanism, I have performed *The Jest,* which contains more sizzling lines and scenes than the ones that sent Mae West to jail. And the Best People and their débutante daughters applauded the Italian text with complete approval.

In high school I first began to realize that other boys wore better clothes than I, that they had money to spend, and that they were sought after by girls—while nobody seemed to pay any attention to me. I then appreciated, too, the sacrifices that my mother was making for me, and I tried to help out by working Saturdays and Sundays in the office of a Los Angeles newspaper, stuffing comics and magazine sections into Sunday newspapers, and counting classified ads.

I developed an inferiority complex, which at that time was a very good thing for me, because I worked furiously as a member of the glee and dramatic clubs in an effort to show the other students that I amounted to something, even though I had only one suit of clothes and couldn't afford to treat the crowd at the corner drug store.

Maude Howell, a beautiful girl, just out of Leland Stanford, came to Manual Arts as a dramatic teacher. All the kids, including myself, instantly fell in love with her, and the dramatic classes were filled to overflowing. She had real talent, and later went to New York, where she played a number of important parts in Broadway shows and then became a stage director—the first woman stage director that New York ever saw. She worked with George Arliss, and when he went into the movies he took her to Hollywood with him. She is still one of the most important members of his staff. When I made *The Prodigal* and *New Moon* in Hollywood, I borrowed her from Mr. Arliss, and she coached my acting and my dialogue.

Miss Howell gave me my first lessons in acting, taught me the importance of exact characterization, and instilled in me an ambition to do a real job on the stage. Had I not had this early training I am sure that my efforts in grand opera would have been less successful, for I have always tried to be an actor as well as a singer.

In high school I sang in the glee club and acted in a score of plays. I played Romeo and Marc Antony and was in Synge's *Riders to the Sea,* and never did learn how to pronounce the author's name.

In the glee club, Glen Meneley, now in lyceum work, was our best singer. Helen Jerome Eddy was our best actress, and after graduating went into the movies at a salary that made your head swim—$100 a week! And Phyllis Haver stepped out of school into a Mack Sennett bathing suit.

I failed to make the glee club the first year. That was my first artistic setback, for, encouraged by my friends, I had expected to be welcomed as God's gift to the Manual Arts glee club. It taught me a lesson. Never since that day have I believed in the gushing praises of my friends. I wait for the morning papers!

At that time I did not have an unusual voice. In fact, I did not develop the spark until after I was twenty-one years old—which may be a note of encouragement, or perhaps of despair, to those fathers and mothers whose children are now going about the house yodeling ambitiously.

As I look back now I often wonder why and how I ever kept at it. I was always struggling to get a part in a play or a place in a high-school concert. There was always somebody who undoubtedly was better than I. No matter how hard I tried in high school I never reached the top.

It must have been my inborn love for singing that carried me on. Certainly, not until years later did it ever occur to me that I might some day sing at the Metropolitan Opera House. Even now I am somewhat dazed by my success, and sometimes I feel that all this surely must be only temporary and that the next time I sing a high A flat my voice will shatter into a thousand pieces.

When I sit down to look in a detached manner at myself I know that it all came about merely because, with the help of others, I did what I wanted to do. And perhaps that's the secret of success.

I was in bad health when I entered high school and my mother was afraid I was tubercular. I did not have the vocal strengh necessary for good singing. I put a horizontal bar in the back yard and learned to perform big drops and little drops and to hang by my heels. I tried out for athletic teams, put the shot, wrestled, played rugby, and swam until I had the lungs of a fish peddler.

Since then I have always been in good physical condition. You can't sing powerfully throughout a performance unless you have a diaphragm like a heavyweight wrestler's. On tour I always carry a folding rowing machine with me, and every morning in my room I row—it seems to me—from New York to Albany.

One of the boys I admired most in high school was Jimmy Doolittle, who turned out to be probably the world's greatest aviator. I was a rather frail, timid boy and Jimmy was the embodiment of all I wished to be. He had a thorough contempt for most would-be actors and singers but still we were good friends. He was a good boxer—later amateur champion middle-weight of southern California—a member of the wrestling and tumbling teams and a dashing, smashing youngster who was not afraid of man, woman, devil, or professor.

Even then Jimmy was interested in aviation. We would argue militantly about whether flying was more important than singing, and I always lost the argument. Rob Wagner, the artist, writer, and moving picture director, taught art and wrestling at high school. I entered his wrestling class, in which Jimmy was the star pupil, and one afternoon tried out for the wrestling team.

Jimmy was standing at one side of the gymnasium.

"Hello, crow," I said.

"Hi, nightingale," he sniffed.

"See what Larry can do, Jimmy," said Wagner.

There was a swish, and I was flat on my back on the mat and Jimmy was walking away brushing his palms. He turned and looked at my sprawling body.

"For gosh sake, sing," he said.

The next day I transferred from Wagner's wrestling class to his art class.

I met Jimmy at Lambs' Gambol in New York a few years ago. He shook my hand and said, "I went to a concert of yours a few weeks ago just to find out."

"To find out what?"

"If that Tibbett kid that used to squawk around Manual Arts was really the same Tibbett I'd read in the papers about. I couldn't believe it. Honest, Larry, you're not nearly as bad as I thought you'd be."

Last year I found myself in trouble in Dallas. Trains were delayed by floods and I had to be in St. Louis for a concert the next evening. Jimmy happened to be in the vicinity and I called him up and asked for help. He responded instantly and, it seemed to me, had me in St. Louis in about twenty minutes.

Soon after we left the ground he yelled back at me, "Y'know, I'm glad of this chance. This is a new plane and I wanted to try it out. It's never been flown before, and a lot of people said if I tried to get 175 miles an hour out of it, the ship would fall apart." He pointed to the speed indicator. We were going 205.

Leaving school, I picked up various odd jobs, acting and singing. I was beginning to find my voice. I did very well in church choirs and at funerals. I got $335 a week, for two weeks out of the month, as a member of the cast of the Civic Repertoire Company. We had guest stars from the movies—Milton Sills, Henry Walthall, Helen Jerome Eddy, and Lionel Belmore—and I stood in awe of these masters and studied their technique as a golfer studies Bobby Jones' swing. I usually played old men with whiskers because I wasn't handsome enough to play heroes.

I had a small part in a company headed by Mr. and Mrs. Tyrone Power, who were giving a program of selected scenes from Shakespeare. After a successful week in Los Angeles, the show was to go on a long tour, but folded after one night in Pasadena. I think dear old superstitious Mr. and Mrs. Power blamed me, for in Pasadena I violated two of the most important rules laid down by actors: I whistled in my dressing-room and then went on the stage before the performance and looked through the peek-hole in the curtain and counted the house—which didn't take long.

I still whistle in my dressing-room and cannot trace any further misfortune to this idiosyncrasy, although it shocks my Italian dresser, who, in spite of all I can do, tries to ward off the hoodoo by forcing me to put on my right shoe before my left one. It seems that when bad luck is hovering around, it flees when it sees a man with his right shoe on and his left shoe off.

When the United States entered the war I joined the navy to see the world, and for nearly a year saw almost nothing but San Francisco Bay from the deck of the training ship, Iris. After four months I had been made an "instructor in seamanship," which was a very fine title for a most unimportant job. I taught the rookies how to row a boat, scrub decks, paint the ship, and tie knots. I also led a ship's quartet in the singing of rowdy songs, regarding which I was more proficient than at the art of holystoning a deck.

Eventually I managed to get a transfer to the Boylston, and was in Baltimore when the war ended. I returned to San Francisco by rail and, instead of being discharged, was sent to Vladivostok on a leaky ship named the Caderetta, heavily laden with

52. Tibbett's dashing Escamillo from the motion picture *Metropolitan*. Courtesy of
Metropolitan Opera Archives.

53. Tibbett on the Packard program for NBC, 11 December 1934. Photo: NBC Photo. From the Editor's collection.

54. Tibbett as Hans Sachs in *Die Meistersinger von Nürnberg.* He only sang Act III, in English, on 12 April 1935, at a gala performance celebrating the 50th anniversary of Walter Damrosch's first New York concert. Sachs was a role Tibbett often talked about, but never sang in its entirety. Courtesy of Metropolitan Opera Archives.

55. Another portrait of Tibbett as Hans Sachs. Courtesy of Metropolitan Opera Archives.

56. Tibbett chats with soprano Lotte Lehmann at a Guild luncheon. The gentleman on her left is Walter Damrosch. Photo: Acme Newspictures, Inc. From the Editor's collection.

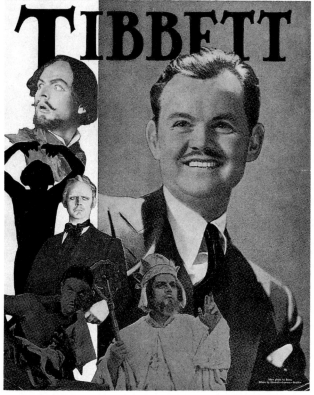

War Memorial Opera House

FRIDAY EVENING, APRIL 26, 1935, at 8:30

Only San Francisco Concert

Tickets at Sherman, Clay Co., San Francisco and Oakland

CONLEY MANAGEMENT

TIBBETT

57. Program cover (front and back) of Tibbett's War Memorial Opera House concert in San Francisco. From the Editor's collection.

THE WORLD OF MUSIC

applauds

LAWRENCE TIBBETT

BUFFALO
The occasion took on gala aspects—auditorium and extra stage seats filled with eager Tibbett admirers. —*Buffalo News.*

COLUMBUS
The walls of Memorial Hall fairly bulged with the press of people that managed to get room inside to hear the most versatile of present-day singers. —*Columbus Citizen*

DETROIT
An enthusiastic audience of such proportion that it filled the auditorium of Masonic Temple and overflowed onto the stage. —*Detroit Free Press.*

LOS ANGELES
When Tibbett sings packed houses are an invariable rule and last night they packed them in on the stage and even on chairs in the aisles until the auditorium would hold no more. —*Los Angeles News*

MANAGEMENT *Evans* and *Salter* NEW YORK

Division: Columbia Concerts Corporation of Columbia Broadcasting System

113 WEST 57th STREET

58. Mr. & Mrs. Lawrence Tibbett (the former Jennie Marston Burgard) at the Surf Club of Miami Beach. Photo: Acme Newspictures, Inc. From the Editor's collection.

59. The baritone with the second Mrs. Tibbett, Jennie, and their son, Michael Edward, on the Tibbetts' "Honey Hill Farm" in Wilton, Connecticut, on 2 July 1935. Photo: Acme Newspictures, Inc. From the Editor's collection.

60. Tibbett and son Michael on the lake near his farm in Wilton, Connecticut, 2 July 1935. Photo: Acme Newspicture, Inc. From the Editor's collection.

61. The Tibbetts at home. From the Editor's collection.

62. Tibbett with his sons (twins) from his first marriage (l. to r.) Lawrence Jr. and Richard, 13; and Peter 5, Marston 7, and Sonny 10 from the first marriage of Mrs. Tibbett. The picture was taken at the Blackstone Hotel in Chicago during the Tibbetts' visit to the World's Fair. Photo: Acme Newspictures, Inc. From the Editor's collection.

63. Tibbett at the Surf Club in the late 1930s. Photo: International News Photo. From the Editor's collection.

64. Tibbett first sang
the title role of
Rigoletto at the Metro-
politan on 28 Decem-
ber 1935. Courtesy of
Kurt Binar.

65. Another portrait of
Tibbett as Rigoletto at the
Metropolitan. Courtesy of
Kurt Binar.

66. Tibbett as Rigoletto at the Civic Opera House in Chicago, on 8 December 1937. He is shown with eighteen-year old Beverley Lane as Gilda. Photo: Wide World Photos. From the Editor's collection.

67. Fred Walker adds the finishing touches to Tibbett's makeup for the role of Méphisto. A sequence from *Faust* was filmed in the MGM film *Under Your Spell.* The New York showing of the film took place on 6 November 1936. From the Editor's collection.

68. A mature Lawrence Tibbett at the crest of his career. From the Editor's collection.

ammunition and supplies for American soldiers and a locomotive for Kerensky.

Six months after she left San Francisco, the Caderetta was back again. It was May 15, 1919. I was twenty-two years old, weary and homesick. I was discharged at once, and four days later, in Los Angeles, married Grace Mackay Smith, who had boarded several years with my mother and whom I had first known in high school.

It was a marriage of impulse and we were fortunate, indeed, that it lasted as long as it did. In 1931, after we had discussed divorce for several years, Grace and I finally admitted that it was no go and that we would be happier apart.

The wedding plans were conceived at a party celebrating my homecoming, and Grace and I were married the following day. One of the guests at the party, Arthur Millier, now art critic of the *Los Angeles Times,* was best man. We had planned a double wedding, but he and his bride-to-be changed their minds. They were married soon after—but not to each other.

I had saved $500. Grace's grandmother, who for several years before and after our marriage sent her fifty dollars a month, gave us a small car as a wedding present. I bought a new suit for $15, and we two crazy kids drove to Portland, Ore., on our honeymoon, and when we returned all that was left of the $500 was $2.35 and a memory of what seemed to us to have been as lavish a honeymoon as any millionaire newlyweds ever had!

My mother, not expecting me from Vladivostok so soon had gone to Dallas to visit relatives and I did not see her until we returned from our honeymoon. She was too poor to give us anything like a motorcar, but her wedding present was some linen for us both, a watch for me—the first one I ever had—and to Grace my mother gave her choicest possession—an enlarged portrait in a gilded frame showing me in a little lace dress at the age of two years.

Although our marriage did not last forever it was an adventure and an important event in my life. When I was married I was a dreamer and wanted to sit under a palm tree and philosophize. If I had no responsibilities I probably would still be sitting under the same palm tree, waiting for the fruit to drop, instead of taking off my shoes and climbing up after it.

Grace had courage, dash, ambition. She was temperamental—much more so than I. She had an unerring sense of comedy, real acting ability. She was witty and would have made a great *comédienne* had she been given the opportunity. Her real ambition, however, was to write, and no less an authority than Rupert Hughes said she had marked ability as a poetess.

We had some very, very good times together—and some awfully rotten ones. We were both mercurial in our dispositions. I had my singing; she had her poetry. When we were both succeeding, all was well, but when I came home at night after a performance with which I was not satisfied, and she had spent the evening searching unsuccessfully for poetic inspiration, we would greet each other sourly, and, like "Mr. and Mrs." in the cartoon, we would argue long into the night about nothing that really mattered at all.

When I was married I was a callow youngster with an idea that a husband should be the head of a family, and without any knowledge as to the way to acquire that position diplomatically. Grace had vitality and force, and at once took charge of me. Manlike, I thought I was henpecked and did my best to dominate, to be the big IT of the family. I thought my singing was something of international importance and that everything else should be subordinated to that. She made me battle for the position of head of the family, and these battles, I think, very often gave me backbone and confidence to step out into the world and keep my head up as I fought for my own career.

I wanted her to praise my singing, and she did. At times she seemed to be the only person in the world who thought I was any good. But, in turn, I did not praise her poetry. I was so selfishly immersed in my own work that I thought I had no time to encourage her art.

I was thoroughly inconsistent. In the first years of our married life I cheerfully—well, perhaps not cheerfully, but at least without complaining *much!*—stood over a steaming tub and washed the twins' diapers, but I refused to get up in the middle of the night when the babies cried.

When we were married, Grace was employed as a stenographer and continued to work for about four months after our wedding. When our twins were born, one weighed 4¾ pounds and the other 4¼ pounds. Today they are fine, strong, healthy boys and the pride of my life.

Both have fine voices and, I hope, will develop real ambitions for artistic careers. I shall be very, very proud if they take a serious interest in making music and the stage their life work.

When I first left Los Angeles to study in New York, I did not have enough money to take the family along, and Grace went to work again in Los Angeles, but after two months found it was better for all concerned if she stayed at home and cared for the twins. My efforts to conquer New York were being financed by loans from a generous patron and, to the small amount of money that I was able to send back from New York, he added enough to keep my wife and children through the critical period, until I made sufficient to support my family and to help my mother a little. It was not until I got into the movies, however—years later—that I was able to pay back the money I had borrowed.

When it became evident that the complete happiness of both our lives could be restored only by separation, Grace and I took the sane, sensible road and she established a residence in Reno and our marriage was dissolved. We share my income and now, enjoying the luxuries that were denied us in our early days, she, as well as I, can pursue a career free from material worry or interruption. She recently published a book of poems and I hope sincerely that she is on the verge of real success.

Soon after we were married, I began to miss the sea. Not that I had any particular love for an ocean life, but I had found that I was enormously stimulated by standing at the prow of a pitching ship and singing into the storm. Singing teachers say you must never open your mouth in the wind, which, I think, is a superstition.

I would get on my bicycle and ride to the hills, climb a sandy peak, and roar into the night breezes.

Ten years later I reported for work at the Metro-Goldwyn-Mayer moving picture studio.

A publicity man, gathering data, asked me, "Where did you come from?"

"Right here," I said.

"You mean, you used to live in Los Angeles?"

"For years and years," I said.

He was a bit astonished.

66

"Well—er," he said, "where did you do the best singing of your career? At the Metropolitan?"

I took him by the arm and led him outside my dressing-room. I pointed to the huge group of buildings in front of us.

"I used to ride a bicycle right across this property," I said, "and—see that hill over there? That's where I sang better than at any other place in the world."

A few weeks later I made a sentimental journey in a motorcar over to that hill and sang into the wind, but it was a flat performance. It was utterly uninspired, and I got no satisfaction out of it whatsoever. The landscape was in no way as magnificent as I had remembered it, and the hill seemed to have shrunk.

Had I ridden over there on a bicycle and pumped my way to the top, instead of gliding up in a motorcar, the view from the heights probably would have seemed worth while. Perhaps there's some pretty sound philosophy about life in general, in that experience. If I had a palm tree under which to dream, I would develop it.

III

THEY PUT ME IN JAIL FOR SINGING

At various times in my early career I was shy and awed at the prospect of appearing with such famous women as Jeritza, Alda, Ponselle, and Bori, but the only leading woman who really had me scared to death was Lupe Velez, in the movies.

After I signed my contract to make *The Cuban Love Song,* they told me at the studio that I was to work with a splendid cast, including Jimmy Durante and Ernest Torrence, which was very good news indeed.

I have never shared with some actors and singers the idea that the worse the supporting cast, the better for the star. An audience, I believe, goes to the theater to see a good show, with good actors in every part, and the star who thinks people like to pay money to see him attempt to put over an entire performance single-handed is riding for a fall. Even in concerts, the successful singer must have the assistance of the most talented pianist he can find.

I once heard an actor complaining that Marie Dressler had stolen his picture.

"I wish," I said, "I could get her to steal one of mine."

Torrence, whose recent death shocked me tremendously, was a real friend and a magnificent actor. Durante is a natural comedian, and in New York night clubs had given me many laughs. Up to that time he had made only one picture, which he stole from William Haines, the star, and I knew Jimmy was working violently to make good in the movies.

"Whom have you in mind for the leading woman?" I asked.

"Lupe Velez," they said.

"Lupe Velez!" I swallowed three times. "You mean the Mexican wildcat who hit a director over the head with a bottle!"

"None other. She will play the peanut vender, and she'll be so hot that she'll melt the steel in the proscenium arch and it'll come blopping down upon the orchestra!"

Up to that time, as leading woman, I had had Catherine Dale Owen in *The Rogue Song,* Grace Moore in *New Moon,* and Esther Ralston in *The Prodigal,* none of whom, as far as I knew, ever hit anybody over the head with a bottle.

"Listen," I said, "there has been a terrible mistake. My name is Lawrence Tibbett. I'm a singer. You evidently have me mixed up with Sam Houston, who licked the Mexican army!"

They said no, they knew who I was and they were going to bill me as the great lover of the Metro-Goldwyn-Mayer lot, and that in the picture Lupe and I had some flaming love scenes which would make the Chicago fire look like a burnt match.

"That," I said, "is out. I'm no great lover. I'm just an opera singer trying to get along in the movies."

We compromised. The great-lover publicity thereupon died unborn, but, if she chose, the dynamic Lupe was to go boiling through the story like Mt. Etna on a rampage.

I went around asking everybody, "What's the best way for me to get along with Lupe Velez?"

I might as well have asked, "What's the best way to jump over the moon?" It couldn't be done.

They warned me, "She's likely to bust out any minute, kick over the camera, and pick up a light and swat you over the head."

When we first met at rehearsal she seemed to appraise me with a challenging eye.

"How do you do?" I said, knowing very well how she did.

She said she did all right, which was contrary to what I had heard.

Then came an inspiration from heaven! I offered, "I understand that you have a lovely voice." I knew nothing about her voice.

"Who told you that?" she demanded.

Something in her tone indicated that, shooting blindly, I had struck a vital spot. I was to learn, thank God, that she did have a good voice.

"Everybody," I answered.

"It is not like my mother's," Lupe said quietly. "Her voice was divine. She was an opera singer in Mexico."—She looked up at me. "Would you sing something for Lupe some time? Something in Spanish, perhaps?"

"Of course," I said, with what little breath was left in my body. "How about now? There's a piano over there."

I felt as Clyde Beatty, the animal trainer, must have felt when he first made a tiger lie down and roll over. Now I believed Congreve— "Music hath charms to soothe the savage breast, to soften rocks, or bend a knotted oak."

I have never worked more peacefully with a leading woman. Flushed by music's success with Lupe, I made up my mind that I would go out and try it on a rock and a knotted oak, but I never got around to it.

Lupe Velez is a great emotional actress. Her only trouble is that she believes what the press agents write about her, and acts off-stage as well as on in a desperate and doubtless tiring effort to live up to her reputation as a firebrand.

Our only difficulty with her was in getting her to sing a song in the picture. Believe it or not, Lupe was too shy! Away from the microphone she sang beautifully. She knew good music, and could imitate an opera singer and sing cadenzas and top notes and hit a clear, free top C as well as many a coloratura. But when the sound apparatus was turning over, time and again, before she finally recorded her song perfectly, she broke

68

down and ran off the set, crying, "Lupe is not engaged to be a singer! She cannot do it!"

Only recently she and Jimmy Durante made a great hit, in person, in the musical comedy, *Strike Me Pink,* and she proved there that she had a fine natural voice.

Durante was a genial, willing, likable roughneck, new to the movies and ready to break a leg for the camera if it would get him a laugh. He was so determined to deliver the goods that he ran around asking advice of everybody on the lot, and believed everything they told him. He was meat for the practical jokers.

One day W. S. Van Dyke, director of *The Cuban Love Song,* after setting the stage for the job and prompting a dozen people, from the chief costumer to Louis Mayer, the big boss, told Jimmy that the next day he was to play a Bulgarian general in a love scene with Lupe Velez.

Jimmy was highly pleased. "Romeo stuff, hey?" he said, spitting on his hands. "Watch Durante!"

Van Dyke told Jimmy to go to the wardrobe department to get his costume.

Jimmy came back staggering under a load. He wore a golden helmet, much too large for him, with eagles on it and a yellow plume four feet long. He had a mighty sword that dragged on the ground. His coat was bright red with yellow epaulettes, and his chest sank under a score of medals. Across his breast were six bright ribbons and around his waist a red, white, and blue sash. His trousers were pink and were almost hidden in patent-leather hip boots, to which were attached flopping spurs that interfered with Jimmy's feet, so that he had to take zigzag steps, like an Indian dodging bullets. Swinging from a gold cord around his neck was a tuba.

The make-up man had painted Jimmy's long nose a bright blue and had put black circles under his eyes and a goatee on his chin.

Jimmy was not in the scenes we were shooting that day, but never worked harder in his life.

"How is it?" he asked Van Dyke.

"Magnificent!" said Van Dyke.

"On de level?" said Jimmy. "I t'ot maybe it was a little loud."

"It's colossal. But you'd better go back and put on blue pants. They're more regal than pink."

The pants changed, he was sent to Louis Mayer. Mayer ordered the medals shifted from the left breast to the right, which, it seemed, was the proper spot for medals in Bulgaria. Irving Thalberg, another big boss called into consultation, sent him to the prop department for a longer sword.

Jimmy, sweating, anxious to please, eagerly obeyed every order, and for half a day ran from executive to costume department, to prop room, to executive.

"T'ink it's better now?" he would inquire hopefully, wiping the perspiration from his eyes, only to be met with further changes.

At last he caught someone snickering. He realized what was going on.

"Hey," he demanded, "what's dis, a gag?"

"It's a gag, Jimmy," somebody confessed.

He grinned sheepishly, then turned toward a mirror, threw back his shoulders, and slapped his chest. "Well," he said, "gag or no gag, I never saw Durante look sweller!"

Torrence, Durante, and I had a big scene in a shell hole in No Man's Land. I sang

69

From the Halls of Montezuma to the Shores of Tripoli, the most stirring military song that we have. It should be our national anthem.

I was supposed to go crazy and try to run over and lick the entire German army. Bombs burst around us, almost burying us in dirt and cork stones. Torrence worked so hard that he fainted, and had to be revived by the emergency crew. A shell exploded in front of me while I was singing, and I finished the song with my mouth full of mud.

There were hundreds of extras, great batteries of lights, and the scene cost thousands of dollars.

We felt that we had done a good job, and the next day asked to see the "rushes," as they called the unedited shots.

"Oh, didn't you hear?" said the assistant director. "The cameramen balled things up, so it isn't any good."

"Do you mean that we have to do all that over again?" I asked.

"Oh, no," he said. "They can't afford it. They've decided to do without the scene."

Jimmy Durante was standing near. He shook a finger in the assistant director's face. "You can't fool Durante," he said. "You guys never was goin' to use the scene! Some day you practical jokers will go too far!"

To this day he may still believe it was a gag to make us do all that hard work for nothing.

It was about this time that I learned that while music may soften rocks and bend a knotted oak, it has no effect upon the heart of a police judge. Nor will it melt iron bars. I was jailed for singing!

Four of us started to sing, late one night, in a Los Angeles restaurant. The proprietor told us to shut up. One of my friends pointed out to the proprietor that I was to sing a few weeks later at the Auditorium, that seats were selling for $7.70 each, and that the restaurant-keeper should be proud to have my voice echoing through his halls. He said it was just a lot of noise to him, and we'd have to "scram" or he'd call the cops.

On the sidewalk my friend, the self-appointed director-general of the party, started a loud quarrel with a passing Negro, and in a moment we were surrounded by policemen, who had been called by someone in the restaurant.

The four of us were locked up in the Wilshire police station, where I said my name was Mervil Lawrence. I might have called friends to get me out, but the director-general said he was a man of great influence in Los Angeles and that he would fix everything—keep the story out of the newspapers and have us freed, with profuse apologies from the police.

He showed me a gold badge to prove his importance and I was impressed, though later I remembered that he had shown the badge to the police and they had immediately taken us to the station.

Since I was sure everything was to come out all right, I looked upon it as a gay adventure. In my cell I sang *The Prisoner's Song, Tenting on the Old Camp Ground,* the prison song from *Faust*—all three parts, soprano, tenor, and bass—and, at the request of a pickpocket, *Frankie and Johnny.*

The other prisoners applauded heartily. I have never had a more appreciative audience than those vagabonds who got a $7.70 concert for nothing.

We went to court in the patrol wagon in the morning. I began to have a few misgivings about the power of my friend who was going to fix everything, and I was quite startled when the judge, instead of apologizing, fined my friend $75 and the other three of us $25 each.

And in the director-general's efforts to reach influential editors to kill the story, he had only tipped them off, and I fled from the courthouse with a newspaper over my head to shield me from the cameras.

Strangely enough, I was still under the spell of my friend's promise to fix the newspapers, and I explained to my wife that I had been up with a sick friend, that my car had broken down, and that I had been rehearsing all night, which assorted alibi seemed to square things until, to my horror, the papers came out with the story and the picture of me with a newspaper over my head. For several days things at home were disquieting.

So I don't sing much in restaurants any more. Nor put my trust in friends who boast about their Power.

It is quite possible that the restaurant keeper was a good critic and was justified in his violent expression of disapproval. I don't sing well after a heavy dinner. My voice loses power and tightens up on the high notes, and on the day of a performance I never eat much until after I have sung.

The problem of what to do about people who say, "Come to dinner and bring your music," is a more serious one than you would imagine. Whether my voice is right or not, I love to stand up and let go, but usually, unless I am among very close friends, I try to beg off.

There was a time when I eagerly sought opportunities to sing for my supper. I wanted experience in singing before people, and sometimes these were the only audiences I could get. Often I used to invite a lot of people out to the house and made *them* pay for their dinner by listening to me.

A great many invitations come from persons I have never seen, or whom I have met casually, and whose only interest in me is that they think they might persuade me to put on a show for nothing. These I reject promptly.

Fritz Kreisler was once asked by a rich dowager to come to dinner and bring his violin.

"Really," he said, "you are too kind. There will be no need for me to bring my violin."

"Why not?"

"It doesn't eat," he said.

Some time ago an experience in San Francisco put an end to my after-dinner singing. I sang at a party there one night, and cracked on a high note. The next day the news was all over town that Tibbett was through. How such news travels I don't know, but my agents in New York heard it a week later. I began to get letters from friends in Atlanta and New Orleans, and Minneapolis and Seattle and Wichita, Kans., telling me how sorry they were to hear that my voice was gone! It was a year or more before I stopped running into the rumor. It jeopardized professional engagements, and got me an offer from a musical comedy producer who said that since he heard I was done as an opera singer he thought I might like to try a show for him. He'd have the music written, he promised, without any high notes in it!

Since then I have been careful to refuse stubbornly to sing after heavy dinners.

When I was in the movies there was a sacred spot on one of the old stages. It was the

71

place where, when I was a struggling youngster, Rupert Hughes introduced me to Mary Garden.

In my early days, the Chicago Opera Company came to Los Angeles every year, and when they sang at the Auditorium I got in for nothing by working as an usher.

In the company were such famous singers as Mary Garden, Muratore, Claudia Muzio, and Baklanoff. I envied them, of course, as a street urchin envies a king, but position such as they held seemed to be so obviously out of my reach that at no time did I have the audacity to hope I might eventually be like them.

At the time I first heard Mary Garden, Rupert Hughes was directing *The Old Nest* at one of the picture studios and asked me if I should like to meet her. He said she was going to visit the studio the next day and that he would introduce me. If I asked her nicely, he said, she might consent to hear me sing.

I floated to the studio. I gulped that I was glad to meet her and, choking, stuttered a request that she let me sing for her. She indicated that she would be delighted to hear me, and told me to telephone her at her hotel the following afternoon for an appointment.

I rushed out to tell all my friends that I was going to sing for Mary Garden! Nobody believed me.

I telephoned her secretary the next day. She had heard nothing about making an appointment with anybody named Tibbett. No, I couldn't speak with Miss Garden; good-by!

I was crushed, angry, disillusioned. My goddess came tumbling down from her temple. To me, then, she was conceited, cruel, and selfish.

And it did not help when my friends asked, "What did Mary Garden say about your voice?"

It was years before I understood that an opera singer cannot possibly listen to all the singers who want an audition. I was only one of a hundred who wanted to sing for her. And had she listened to me, there was nothing much that she could have done except, perhaps, to say that I wasn't as bad as most singers. Probably the day I called was the day of a performance and, as all singers must do, she had shut herself in to rest and practice.

Profiting, however, from that experience, I have always tried to listen to as many young singers as possible. It can't be done on the day of a performance, but when I have a day to spare in a city I listen to as many as time permits. Out of the hundreds that I have heard not many have had voices of promise. Many, when I advised them to give up their ambition for a career, were quite angry with me.

Twice, through no fault of mine, I have had to break my promise to hear young singers. I know they were hurt, as I was hurt when Mary Garden broke her promise to me. I felt worse about it than they did and I wrote them trying to explain, but I'm sure they will never forgive me. At least, not until they rise in their profession and pardon me, as I, understanding at last, pardoned Mary Garden.

A few years ago, when I was singing in a Western city, a woman, well past thirty, came to me with her father, a traveling evangelist. She had a beautiful native voice; she sang accurately and naturally but with absolutely no feeling. Once there had been a great voice in that throat, no doubt about that. Properly trained, as a girl, she might have developed into one of our finest American singers.

After she sang for me she asked whether I would advise her to go to New York to study. She had some money of her own now, she said, looking defiantly at her father.

It was too late to save her voice and, as kindly as possible, I told her so.

"Good," said her father brutally. This man who had announced that he was a Representative of God gloated, "I told you he'd say that. And it's better for all concerned. You keep on with me in the Lord's work and don't go gallivantin' around in theater business."

"Singing," the girl said quickly, "singing to people, making them happy, is just as divine as saving souls." She turned to me. "Isn't it, Mr. Tibbett?"

I said that I believed it was.

"Nonsense!" said the evangelist.

Then it came out that she and her father were at war because he had forced her to give up her voice to revival singing. Since youth she had wanted to leave him to study, but sullenly had obeyed his command that she stay with him to help save souls.

He took her by the arm and led her away. She said not a word but looked back at me with despairing eyes that still haunt me. It was as if I had condemned an innocent woman to life imprisonment.

I wish that I had lied and told her to go.

In introducing me to Mary Garden, Rupert Hughes was performing only one of many kindly acts. Over and over again he helped me enormously. He is best known as a writer, but is a talented musician as well. He plays the piano with professional skill and has composed a number of beautiful songs, many of which I have sung in concerts.

The Ebell Club, a woman's organization, brought us together. Hughes was to talk on music before the Club and as part of the program was to present some of his songs. Some of the club members suggested that I do the singing, and I went to see him. Quite frightened in the presence of this famous man, I sang for him. He played the accompaniment, and when we finished he leaned back and looked at me and said, "You have one of the most beautiful voices I have ever heard."

I was greatly pleased, of course, especially because I got the job. I took it for granted that after I sang at the Ebell Club, Rupert Hughes would forget all about me. I was astonished, therefore, when he invited my wife and me to dinner at his home.

At dinner he asked, "What do you intend to do with your life?"

I didn't exactly know. There didn't seem to be much money in singing, so I had thought I might become an orchestral conductor, a position which not only paid well but was highly honored and was a thrilling artistic expression. I had bought a book on conducting and had practiced for hours in front of a mirror, leading a phonograph like nobody's business.

"You have a career in that voice," Hughes said. "You ought to go to New York."

I had heard so many dreadful singers praised that I had learned to scoff at compliments. But I realized that Hughes was no flatterer and that he knew music.

"Lord!" I said to myself. "What if he's right!"

"New York?" I asked aloud. "In order to amount to anything I'd have to study in Europe, wouldn't I? And if Europe were as close as Catalina Island I wouldn't have enough money to get there."

"New York," Hughes said firmly, "is the music center of the world. American singers will soon come into their own and a foreign reputation won't mean a thing.

73

Borrow the money. Some day, with that voice, you'll be able to pay it back."

I thought about it for a week, and then went to James G. Warren, a wealthy business man and one of the kindest, most lovable gentlemen I ever knew. He was president of the Orpheus Club, a men's choral organization in Los Angeles to which I had belonged for several years.

When I told him timidly what I wanted to do he said he would be glad to help. A few weeks later, when I was ready to go, he wrote a check for $2,500, which was the first of many loans through which he helped support me and my family during the critical years. I took out life insurance policies that would pay him back if I died, but that was all the security I could give.

I was twenty-four years old. I promised Mr. Warren and myself that if I hadn't achieved something by the time I was thirty, I would return to Los Angeles and sell trucks for a friend who told me he would give me a job whenever I forgot this singing nonsense and decided to go into a respectable business.

Mr. Warren said he would send me to Frank La Forge in New York, with whom Mr. Warren's daughter, Eleanor, was studying. La Forge was coaching Frances Alda and accompanying Matzenauer and other famous singers in concert work.

In an effort to raise more money, I gave a farewell concert in the Gamut Club auditorium. Rupert Hughes not only accompanied me when I sang a group of his songs, but bought $300 worth of tickets, using only four of them. About 150 persons came to hear me in the auditorium that seated 800. I made $375 on the concert.

Bearing letters of introduction from Rupert Hughes and Mr. Warren, I left my family in Los Angeles and set out to make my fortune. Except for my trips during the war, it was the first time I had ever been outside the state of California, and I was scared to death. I was thrilled, too. Ahead of me was adventure in a great city!

For the first year, however, my adventure was confined mostly to singing in the North Avenue Presbyterian Church in New Rochelle, N.Y., for $75 a month.

I began paying Frank La Forge $12.50 for a half-hour lesson twice a week, and spent $2.20 twice a week for standing room at the Metropolitan Opera House, but soon realized that at that rate my money would quickly vanish. I gave up the opera except on rare occasions, and La Forge, who had taken a real interest in my voice, agreed generously to help me get concert engagements, by means of which I could pay for my lessons.

I was even more fortunate than I realized in being in the hands of a real teacher. I escaped being caught in the singing-teacher racket, which is one of America's greatest fakes. Probably in no profession are there so many incompetent instructors as in music. All over the world they are obtaining money under false pretenses, wasting the time, often actually ruining the careers of potentially successful singers.

They feed their pupils impressive bunk. They say your top notes should come from the bottom—that you sing them from the base of your spine. Others tell you the high notes should come out of the top of your skull. Some teach the singer to pull his tongue back in his throat, or to leave it flat in his mouth. They tear apart the simple art and tell pupils to use this muscle, then that.

Singing is a natural process, as natural as speaking, and a teacher who tries to make a pupil produce tones by thinking only of muscles and chords is as incompetent as an athletic coach who expects to make a man win a 100-yard dash by yelling at him, "Now wiggle the right calf muscle! Now push with your left toe!"

Bad teaching, of course, is worse than no teaching, and there are times when I believe that the person with the average voice who studies with the average teacher may progress farther if he has no instruction at all. Go to Sunday school and listen to the kids sing, and you will learn more in an hour than a great many instructors can give you in a lifetime.

About the only way to tell a bad teacher from a good one is through your own common sense. If he makes singing a mysterious process, if he begins to deal in hocus-pocus, quit him.

One day, after I had been studying about six months with La Forge, like a thunder-bolt he said, "I think you ought to try an audition at the Metropolitan."

I was flabbergasted. "I don't know any language but English," I protested. "I don't know any rôles and, besides, my voice isn't big enough for the Metropolitan."

"There's no harm in trying," he said.

The auditions were to be held in April, three months away. We started to work on arias—Iago's *Credo* from *Otello,* Valentine's aria from *Faust,* and *Eri tu* from Verdi's *The Masked Ball.* The aria I sang best, I thought, was the prologue from *Pagliacci*—which I have sung in public more than a thousand times—but that's what every baritone wants to sing, and La Forge said we'd try to use it but he was afraid the judges at the Met wouldn't stand for it.

La Forge made arrangements for the audition, and finally the day arrived. We walked out on the stage. Out of the dark auditorium came a voice: "What will he sing?"

La Forge, at the piano where he was to play my accompaniment, cleared his throat and said hopefully, "The prologue from *Pagliacci.*"

"Didn't he bring anything else?" said the voice wearily.

We had lost our first battle. La Forge put the music for the prologue aside and opened *Eri tu.*

In the beginning there is a high F sharp. My voice cracked on it. My knees were shaking as I struggled through the aria.

"Sing something else," the voice said.

I sang Valentine's aria from *Faust.*

"Thank you," came from the blackness of the auditorium.

So we went home and waited for the Metropolitan to send for me.

We waited three weeks, and finally La Forge telephoned Madame Alda for help. She told him to bring me over, and in her apartment I sang for her.

"Pretty tight on top," said Alda, "but a good voice. I'll phone Gatti."

Gatti-Casazza, general director of the Metropolitan, was then her husband.

Gatti didn't remember anything about my audition, but on Alda's recommendation said he would hear me again.

At the second Metropolitan audition I sang Iago's *Credo* from *Othello.* When I finished, that spooky voice asked me to wait.

They offered me $50 a week, for 22 weeks. Before I made my decision, La Forge called Alda and told her about it.

"It's not enough," she said, "for a man with a good voice and a wife and two children to support. I'll phone Gatti."

She called back. "It's all right now," she said triumphantly. "They'll pay you sixty."

75

I signed a contract—one of those option affairs by which, if they chose, they could keep me for four years, at $100 a week for the second season, $125 for the third, and $150 for the fourth. The contract tied me up tight. I could sing in concerts but, without the Metropolitan's permission, no radio, no musical comedy, no movies. Years later, when I appeared in the movies, I had to pay the Metropolitan percentage of my earnings.

I noted another strange clause in the standard operatic contract. I was forbidden to wear a hat or to carry a cane at rehearsals. I was to learn later that Gatti had inserted that role in all contracts because opera singers had turned rehearsals into formal social events and appeared in high collars, silk hats, frock coats, spats, and gold-headed canes and, all dressed up, merely walked through their parts. He made them report in old clothes so they would loosen up and work.

I left Gatti's office with some assurance that I was under way with my career. At twenty-nine, if the Metropolitan took up the options, I would be making $150 a week for twenty-two weeks out of the year. Perhaps I wouldn't have to sell trucks, after all.

As we crossed the dark stage after leaving Gatti's office, a man smiled and bowed to me. "I heard your audition the other day," he said. "May I compliment you on the way you sang the *Credo*. Iago is an old rôle of mine."

I stammered my thanks, and as we left the opera house, I asked La Forge, "Who is that man?"

"That's Scotti," said La Forge, and I almost swooned.

Antonio Scotti, who retired last January at the age of sixty-four, became one of my good friends at the Metropolitan. He was a real actor, and had no use for opera singers who played blatantly to the audience.

"Imagine that the stage is a four-walled room," he told me once. "Keep your face to the audience when the action permits it, but don't be afraid to turn and sing to the back drop. You're performing a play, not singing a concert."

It was in May, 1923, that Scotti so generously praised me, a rank beginner. In January, 1925, on that same stage, I was to experience the greatest moment of my life, in a performance that had been arranged to glorify Scotti, and overnight to find myself turned from an unknown into a Metropolitan star!

Falstaff had been revived as a tribute to Scotti. In the grand revival were Alda, Gigli, Bori, and Kathleen Howard. I was cast as Ford, a secondary rôle.

I got the rôle because Vincente Ballester, the Spanish baritone, who died a few years later, became ill. It was the old, old story of the understudy who gets a chance to make good.

In rehearsal, surrounded by a horde of the greatest names in grand opera, I was at first a stumbling incompetent. I balled up stage directions which, in Italian, had to be translated for me. At one time I was so bad that somebody went to Gatti and said I would never do. Gatti came down to the stage, watched me rehearse, and then talked with Tullio Serafin, the conductor, who had put me in the rôle and was coaching me. Serafin believed in me, and it was only his protest that kept Gatti from throwing me out.

At first I seemed to upset everybody's disposition, and most of the time I was apologizing for some outlandish error that held up the rehearsal.

Other members of the cast were making mistakes, but they laughed them off and nobody seemed to complain. After three of the five weeks of rehearsal were past I discovered a great truth about human nature. If you admit your weaknesses, if you continually apologize, people instinctively scold you—whether it is at a Metropolitan rehearsal or at a contract bridge table. If you never confess your sense of inferiority, if you airily wave aside your errors as if they amounted to nothing, people sneer at you not at all.

I stopped apologizing. Instead of moaning at a stupid error, I merely grinned and shrugged my shoulders. No longer did the stars bark at me. I began to get the hang of the part, and made up my mind to do or die.

The night of the opera I set myself and let go with all I had. In my aria in the second act I tore my heart out. Some subconscious force lifted me up, cleared my throat, and my voice was never better. It is the scene where Ford learns that his wife has been untrue to him and is in love with Falstaff. I went through the scene with terrific desperation, power, and abandon. When I finished I knew that in my furious effort to make the audience pay some attention to me, I had acted the scene well and had sung, for me, superbly.

Marion Telva, who played Dame Quickly, Scotti, and I took a bow. The applause shook the opera house. Then Scotti took a bow alone. Then the three of us again. Then Scotti and I. Then Scotti alone. The applause did not die down.

At last I went to my dressing-room, two flights up, powdered my perspiring face, and came down for the next scene. The applause was holding up the performance. I stood in the wings watching Scotti with envy, hoping that some day I might merit such acclaim. A man came running to me.

"Maestro Serafin," he said, "wants you to take a curtain call alone. The audience is calling for you!"

"For me?" I said. I looked at Gatti, who was standing in the wings across the stage, back of the curtain. He waved me toward the center of the stage. "They want you, not Scotti!" he called. As I walked toward the opening, through the curtain came muffled cries from the audience. At first I couldn't believe my ears.

"Tibbett! Tibbett!" they were crying. "Bravo, Tibbett!"

Alone I stepped out in front of that audience, the audience that had come to cheer Scotti. A thundering wave of applause and cheers smashed me in the face. I almost fainted. I still get goose flesh all over my body when I think of it. Thirty-five hundred persons had their eyes on me. They were cheering *me*! Not Scotti, nor Alda, nor Bori, nor Gigli, nor Kathleen Howard, but ME! There's no thrill in all the world like that!

After the performance Mrs. Tibbett, La Forge, and I went over to a restaurant and had some soup.

"I think you'll get some pretty good notices," La Forge said.

"I hope they do more than to say I was 'adequate,'" I said, and treated myself to another bowl of soup.

I still didn't realize what had happened. The next morning my wife woke me up by shouting excitedly, "The hall outside is full of reporters and photographers! Look at the papers! On the *front page*! You were the hit of the performance!"

Then I believed in Santa Claus!

WHY I QUIT MAKING FUNNY FACES

When I went to Hollywood in 1929 to make my first motion picture, *The Rogue Song,* it was against the violent protest of most of my friends. They said the movies were a thing depraved and that I had become money-crazy and was wrecking my career for gold.

I disarmed my advisers somewhat by confessing that perhaps I was money-crazy. I owed a good many thousands of dollars to friends who had financed my career, and here was a chance to pay back every dollar. If that is being money-crazy, so be it.

The Metropolitan Opera Company was then engaging me for twenty-two weeks out of the year. I was making some money on concerts and from phonograph records. I had been fortunate in turning out a good record of the Prologue from *Pagliacci,* and the royalties the first year had totaled nearly $10,000.

It might seem to the public that I should have been rolling in wealth, but most of an opera singer's money goes for commissions to managers, musical coaching, traveling expenses, accompanists, wigs, advertising, entertaining, pianos, music, and heaven knows what else.

The movies offered me a great deal of money, and I accepted. Some of my colleagues at the Metropolitan as well as some of the newspaper critics predicted that I would be ruined as an artist.

"Look here," I said, irritated by their smugness; "I believe that the best actors in the world are in the movies. No less an artist than Lionel Barrymore is going to direct my first picture. When I come back here, thanks to the movies, I hope to be a better artist than I am now."

"Poor Tibbett," they said. "He's already gone Hollywood! His operatic career is ended!"

Last January, at the première of the opera, *The Emperor Jones,* the critics and the audience were enthusiastic. They gave me twenty-two curtain calls.

Eugene O'Neill's powerful and unique play, set to music by Louis Gruenberg, is almost a monologue for the Emperor. The lines are spoken on the music and it is primarily an acting part, as the cocksure, bullying Pullman porter turns into a terror-stricken, whining fugitive. Whatever success I had in acting that part was greatly enhanced by the lessons I learned in Hollywood.

I must admit that when I first went to work in a motion picture studio, I began to wonder if things were going to come out all right, after all. The first voice tests were not so good. I sang so loud that I blew out a light valve in the recording apparatus. I have no idea what a light valve may be, but, after I finished a song, people began running around yelling excitedly and telephoning for help, and when I asked what it was all about they said accusingly, "You blew out a light valve!" I shrank into a corner, afraid to ask what a light valve was, for fear I should learn that I had caused damage amounting to thousands of dollars and that they were going to make me pay for it. I learned later that, whatever it is, it costs about $45.

We got the sound straightened out, but the camera tests and the make-up almost caused me to run down to the ocean and drown myself in shame. They had to learn how to light me. They studied both sides of my face, from all angles and altitudes. I stood on a stage, while a dozen men and women, frowning and muttering, looked me over as though I were a horse. Electricians fussed with lights, cameramen held their hands in front of their faces and glared at me through spread-out fingers, now eying me from the floor, now from a perch on a chair, to see whether there was any way to shoot this guy so he'd look somewhat human.

They advised me to grow a mustache, which I started at once and found that the hair grew luxuriantly on the left side of my lip but hardly at all on the right. They fixed that by patching in some false hair. Eventually the right side caught up and I was able to abandon the false half-mustache.

They said all leading men must have wavy hair, and sent me to a hairdresser for a permanent wave! I made the appointment for very late at night and stole into the hairdresser's through a side door so no one would see me, and sat for hours with my hair wrapped around those diabolical hot electric gadgets. I was ashamed to go around Hollywood dolled up in such a manner, and whenever I had my hat off I expected at any moment to be mistaken for Mary Pickford.

They said my ears stuck out too much, and pasted them down with glue and tape.

It was all new to me, and I took orders without protesting until I went on the stage for my first scene. Lines were marked on the stage, showing me where to stand and where not to walk. My hair was curled, I wore half a false mustache, my ears were pasted back. It was a hot day; the picture was being made in color and the batteries of lights were like an open furnace. I was bundled up in a Russian costume meant for sleighing in Siberia. I had learned my lines for the first scene.

"What do you want me to do?" I asked Lionel Barrymore.

"Just act natural," he said.

"Act *natural*! Under those circumstances!

"Just be yourself," he said.

"O.K.!" I said. I tore off the Russian fur hat and slammed it on the floor. I started to unbutton the coat. I saw then that Lionel was grinning at me.

"That disrobing scene, Mr. Tibbett," he drawled, "doesn't come until later in the picture. If you don't mind, we'll shoot the scenes in their proper order."

I stopped short. Then I laughed. He laughed. Everybody on the stage laughed. I put on the fur hat and started to work. I believe that is the only time in my life that I ever exhibited any of that much-talked-of and seldom-seen emotion called operatic temperament.

It wasn't long before I became accustomed to all my make-up. I had only one mishap. After *The Prodigal* was finished, when executives were looking at it in the projection-room, one suddenly shouted, "Look! His ear!" They looked. In the midst of a love scene, my right ear suddenly popped out like a swinging door. The glue had let go, and up to that time no one had noticed it. I thought it was a quite interesting magical effect—an ear coming out of nowhere—but they made me do the scene over again.

I had been in Hollywood only a few weeks when I engaged my first man-servant. He was a distinguished-looking young man with a foreign accent, and he acted as my dresser and valet at the studio and occasionally helped serve dinner at home.

A week after I had engaged him I discovered he was a Russian count—a real one, according to other refugee Russians in Hollywood. It didn't seem right for a real count to be pressing my pants, and I told him so. He said he needed the money and was very

79

happy to work for me.

I protested: "When you are around here, you mustn't act so much like a menial. Though you are working for me, I'd rather have you consider yourself somewhat as one of the family."

He thanked me and said he would.

That evening I had a number of guests, and after dinner they wandered out into the garden. After a while Elsie Janis, the actress, came up to me and said, "What's the matter with this butler of yours? He just asked me to take a drive with him down to the beach!"

A moment later Helen Wills Moody, the tennis champion, said my butler had invited her to play tennis with him the next day, and Basil Rathbone, the actor, told me he hoped he hadn't hurt my feelings, but he had just turned down my butler's suggestion that the party was getting dull and that they ought to start a bridge game.

I explained to the count that while I did not want him to act exactly like a menial, I had not intended that he promote himself to co-host. He became quite abusive and said that he didn't think much of me and my guests, anyway, so we parted company.

Although I had grown up in Los Angeles, I didn't know much about life in a movie studio. I took things as they came and made no complaint. Other stars said I was foolish because I didn't go around demanding things. You weren't respected, they said, unless you demanded things.

"What things?" I asked. "I have everything I want."

"Make them give you a better dressing-room. Ask for John Gilbert's."

My dressing-room was all right—much better than anything I ever had at the Metropolitan—but just as a try-out I went into the front office and demanded John Gilbert's dressing-room. It was not in use at that time.

I got it at once.

"How long," I asked myself, "has this been going on? Just ask, and you get!"

I made up my mind that if the way to become respected on a movie lot was to ask for things, I'd build myself into a god. But after I got the dressing-room, I sat and sat and thought and thought but never could think of another thing to ask for, so I guess I wasn't respected very much.

When I finished *The Rogue Song,* one of the officials told me, "We're suppressing in our advertising the fact that you're an opera singer. I hope it won't hurt your feelings."

It didn't hurt my feelings particularly, but it aroused my curiosity.

"You hired me because I sang at the Metropolitan, didn't you?" I asked.

"Yes."

"Then what's the idea?"

There's a curse on opera singers," he said. "Caruso made a couple of pictures years ago, and the first one was such a flop that they never released the second."

"That was a silent picture," I said. "And, anyway, didn't Geraldine Farrar do well in the movies?"

"She was a woman. That's different. Men opera singers"—he held up his hands—"no good. The movie fans think they're fat and speak in a foreign language and smell of garlic. We'll bill you as a new singing star and forget the Metropolitan."

The Rogue Song played for five months at the Astor Theater in New York, and I was advertised there as a Metropolitan Opera star. But in all other theaters throughout the

69. Tibbett as Guido in Richard Hagemann's *Caponsacchi*. The American première at the Metropolitan was on 4 February 1937. Courtesy of Metropolitan Opera Archives.

LAWRENCE TIBBETT

70. Tibbett's picture postcard photograph sold in London at the time of his European tour in 1937. From the Editor's collection.

71. Tibbett in the title role of Eugene Goossens' opera, *Don Juan de Mañara*. Tibbett created the role at the world premiere at Covent Garden, London, on 24 June 1937, at the composer's explicit request. Courtesy of Metropolitan Opera Archives.

72. As Iago in *Otello* which Tibbett first sang in San Francisco on 28 November 1936.
Courtesy of Kurt Binar.

73. Tibbett as Iago, Eidé Norena as Desdemona, and Giovanni Martinelli in the title role in a London performance of *Otello*. Courtesy of Metropolitan Opera Archives.

74. A Ray Lee Jackson studio portrait of Lawrence Tibbett. From the Editor's collection.

75. Three baritones with the terminally ill soprano Alma Gluck. From l. to r.: Richard Bonelli, Lawrence Tibbett, and Frank Chapman. From the Editor's collection.

76. Tibbett and soprano Kirsten Flagstad. From the Editor's collection.

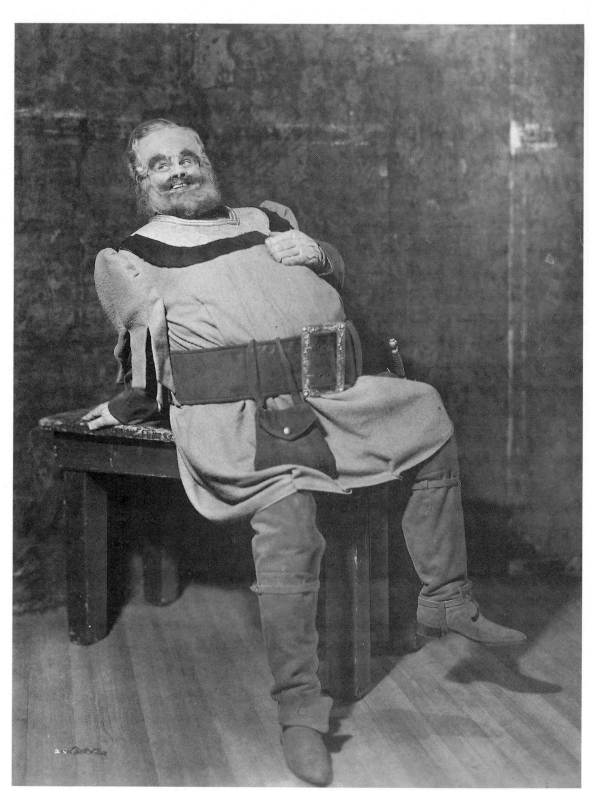

77. In his forty-third year Tibbett gave up Ford for the title role in Verdi's *Falstaff*. He first sang the role on 16 December 1938. Photo: Wide World Studio. From the Editor's collection.

78. John Falstaff (Tibbett) with his servants: Pistol (Norman Cordon) and Bardolph (Alessio de Paolis), at the Metropolitan. Courtesy of Metropolitan Opera Archives.

79. Student concert managers (l. to r.) John C. Collins, William R. Moran, and Elinor Hall with Lawrence Tibbett after a Stanford University Memorial Auditorium concert on 24 January 1940. Courtesy of William R. Moran.

80. Tibbett at the artists' entrance of the War Memorial Opera House in San Francisco (1941). From the Editor's collection.

81. Tibbett as Figaro and Bidù Sayão as Rosina in *Il Barbiere di Siviglia* at the War Memorial Opera House. From the Editor's collection.

82. Tibbett as Figaro in *Il Barbiere di Siviglia,* a role he performed only once in his career, on 22 September 1941, at the War Memorial Opera House in San Francisco. Courtesy of Metropolitan Opera Archives.

83. Captain Harold Greene accepts cartons of records from (l. to r.) Vaughan Monroe, Gladys Swarthout, and Lawrence Tibbett. The artists and RCA Victor donated the records to the Armed Forces in Alaska for the entertainment of the troops. (December 1942). From the Editor's collection.

84. Tibbett as Don Carlo in *La Forza del destino.* He first sang the role on 9 January 1943. From the Editor's collection.

85. Tibbett, Mrs. Walter Sands Marvin, and Lauritz Melchior at a Guild luncheon. From the Editor's collection.

86. Host Sinatra with his guest Lawrence Tibbett on "The Frank Sinatra Show," on 21 March 1945. Photo: CBS. From the Editor's collection.

country my supposedly shameful connection with grand opera was carefully suppressed. Laurel and Hardy were in *The Rogue Song* and at that time had not reached anywhere near their present popularity. Any conceit that I might have had regarding my box office value as a movie star was quickly eliminated when, passing through a small Western town on a train, I saw on a theater canopy: "Laurel and Hardy in *The Rogue Song.*"

It was not until I had made two motion pictures that theater officials generally looked upon me as a star and advertised my name without much reluctance.

The movies began to improve my acting the minute I saw the shots of the first scenes. To my utter astonishment I discovered that every time I took a high note I looked at the end of my nose and crossed my eyes! I was twisting my mouth into queer shapes, and when I pronounced certain words they didn't sound at all the way I expected.

I was using Operatic Gesture No. 1—the right hand above the heart, the left hand extended skyward—to mean anything! I used it for "I love you very much," "It looks like rain," "Good night, Mother," and "No, I don't believe I'll have any more spinach."

I learned that action is not necessarily acting. Lionel Barrymore taught me to *think* of an emotion and to use only enough gestures to get the idea over. He knocked out of me forever, I hope, almost everything I had learned to imitate in bad operatic acting of the old school.

I believe that the secret of Greta Garbo's success as an actress lies in the fact that she can stay still and concentrate on an idea, and hold your interest, longer than any other actor I ever saw.

I lied when *Who's Who in America* first asked me for biographical data. I said that I made my opera première at the Metropolitan as Valentine in *Faust*. I was loath to confess that I had made so little impression on the operatic powers that they launched me in what is probably the most insignificant rôle in opera.

I played one of two monks in *Boris Godunov.* We sang about twenty bars of music in Latin, most of it off-stage. I didn't even put on makeup. We walked on the stage, were pelted with stones by a mob, and retreated. Then we took off our monks' costumes and went home.

Unimportant though it was, I was well satisfied. I was quite proud to have started my career with Chaliapin, who sang Boris. Chaliapin, I believe, is the greatest operatic performer we have ever had. His was a magnificent personality and he was the strongest single influence in bringing to the operatic stage real acting, as opposed to operatic acting.

As Chaliapin tops the singing actors, so does John McCormack lead in his line. McCormack is my favorite concert singer and he is a good friend of mine.

Several years ago at the Bohemian Grove, near San Francico, John and I got into a friendly argument as to the merits of our respective B flats.

"I can sing a better B flat than you can," I said, and produced a sample.

"Maybe so," he grinned, "but I get more money for my B flats than you do."

Which ended the argument.

My performance of Valentine was my second appearance at the Metropolitan. Three days before the performance I was notified that because of Vincente Ballester's illness I had been assigned to the rôle. Coached chiefly by Wilfred Pelletier, assistant conductor, working day and night, I learned the part. With the help of the prompter, I got through the opera without serious mishap, but to this day the music of *Faust* makes me catch my breath, and when I make my first entrance over the bridge, as Valentine, my knees shake most deplorably.

After I appeared in *Faust* I was visited by a swarthy man who runs a claque at the Metropolitan. For $25 he guaranteed to deliver at least two bows at any performance.

I asked the Metropolitan officials about it and they told me not to waste my money. It was then that I heard that every opera house has a claque of its own—a body of men and women, spotted in strategic parts of the house, who lead the applause and make sure that it comes at the right time.

A claque cannot rouse an audience that has not been stirred by a performance. But for a worthy performance it can get applause under way. Americans will join in applause but seldom will initiate it. However, an audience quickly resents an obvious effort to stimulate applause and, frowning, sits at once on its hands; so the claque must only suggest and never blatantly lead.

An opera singer cannot live without his bows, which he counts as a kid counts his new agates. There is a technique in bowing to an audience which it took me several years to learn.

Mrs. Paul Cravath, who was Agnes Huntington, a famous singing actress, gave me my first lessons in taking curtain calls.

"You're popping out and in," she said. "Stand still when you get out there. Let them see you! Look at each person in the opera house and make him think you're a good friend of his. And, after you step back, don't wait until they *demand* your presence. When the applause seems to be dying, take another bow!"

Grand opera seems to stir audiences to greater enthusiasm than any other theatrical effort, and, because I had become accustomed to the urge of the audience, when I contracted to sing regularly over the radio I found myself in the most difficult work I had ever attempted.

The inspiration of an audience is a definite physiological stimulant. When I sing to a radio microphone I feel like a football player who is charging through a line in front of empty stands.

I shut my eyes and try to pretend that I am singing to an audience. I act the part that I am singing, and when I finish I try to imagine that somewhere somebody is applauding.

Unless he has had years of radio experience a singer usually suffers instinctively a distinct shock like a slap in the face when his song ends and nothing, *absolutely nothing,* happens! For a moment, until you realize where you are, something clutches at your stomach, and in the deathlike silence you think, "Gosh! Not a sound! Am I as bad as all *that*!"

It is rather disturbing, that twenty-four-hour wait until the mail man comes in with the applause.

The task of choosing songs for the radio audience is a difficult one. Requests are divided rather evenly between popular and classical music, so I attempt to solve the problem by singing a little of every kind.

This was a problem that confronted me when I first sang over the radio—in Los Angeles in 1922. I was honored by being invited to sing for Station KHJ. I worried for days, and finally selected a program of operatic songs that I decided would be worthy of this great occasion. Millions, they told me, would listen in.

I sang, and got along rather well and felt that I must have become famous overnight. The next day I waited for congratulations, but none of my friends had radios and not one had heard me. It was a great shock. I went around asking utter strangers what they thought of Lawrence Tibbett's radio début, and all they said was "Huh?" To this day I have never found even one person—out of the audience of millions that I imagined was listening breathlessly—who heard me over KHJ in 1922.

When I began to sing regularly at the Metropolitan, Rupert Hughes tried to get me a summer job in opera in Chicago. The impresario told Hughes, "I never heard of him. I couldn't use an unknown."

Two years later this impresario said to Hughes, "I heard Lawrence Tibbett recently. He's great!"

"Why don't you engage him?" Hughes asked.

"He's too expensive. I need a baritone, though. Perhaps I could place that friend of yours. What was his name?"

"Tibbett," said Hughes.

I started at the Metropolitan at a salary of $60 a week. They gave me a bonus of $1,500 for my second season, in which I first did Ford in *Falstaff,* but they raised my salary to only $90 a week, instead of the $100 my contract promised.

My wife and the twins had joined me in New York and the expenses were high. I had practically thrown away $750, which was the cost of giving a recital.

During the first season at the Metropolitan I had a mild attack of influenza and got out of bed to sing with Jeritza in a scene from the last act of *Carmen.* The company was doing a program of big scenes from various operas. I sang Escamillo, the toreador, who has very little to do in that scene. But it was my first year in grand opera, and to appear as the toreador with Jeritza in any scene at all from *Carmen* seemed to be an opportunity for which I could justifiably risk my life.

The day after the performance I had a relapse and went to a hospital, where they said I had spinal meningitis. They were wrong, but I wasn't back at the Metropolitan for three weeks. Rupert Hughes happened to be in New York and came to see me. I was broke, and he lent me $300 to pay my hospital bill. Luckily, I have never been ill since then.

I was fortunate that the Metropolitan kept me, and thus gave me the opportunity, in my second season, to sing Ford. At the end of my first twenty-two weeks they told me that they didn't want me particularly and offered me $75, instead of the $100 that the option called for. After my tearful protests, they raised it to $90, which I accepted. It was then that I learned what "option" means. I was so inexperienced in legal language that I had thought I had a four-year contract at certain definite figures. I discovered that the Metropolitan had an option to do with me about as they chose. The only option I had was to take it or leave it.

They had an idea that my health was bad, and at the Metropolitan they don't want singers who are likely to become ill just before a performance.

The newspaper publicity that I received for the *Falstaff* performance started a rumor that the Metropolitan had raised my salary to fabulous figures. There were other stories, to the effect that I was to take Scotti's place immediately, that Scotti and I were at swords' points, that he was jealous of me. Newspapers said he had tried to prevent me from taking a bow when the audience applauded for me.

When these stories appeared, Scotti came to me and said, "I hope you realize that I wouldn't do anything like that." And certainly in the enthusiasm and excitement of the moment neither Scotti nor I had realized the situation.

A few weeks later, when I was singing at the Metropolitan, William M. Sullivan, my attorney, sat in a box with, among others, Mrs. Lawrence Townsend, a distinguished patron of music and wife of the former ambassador to Belgium, and Rufus L. Patterson, the tobacco man. Patterson said, "After his success in *Falstaff* I suppose Tibbett's troubles are over. The Metropolitan must be paying him a large salary now."

Sullivan told him how much I was getting.

"That's a shame," Patterson said. "We'll have to do something about that."

Unknown to me, Sullivan had already discussed with Mrs. Townsend the fact that my income did not in any way meet my expenses. When Patterson offered to help, Mrs. Townsend and Sullivan organized themselves into an informal committee, and a few days later they received nearly $4,000.

Among the contributors were Mr. Patterson, Mrs. Ida A. Polk, Mrs. Charles B. Alexander, Mrs. Marius DeBrabant, Mrs. William Crocker, Mrs. Charles E. Mitchell, and Clarence Mackay. It was their tribute to a young American artist, they said, not a loan. I insisted upon accepting it as a loan, or having the privilege of repaying my debt of gratitude by singing at their homes.

When I sang *The King's Henchman,* at its première in January, 1927, I first *felt* the strong concentration of an audience on the story. Edna St. Vincent Millay wrote the libretto and Deems Taylor the music. It was the first time I ever sang in English at the Metropolitan, and at the end of the performance, I made up my mind that I would crusade actively all my life for opera in English.

Edna St. Vincent Millay wrote a beautiful and singable libretto for *The King's Henchman,* though some of the patrons of the opera were shocked when the Henchman sang right out in English a complaint that his feet hurt him.

Miss Millay is a tiny, brilliant, energetic person and in rehearsals won a battle from the entire staff of the Metropolitan Opera Company. The opera ran a little long, and the conductor and stage manager decided to cut out my last aria. Deems Taylor protested, but finally gave up. I said I thought they were all wrong, then was forced to surrender.

So they cut the aria.

Miss Millay came to a rehearsal the next day and missed the aria. Taylor told her what had happened.

She gritted her teeth. "They won't cut that out of *my* opera!" she declared.

The Metropolitan staff had conquered many a woman opera singer, but never before had gone into battle with a poetess. I could have told them something about the futility of arguing with a poetess! For the first time in the history of the opera a woman had the maestros scared to death.

"That is the best scene in the opera. If it goes out," she said, "the entire opera goes out. We stop right now!" And they knew that she meant it.

The aria stayed in. And she was right. It turned out to be the peak of the performance. . . .

And now I come to the most important event in my life—my second marriage, which brought me quiet, sympathy, inspiration, and companionship such as I had dreamed of, but which I thought actually existed only in those vague promises of Hans Christian Andersen: "And so they lived happily ever after."

It was in San Francisco that I met the present Mrs. Lawrence Tibbett. I had gone to a reception to meet Herbert Hoover, then Secretary of Commerce, who was the guest of honor at the home of George T. Cameron, owner of the *San Francisco Chronicle.* I was in San Francisco for a holiday at the Bohemian Grove, where, during my vacation, I sang *St. Francis of Assisi.*

At the reception I was asked to sing, and I did, gladly. After a number of encores I felt that I had given my voice all the use it should have that evening and decided that neither wild horses nor Herbert Hoover could make me sing again. Then a lovely lady approached me. She had read of my success as Ford in *Falstaff,* she said. She had followed my career through the newspapers. Wouldn't I please—And I found myself singing her favorite song, *Drink to Me Only with Thine Eyes.*

She was Mrs. Jennie Marston Burgard, a New York girl, living in San Francisco, the daughter of Edgar L. Marston, a retired banker. She knew music, was fond of the opera, and we instantly became good friends.

On January 1, 1932, the year after my first marriage was dissolved, we were married. Our son was born in August of this year. Because we agree that the life of a successful artist is the happiest of all, combining as it does avocation and vocation, we shall do everything possible to develop his interest in the arts.

Since our marriage, ours has been a tranquil life, born of complete understanding. My wife is interested most in my career, and we like to do things together, whether it is a motoring trip in Europe or a midnight jaunt to Harlem. Whenever possible, she travels with me on tour, and is at the opera every night that I sing and usually is the first to greet me in my dressing-room after a performance.

We avoid as far as possible elaborate social functions. We are not hermits, but we do enjoy each other best and we have more fun sitting quietly at home, discussing intensely and at great length what probably to most people would seem to be quite trivial subjects, than we would have at a formal dinner party where men and women debate the affairs of the nation.

My wife has a fine mind, a marvelous sense of humor, and a sound feminine instinct which saves me from many a blunder. Like me, she abhors sham and pretense, and, as much as my life will permit, we try to live the sane, happy, normal life of two newlyweds in an average social circle in the average American city. I feel quite sure that our honeymoon will never end.

Many men, I think, all their lives dream of an ideal princess. For some the dream never becomes a reality, the princess is always far away, just out of their grasp. To those men the promise of a happy life is only half fulfilled. I am extremely fortunate in that, beyond the shadow of a doubt, my dream has come true. Like the two in the opera—here is my Isolde. . . .

As I write this, the Metropolitan is about to start another season, cut from a brave twenty-four to a pitiful fourteen weeks. Philadelphia and Chicago, once great opera centers, have practically given up the ghost.

I love opera. It is the most extravagant and idealistic gesture that man has made in the theater. But opera as it is today, I am afraid, cannot survive.

Opera must take off its high hat. It must present its librettos in English, and those librettos must be sung by artists who have learned to enunciate the English language so that it can be understood—which is as we speak it, simply and naturally.

It is too much a spectacle. Opera houses are too large for a keen emotional contact between the audience and the actors.

The opera is suffering from tradition. The long gray beards are tripping it up. It needs a housecleaning and some showmanship. It is still trying to make the people adapt themselves to the old-fashioned opera, instead of adapting the opera to the modern-day music lover.

The whole structure of opera must be Americanized if Americans are to support it in the long run.

Most of the old patrons of the opera, themselves, are fed up with its antique art. The rich and the society leaders—no longer quite so rich—who made opera-going the fashionable thing to do, are withdrawing their support. And now that opera needs audiences, it finds that by being snobbish it has alienated the great middle class of music lovers. Even if opera houses should reduce their admission prices to the fees charged for a good musical comedy, which ought to be done immediately, they would have trouble in drawing the crowds.

The Metropolitan needs the patronage of only 3,000 persons at each performance in order to be successful. If 1,500 men and their wives, out of the millions in New York and vicinity, decide to go to the opera tonight, they will fill every desirable seat at the Metropolitan and most of those worthless ones, high up, 'way back and against the wall, from which the disgusted and hornswoggled purchaser can see no more of the stage than if he had bought a seat on a barrel up an alley in Hoboken. I know about those seats. They are the ones that were handed to me when I first came to New York.

But those 1,500 couples won't go to the opera tonight, and half the opera house is likely to be empty. The opera's worship of foreign gods and its overaccentuation of the social side has driven to concerts, to the radio, and to musical comedy hundreds of thousands of music lovers who, even with opera as it is now produced, would thoroughly enjoy it.

Grand opera today is still truly grand—but fine singing, splendid orchestras, and artistic stagecraft are not enough to bring in the dollars of the average man, whose dollars opera must have in order to survive.

The old fogies, when I argue this, say I am crazy. But I wish some forward-looking impresario would try it. Let him get a great American librettist to translate such classics as *Tristan und Isolde* and *Tosca* and *Carmen* into English. Let him charge not more than $3.30 for the best seat in the house and tour the leading cities of the United States with a company of singers from the Metropolitan, including, I hope (if this insubordination doesn't cause me to lose my job!), Lawrence Tibbett.

Would you be there?

PART 3
Selected Articles and Interviews

Everything Counts in Your Musical Success—an Interview with Lawrence Tibbett

FROM *THE ETUDE*, VOL. 44, P. 411–2, JUNE 1926

It may seem extravagant to say that everything one does counts to advantage in one's musical career; but, as I see the subject in the view of my own experience, this is unquestionably the case. The main thing in any musical career is a high ideal. This accompanied with patience, confidence in one's star and incessant industry, usually accompanies more than one really anticipates. In my early youth, when I was engaged in musical, dramatic and cultural studies and activities, I was really not ambitiously dreaming of a day when I might be singing important roles with the Metropolitan Opera Company, in New York. In fact, I hardly know now how it has all come about except that I worked everlastingly and did my very best in every situation and in every occupation that has confronted me.

"I know that there are thousands of young people who find themselves in some phase of work which they feel is very distasteful and very much a waste of time. Consequently they get disgruntled and mope over their work. That is one of the sure ways in which to fail. No matter what you are doing or where Fate may place you, do your level best. The experiences you are now having may be the very finest things to bring out certain qualities in your character, your 'make-up,' your soul. Fate is a mysterious thing. It seems to favor those who keep thinking of the best in themselves and in their fellow men, who never cease working and who possess optimistic patience.

"Since this conference must necessarily be more or less personal, let me say that from my childhood I have always been a devoted worshipper of beauty. It meant little whether it was the beauty of nature, of art, of the theatre, or of music. Beauty fascinated me. I have noticed that with this goal every experience seems to be taking a

89

formative part of my life. Sorrow, joy, travel, financial strain, everything has been like some great hand in shaping my career. Sorrow came to me at a very early age when my father, whom I adored, went upon his duty as the sheriff of Kern County, California, in quest of some notorious highwaymen and robbers. They were located in a Chinese Joss House. The doors were battered down and my father entered alone. The robbers' aim was true and my fearless father was brought home dead. This was my first great sorrow, but it gave me a very different aspect upon life. It made me think of the seriousness of the great adventure through which we are all passing and how necessary it is to do one's bravest and best at all moments.

"My mother wanted me to become a physician, and I then aspired to be a writer. Singing, music and acting always fascinated me. At the age of twelve, I commenced to sing. I also studied the piano for two years in Los Angeles. The advantage of getting this acquaintance with music at an early age has been of very great importance to me in all my later life. I went to the high school at Los Angeles. This school had also what was the equivalent of two years of college work. Thus I had five years of Latin. All this has been useful to me since then, as Latin has proven of especial value to me in acquiring other languages. I studied some harmony and composition in high school. While at the school, I became interested in theatricals and took the leading roles in the school performances, which were usually conducted on a very fine scale.

"I then joined the Hollywood Community Theater. I acted with this and other companies for three years, playing in many of the great works of Shakespeare, Lord Dunsany, Kreymborg, Ibsen, Mary Austin, Shaw, Oscar Wilde and Anatole France. Later I joined the company of Tyrone Power in Shakespearean repertoire. This was most valuable experience for me, as the general character of operatic productions was changing all the time. Time was when the opera singer could make gestures like a railroad semaphore, and 'get away with it.' The new school of opera demands actors, and fine actors, as well as singers. There is no place where one can get dramatic experience like the school of the stage itself. Of course, I didn't know it when I was acting in the Community Theater, but I was actually training myself in the best possible way for the Metropolitan.

"Meanwhile, I had been singing whenever I had the opportunity. At the age of seventeen I commenced singing in choirs. I sang for over eight years. My first position as a choir singer paid me five dollars a month and the amount seemed enormous at the time. It meant spending money for a lively youth. Later, I received forty dollars a month, then one hundred dollars a month. I also did recital work and became a member of the Gamut Club Quartet and of the Orpheus Club. The leader of both, Joseph Dupuy, was my first teacher and an excellent drill master he was in music of this type. This choir work I now look upon as an immense asset in my career. It introduced me to some of the most beautiful and spiritual of music and had an unquestioned effect in developing my conceptions of musical art. I sang the solo roles in *Elijah*, in *Messiah*, in *The Seven Last Words* of Dubois, in the *Crucifixion*, *The Holy City*, and in numerous other works familiar to all good choirs. I know of students aspiring to go into opera who turn up their noses at church choir work. This is nonsense. The church choir gives one spirit of reverence and poise and reserve which may be needed at any time in the career of the operatic singer.

"You see, everything really does count! Studying the piano, going to orchestral concerts, studying through the talking machine, everything. No honest effort is ever wasted. I even made a study of orchestration and read Berlioz assiduously. The more trained intelligence and experience one can bring to the opera, the more welcome will be the singer. Everything depends upon how you do what you are doing at the time. Church music, for instance, affords a magnificent drill in reading at sight. But it does more than that. The great music of the church is vital and very much alive. I gave to the music of the church the same vital expression and the same intense interest that I would to an operatic role. I never sang it as though I were wearing a pall of mock sanctity.

"For a time I sang the Gilbert and Sullivan operas, with a very fine light opera company in California. This too was a valuable experience. Comedy is often more difficult than tragedy, and in Grand Opera it is greatly appreciated, when appropriate. The deft touch that comes with experience in Gilbert and Sullivan is a very much worthwhile form of practice for the larger proscenium.

"These experiences may seem quite enough for a young man; but there were others and many of them without which it seems to me that it would have been impossible for me to bring to my art that meaning for which every normal audience craves, and which it identifies as a human quantity. By this I mean that far too many performers and singers have seen very little of life itself except by observation. For a time, I was a cowboy on my grandfather's ranch, doing all the work of a cowboy. Again, I worked as a farmer in the hayfields. At another time I worked on an orange ranch. Once I was assistant engineer, working in overalls with a large stationary engine. During the war, I enlisted in the Naval Reserves and was at different times quartered in Vladivostok, Japan and China.

"All these experiences did two things for me. First, they helped to build up my vitality. Vitality, according to Charles Frohman, is the secret of the success of most performers. You may be a wonderfully gifted artist; but if you have not the supreme good health and the strong physical and mental activity that go with it, you will find that the public may not pay much attention to you. The artist should make health a regular part of his business. Health practice is just as necessary as scale practice. The singer especially must come to his work with a body rested, fresh, spontaneous, and with a good digestion. Late hours, bad air, poorly digested meals, spell failure in the long run. The spontaneity that comes with fine health is quickly identified by audiences.

"Second, my varied experiences gave me an opportunity to see men and see life. They built experiences ranging from the most trivial to the most tragic and gruesome, as for instance when I looked into a store-room in Vladivostok and saw scores of soldiers who had been killed in action, now frozen stiff and piled up like cord wood waiting the time when the granite ice would permit the digging of graves. It is impossible for one of trivial domestic experiences to imagine those extreme conditions which mark human existence. Again, audiences are quick to sense this and they seem to be able to divine physically whether the performer is merely feigning things, or whether he has lived a wide and varied life.

"In addition to other happenings, I decided to get married, and without very much idea of where our support was likely to develop. That does not matter much with a fellow who is convinced that he has found the finest girl in the world. I received great encouragement from the famous baritone, Emilio de Gogorza, the writer, Rupert Hughes and a prominent Los Angeles business man, James G. Warren. From the latter

I borrowed money, with my life insurance as collateral, and my wife and I set out with our twin boys to attempt to get a start in New York City. My intent was to become a recital singer, as I had no idea that I had Grand Opera possibilities.

"In the great metropolis, I became a pupil of Mr. Frank La Forge. Mr. Lawrence Evans of Evans and Salter, heard me sing and encouraged me greatly. Finally Mr. La Forge said that he thought I ought to try for Grand Opera, and that he would arrange an audition and also play for me then. I had my auditions and made my debut in *Faust* in the latter part of 1923. Nothing of much moment happened until the eventful *Falstaff* performance when I could hardly realize that all the applause was intended for a newcomer. It was then, however, that I saw that everything I had done in my life had counted toward what I was able to put into that performance.

"Personally, I lay very great stress upon daily work for the voice, just as daily exercise keeps the athlete in fine condition. When I am singing and rehearsing daily, I do not give so much time to vocal exercises. When I am not, I usually practice about two hours a day. In fact, the singer must make a business of singing, and his business starts from his physical culture exercises in the morning, and his cold bath, to the very last moment of the day. For my voice, Mr. La Forge and I find that practice on the vowel 'ay' as in may is best. This vowel is brilliant and sharp and seems to approximate the vocal chords in my voice better than any other. Mind you, another voice might require a different vowel, in the judgement of the singer and teacher. With me, the vowel E seems to raise the tongue high and tighten the jaw. Therefore, I avoid much use of E in practice. I always start in at middle pitch and sing softly and clearly for about ten or fifteen minutes. Then, when my voice is warmed up I try a few high notes, but I never use them in ordinary practice.

"The exercises I use are those worked out under my teacher, Mr. La Forge. These are of the simplest form.

92

Ex. 6

"Their efficacy lies in the way they are done. Two principles predominate: relaxation and support—positive and negative. The positive is the diaphragmatic breath support, and the negative, the relaxed throat and neck."

Youth at the Top:
Lawrence Tibbett, Baritone

by

John Hyde Preston

FROM *WORLD'S WORK,* VOL. 59, P. 36–8, SEPTEMBER 1930

One day late in 1922 another young man from California arrived in New York, to "see what the hell." He was tall, this young man. He had broad shoulders, a California sunburn, some meager luggage, scant money, and a baritone voice. He also had a young wife and two babies, but they had been left behind, safe from the buffets of his fortune, in a ranch house in the Los Angeles hills.

Lawrence Mervil Tibbett laughs now when he thinks of that first day in New York when he was twenty-five years old. Nobody knew who he was. Nobody cared who he was. He was as obscure as the million-and-first snowflake that falls in a blizzard. He laughs now because he realizes what a mad chance he took.

He is casual about those early days of struggle. He will say he was lucky. He will say he got the breaks. He prefers to talk about the good times that he had, about his childhood in Bakersfield, where he was born, and those gay days of his early youth when he lived on his uncle's ranch in the mountains.

"When I was about nine I wanted to be one of two things—a cowboy or an actor. The acting bug got into my system early. I don't know why. I guess drama was in my blood. I could always fight better if I had an audience. When I got a little older I used to play parts in school performances. . . . Where did I go to school? Oh, all around, any place, I wasn't much of a student. I cut up all the time."

He was tall and gawky in those days and his elbows stuck out, but he loved the romantic parts and always got them. The girls thought he was magnificent, but people who knew about acting reserved their opinions.

"Honestly, I can't remember when I first began to sing. I guess I have always sung. I

94

used to bellow songs all over the place. I had music lessons as a kid, but I never took them very seriously. But as I got older I found that I liked learning songs, so I worked like the deuce to learn as many as I could. It was just for my own fun. I never thought of being a singer. Not until I was about seventeen at least. Then somebody heard me one day and said my voice was worth training. I thought it was a huge joke. But I let them take me down to see Joseph Dupuy in Los Angeles. Dupuy was a well-known teacher. He liked my singing and agreed to coach me.''

Young Tibbett, however, got on too fast for Dupuy. Dupuy was wise enough to see as much, and turned his young pupil over to Basil Ruysdael for more advanced instruction. Tibbett was nineteen then—tall and thin and wiry.

There was no holding him back; he wanted to try every song known, the more difficult the better. But soon found himself up against a serious obstacle, the mysterious horror of foreign languages. He had no tongue for them; he hated the very sound of them. Though he labored like an ox to master them, he only stumbled and sprawled. A hopeless task. What was the use of learning them anyway?

Here, for the first time, Lawrence Tibbett butted head-first into the wall of ''tradition.'' The idea of this rut of culture revolted his whole being. Tradition be damned, he insisted; but Ruysdael sadly shook his head. So Tibbett, sweating and scowling, set to work to memorize arias and Lieder, word by word. He could never undertake a whole language. To this day he never has.

1917. Tibbett was twenty. He had been progressing at awful speed. His range was getting broader, his voice steadier. His collection of memorized foreign songs and arias was amazing even Ruysdael. He thought his young pupil should give a concert. His young pupil didn't think so, but he was not going to protest. The concert was arranged. A few people came and applauded with unassuring enthusiasm. A few papers mentioned him next morning with a sort of damp approval. That was all of concerts for a while.

1917 advanced. March came. There was the sound of guns in the distance. April came. There was the sound of men marching and women weeping. America was going to war. The young man of twenty with the baritone voice strolled down to Los Angeles harbor and gazed at the noses of massive dreadnoughts standing in the tide out there on the brown-green waters of the Pacific. He wandered back to town. He went into a navy recruiting station and signed up.

''We went all over the Pacific,'' he says. ''I was given a job as instructor after a while. I didn't know what I was teaching, but that was all right. Nobody minded. We went to China and Japan. Then to Hawaii.''

The weary months dragged on into 1918. There were more cruises. Then November. And war's end.

Lawrence Tibbett got back into civilian clothes with singular speed and enthusiasm. Immediately he returned to the studio of Basil Ruysdael and commenced sweating once more over countless bars of song. War was forgotten. Music was all of life—except for a girl Tibbett met in California. She was young and gay and enthusiastic, and she understood and sympathized with his great ambition. Her name was Grace Mackay Smith.

At least that was her name until the spring of 1919. Then it became Mrs. Lawrence Tibbett.

Two years passed. In that time twin sons were born to the Tibbett household. The

95

proud father soon discovered that his occasional appearances on the concert stage could never support the extra burden. He told Ruysdael of his predicament. Give up singing? Never! insisted Ruysdael. No, he must take his chance; it was too hale a one to miss. Why didn't he go to New York?

Tibbett thought constantly on it for weeks, beset by gnawing doubts. Would he? . . . could he? . . . did he dare? Then suddenly, one night, he made up his mind. He would go—and he would succeed!

In New York he started immediately to study under Frank La Forge, the famous teacher of voice. Six months later La Forge said:

"Why wouldn't it be a good idea for you to get an audition at the Metropolitan Opera?"

Tibbett thought he was joking at first. An audition at the Metropolitan—what a riotous idea! An American who didn't even know a foreign language! Why, they would kick him out on sight.

La Forge insisted. It wouldn't do any harm to try his luck, would it? No, it wouldn't do any harm to try.

About a week later, Lawrence Mervil Tibbett, twenty-five, baritone, of Bakersfield, California, was singing a memorized aria before the grave, important, merciless heads of the Metropolitan Grand Opera Company. He was half-nervous, half-amused, standing there with that awful silence out in front. His knees shook; all the blood was pounding in his head, but his voice was as steady as the sea. Finally, after what seemed as long as eternity with fifteen minutes added, it was all over and he went home. He was sure he would never hear anything of it. He didn't think his voice was big enough for grand opera. No, the audition would come to nothing.

A few days later a message came. At first Tibbett could not gather its meaning, but only at first. Then he delivered himself of a whoop—then another and another. He had been accepted! Accepted! He, Lawrence Tibbett, was on the roster of the Metropolitan!

He sent a telegram to his wife, who was still in California with the children. Applause thundered around him. For a few weeks he stayed on in New York, in a state of drunken ecstasy, and then took the train across the continent to get his family.

But Lawrence Tibbett, back again in New York with his family, first appeared in a small role in Faust on the stage of the Metropolitan Opera House. Giulio Gatti-Casazza, that great impresario saw that his young singer couldn't act. His elbows stuck out all around him, as they had in the old school days; he walked too fast or too slow; his exits and entrances were muddled and clumsy.

Gatti-Casazza told him of his bad fault. That judgment was at once a warning and a command. Tibbett struggled on to get some grace into his unwieldy movements, to control those elbows, to accomplish the perfect gesture, to make dramatic entrances and dramatic exits. It was a long pull, but finally its effects began to show. Gatti-Casazza quietly registered his approval by giving Tibbett better roles and more performances.

A year passed. Lawrence Tibbett now felt himself a fixture at the Metropolitan, though not a very important one. His parts were small, and his plaudits were few and very lukewarm.

Then the night of January 2, 1925. A special performance of *Falstaff* was being given in honor of Antonio Scotti, who sang the title role. Tibbett was playing Ford—a

87. Tibbett as Michele in Puccini's *Il Tabarro*, a role he first sang on 5 January 1946. Courtesy of Metropolitan Opera Archives.

88. Another portrait of Tibbett as Michele. Courtesy of Metropolitan Opera Archives.

89. Rigoletto was Tibbett's main "export" role. Here he is shown with Emilia Carlino as Gilda, at the Royal Opera House in Rome. Following the final performance (6 June 1946), Tibbett was presented with a memorial by the chorus of the company. Photo: Acme Newspictures, Inc. From the Editor's collection.

90. Tibbett as Captain Balstrode in Benjamin Britten's *Peter Grimes*. His first assumption of the role came late in his career, on 21 January 1949. It was followed by the silver jubilee celebration of his Metropolitan debut. Courtesy of Metropolitan Opera Archives.

minor part, though better than most of the others he had been singing. It was a select audience that night, a very critical audience for some reason, even in the face of that much-bejeweled house. He knew he was singing especially well and that he was attracting notice.

The opera was progressing. The first act was over. It was now the end of the first scene of the second act. Tibbett, alone on the stage, was singing Ford's soliloquy—that mortally sad, grief-stricken lament of the betrayed husband. He finished. The curtain fell. The great house was hushed, ominously hushed, for a moment. Then, suddenly, came a smashing burst of applause, like the ocean rushing through a broken sea wall, getting louder, rising, until it became a storm.

Scotti came out with the soprano. The curtain parted. Tibbett joined hands with them, and the three took the calls. Then Tibbett retired. Scotti and the soprano remained. They took call after call. But the applause did not for a moment diminish. On the contrary, it got steadily louder. Nobody could understand why, but they judged it was for Scotti. The great baritone went out again and again, but nothing could satisfy the audience. The noise became deafening. Serafin, the conductor, came to the orchestra pit to resume the opera, but he was shouted down. The house was in uproar.

The other night, five years after, Tibbett told me the story of that exciting evening in detail.

"Frankly," he said, "I had no idea what it was all about. They had gone mad out there. I thought it was for Scotti. I started upstairs to change my paint, but halfway up I heard a voice from the house yelling 'Tibbett! Tibbett!' I thought it might be some foolish friend who had become excited in the turmoil. I hesitated for a moment and then went on up to my dressing room. When I closed the door I could hear nothing, because of the noise of traffic in the street below.

"I had my costume half off and was sitting by the mirror removing grease paint, when suddenly the door opened and one of the fellows rushed in and grabbed my arm excitedly. 'Gatti wants you down there. Hurry up!'

"I grabbed up some clothes and went out. I thought I had done something wrong and was going to get called down. I was scared all through. Then I heard that thunderous roar still going on. I went downstairs. Everybody was running around. Gatti was there. I said to him: 'What has happened?' They want you out there; they're calling for you.' I paused for a moment. The din was terrible. Then I heard calls of 'Tibbett! Tibbett!' I looked at Gatti. 'Shall I go out?' I asked. He nodded.

"I started onto the stage, but the big curtain was down and I had to go around in front of it. That curtain is only for stars, you know, and I had never been out there before, so I guess I looked pretty silly when I emerged. I was only half dressed besides.

"They all went wild then. They threw silk hats and stamped on the floor. I felt very embarrassed. I didn't know exactly what to do. I just stood there and smiled and felt dizzy. They made me come out about fifteen times. Once Scotti came with me and patted me on the back before 'em all. That made 'em crazier. But pretty soon they got tired and stopped. That was a great relief. They had been yelling for twenty minutes.

"When the opera was all over, my wife and I and a few friends wanted to celebrate, but we didn't have much money. So we went to Child's and drank soup, and tried to guess what might come of an ovation like that. It was only when we saw the papers the next morning, with their glaring headlines, that we understood what it really meant. Those newspaper fellows really put the thing over. It was wonderful of 'em."

Tibbett literally woke up to find himself famous, if any man ever did. The idea of the young American singing his way to glory, took the whole country by storm. But few people knew then that Tibbett was the only man in the history of the Metropolitan Opera who ever jumped from being a singer of small roles to being one of the world's greatest baritones—all in one short night. All the others had worked slowly up; Tibbett took one flying leap and landed on top of the pile.

Through all this glory Tibbett has been modest. Among the florid, gesticulating foreigners at the Metropolitan, his tall, quiet figure is unmistakable and almost strange. He still loves his own language best of all, and holds Deems Taylor's *The King's Henchman* as his favorite opera, the one in which he finds the most pleasure as a singing man. He is always moving ahead, impatient to be trying something new. He laughs at tradition in music.

"All the best in a tradition," he will say, "is used up before it becomes a tradition. After a fine thing is dead, what is left is called 'traditional.' It's a great joke. To hell with it!"

For a man in his early thirties, Lawrence Tibbett has gone far, especially when you consider that his is an art which, until very recent years, has not been kind to native artists. And he will go farther. His imagination and independence will carry him into unexplored places. One feels confident of progress in him. For he has the searching vitality, the enthusiasm, the hatred of repetition, and the restlessness that denote the true artist.

A Talk on the "Talkies"

by

Lawrence Tibbett

As told to R. H. Wollstein

FROM *THE ETUDE*, VOL. 49, P. 539–40, AUGUST 1931

Since the release of my talking pictures, I have received hundreds of letters from music students all over the country, telling me that they consider it an advantage to observe the methods of an operatic singer "at close range." Letters of this sort make it clear that the sound films, which are produced solely as a means of public amusement, can be of immense help to the student and the young singer. They can assist them in many ways.

First, there is the angle which my correspondents so kindly called to my attention. One says, "I watched your breathing"; another "the close-ups were a good object lesson of production methods"; and a third, "when you opened your mouth, I could even watch what your tongue was doing"! I confess that this last staggered me a bit. I had no idea that, when I was trying to play my part as romantically as possible, spectators were going to watch the vibrations of my tongue, that highly useful, though none too ornamental, factor in the singer's art. But even if it rocked my vanity, the incident demonstrated the manner in which the talkies can serve the art of music.

If an object lesson of this sort can be derived from ordinary talkie entertainment, the facilities of the new art can be utilized further. I believe that it would be an excellent thing if the greatest musicians of our day, both vocalists and instrumentalists, were to make short sound-films, of one or two reels, demonstrating the individual characteristics of their methods. Explanatory comments would add greatly to the usefulness of such demonstrations. Think what a boon it would be if the students of today could benefit from the authentic recordings of Caruso, Melba, Patti, Jenny Lind. The students of tomorrow will doubtless be able to learn their lessons from talkie recordings of the authorities of today.

If the equipment for showing such films were too costly for the average studio, they could be exhibited in the larger conservatories, at public museums and at educational centers. Master lessons setting forth the methods and the physiological motions of recognized artists would be an invaluable aid to music students, and the talkies will undoubtedly make them available.

The great advantage of the talkies is that the entire audience has as good a view as those who sit in the first ten rows. Whether the film gives a definite vocal lesson, or whether it is a regulation picture, featuring some well-known singer, in whose working methods individual members of the audience may be interested, the magnified "close-ups" make it possible for the demonstrator or actor to get his message or his methods across to his public with far greater precision than he could hope to achieve from the stage or the lecture platform.

Still, the business of teaching music and singing methods covers only one angle of the role which the talkies are playing in the lives of our younger singers. Obviously, there is a great career in the talkies for hundreds of today's students. Quite naturally, "names" and "box-office draws" will always be given preference where big parts are concerned. But the talkies—as well as the radio—are opening an entirely new field of outlet to young purveyors of the commodity of music.

Which brings me to a consideration of what is called talkie (or radio) technic. It has been suggested, even in vocal studios, that the talkies require a special vocal technic which differs from that of the concert platform or the operatic stage. The argument is that the singer does not depend entirely on his own powers in "getting across" his effect: that the elaborate system of controls regulates volume and even quality of tone to such a degree that the singer is called upon solely for the production of the tone, and its nuancing is made effective by mechanical regulation. *This is absolutely false.* I should be inclined to warn students against agents or even teachers who put forward such a view.

There is no such thing as radio talkie technic. Either your singing methods are right or wrong. If they are wrong, your defects cannot be glossed over by mechanical controls. If they are right, they are applicable to any field of singing. When I prepared for talkie work, I was given any amount of advice, about reducing tone volume and so forth, but I did not heed it.

I sang before the microphone exactly as though I had my Metropolitan audience before me. As far as the *tone* is concerned, a *piano* tone will retain its basic quality of a *piano* tone no matter how greatly it may be amplified by mechanical means; and the audience that is asked to accept such a mechanized substitution is not being fairly dealt with.

As far as the *singer* is concerned, his performance loses in vitality as soon as he allows himself to be bound by artificial and repressive methods. Incidently, it is this false concept of a separate technic which is responsible for the disappointing performances of many radio stars, who essay concert appearances on the strength of an "air success." The only method that is tolerable for talkie work is the best and soundest singing method possible, used without stint or self-saving.

There is a branch of talkie work, however, which does require a highly special technic, and that is the acting. I believe that movie acting entails far greater problems of adjustment than movie singing. The talkies, by their very nature, lack the scope of stage. When a spectator looks at the stage, he is always at the same distance from the

100

entire action taking place there. In the movies a constantly equal distance between spectator and screen would prove monotonous. The scenes are constantly broken up by close-ups, by medium shots (which show part of the scenery, and perhaps three-quarters of the players), and long shots (which focus on the scenery primarily and reduce the size of the players). These breaks in the scene afford the spectator an ever-shifting view of the action instead of an oversight of the stage as a whole. This involves an entirely different acting technic. The actor who is used to playing scenes as a whole must accustom himself to playing a "three-minute shot" one day, and resuming the actions at the same point, in the same mood, and with the same facial expression some four days later.

Further, the scope of all gestures must be reduced. In the operatic acting to which I am accustomed, large sweeping gestures are the order of the day. The first time I tried a broad sweep of the arm in the films my arm was cut off at the elbow. The film-band, which is so powerfully magnified on the screen, is in reality no larger than an oversize postage stamp, and all gestures must be confined to fit within its limits. That is why most of the emotions depicted in the movies must be conveyed through facial pantomine and eye work. A two-inch wave of the hand must take the place of the operatic sweep of arm. The next time you visit the talkies, notice how the actors walk on and off the scenes, but remain more or less still in the scenes themselves, as far as large-scale motions are concerned.

The advantage of this is that the important moments can be emphasized to a greater degree than on the stage, and that the acting is, perhaps, more precise. The disadvantage is that the actor's emotional continuity is constantly broken into, and when it is resumed, eventually, mechanical methods must be called into help. In "The Rogue Song," for instance, I had to sing a song that lasted about four minutes. In the talkies, this is a long scene. It was intensely hot, and the lights beat down on me like concentrated fire. Almost immediately, I began to perspire, and, in another moment, the beads of moisture were rolling down my face so that they were in danger of showing in the film. The scene had to be stopped, to give me a chance to wipe my face.

This interruption meant that the sound track had to be cut and resumed at the very note at which I had left off, and the film band, too. Giving me the note in the music was simple enough. Cutting the action, though, involved quite a procedure. First, my feet had to be outlined in chalk at the exact spot where I had been standing. Then, my fingers had to be marked on my uniform, in the place where I had placed my hand on my heart. Next, the director made careful note of the angle of my head and the expression of my face, and then, at last, I could stop to wipe away the perspiration from my face. It is well to draw points like these to the attention of students in operatic classes, who may think that acting is acting!

There is no doubt that the talkies will soon bring entire operas and concert recitals to the movie public at movie prices. This has not been done yet, because at present no widespread demand exists for this sort of entertainment throughout the country as a whole. To date music thrives as a popular amusement only in Germany and Italy. But the music which has been given our public has been so enthusiastically received that a greater demand is being created everyday. As this demand grows, there will be more opportunities for talented young musicians. Small indications point the way towards it already. The Metro-Goldwyn-Mayer studios employ a capable vocal teacher on yearly contract to build voices and improve the singing and talking methods of the actors already affiliated with them. Some years ago there were hundreds of musicians of ability, but of less stellar renown, who toured the country, giving performances at less than stellar fees. The number of these has fallen off tremendously during the past five years, and many of these musicians are working in the radio and talkie studios.

I believe that opera will have to be adapted and modified to suit the structural needs of the talking films, since long shots of an entire opera straight through would be monotonous. I have no reason to doubt, though, that strictly musical work in the talkies is on the increase and that they offer a definite career for young people with trained voices. The talkies are America's best chance of popularizing good music and of affording the remote districts of our country a chance to see and hear the best. This value of the talkies cannot be overestimated.

There exists, at present, two obstacles to the popularization of good musical performances, and the talkies have it in their power to do away with both of them. One of these is cost. The best seat at a movie cost less than the cheapest at an opera or at a good recital, and affords the spectator better visual and acoustic facilities. The other obstacle lies in the inexplicable but none-the-less actual psychological fact that the average person still feels a bit shy of "high brow" art, as such. The man in the street who whistled *I'm Always Chasing Rainbows,* some years back, would have needed a bit of urging to spend money on a piano recital which included the Chopin *Fantasia Impromptu* from which the rainbow song derived! Of course, this *oughtn't* to be so, but it *is.*

The painless popularization of good music, through the far-reaching media of radio and talkies, can cure and is curing this hesitancy. By painless popularization I mean that the psychologically expert talkie producers are giving the public good music, simply as music, without frightening them off by "high brow" labelings. When my own talkies first came out, the M-G-M people were careful not to advertise me as "baritone of the Metropolitan Opera Company." There is a vast section of the country's movie public to whom such a billing would have meant "something for the high brows—something for the swells—something to keep away from." Instead, I was billed simply as Lawrence Tibbett—a new actor who sings! And those very people who might have been shy of a Metropolitan Opera baritone came to hear this Tibbett person and, I am grateful to say, liked him, too!

After the entire movie public has heard three or four or five Metropolitan Opera singers, and found that it need not be afraid of them, the form of advertising may change, and good singing will be on the highroad to painless popularization. The main thing, after all, is to get good music and good singing before the people, and there is not the slightest doubt that this is taking place. The public is being put into closer touch with good musicianship, through an eminently popular medium. That is one way of building a musical tradition.

I have frequently been asked about the type of voice that "takes" well in the talkies. Just as some faces photograph better than others, regardless of the comparative pulchritude of the faces, so some voices record better than other, regardless of the inherent merits of the voice compared. Just what the qualities are, which make voices "take," is not definitely known. As a rule, though, men's voices take better than women's, which might lead one to suppose that the reproducing mechanisms are kinder to the voices of heavier timber. As a rule, this is true in radio work, too.

On the whole, then, I can say that the talkies offer a splendid chance of a career to young, fresh, trained voices. Beginners might do well to look into the matter, remembering, of course, that they will be allowed to begin only in the smallest way, despite their years of study and training. They should remember, too, that talkie work is no haphazard affair, with which to toy as a stop-gap. The talkies are proving themselves a potent force in the nationalizing of good music, and aware men direct their destinies. They want the best only. That is why only the best singing technic will be able to succeed and endure there. Aspirants for honors must not let themselves be led astray by catchy, quick-success methods of "talkie technic." There are none!

The only drawback I found in talkie work was the missing stimulus of an audience. It is quite true that the impersonal glare of camera lights and microphone proves more disconcerting than the focus of thousands of eyes. Anyone who is used to facing audiences grows accustomed to the psychic influence which emanates from those thousands of heterogeneous units which combine to form that precious factor—*My Audience.* Their coldness can depress you, their enthusiasm buoys you up, and the feeling of contact with them makes you live more keenly. In the talkies, you face only the eye of the camera, lights, microphones, and mechanics, all busy on their own jobs. No one is under your spell! You have no means of gauging the goodness or badness of your effect on people. And you miss that gauge of your efforts which rises so subtly to meet you on the stage. Still, that obstacle can be surmounted by mental training. The young people who begin talkie work without stage experience will not feel it at all. And to them I say, "Do your best; aim at the highest vocal standards; stand by them unswervingly—and watch the talkies!"

Opera Can Be Saved by the Movies

by

Lawrence Tibbett

As told to H. H. Taubman

FROM *PICTORIAL REVIEW,* FEBRUARY 1933, P. 8–9, 68

Opera in this country is in grave danger. This fact can no longer be blinked at. The depression has written this on the wall in burning letters for all to see. The Chicago and Philadelphia Operas, two of the major companies in the country, have suspended entirely, and the Metropolitan Opera has been forced to reduce its season from twenty-four to sixteen weeks, with the future of the company even on this basis, in extreme doubt. I am "for" opera. I love it so much that I would like to see some of the deadwood cleared away, and it is for this reason that I am going to speak frankly.

What is the trouble with opera? Can its defects be eradicated? If so, just what are the steps to be taken? These are some of the questions that those of us who are laboring in the vineyard are considering.

The American people as a rule are frightened by opera. It is a sad thing, yet it has its basis. They are frightened by many things—by the manner of presentation, by another and alien language, and by acting of a different school. They are not yet wholly accustomed to hearing their language sung. Their background does not make them sympathetic immediately to opera. The art has no national history. To the average American it is an exotic, a thing for the few.

It is unfortunate that these things be so. But these barriers need not exist! They should not exist! If opera is to live something will have to be done, and done soon. The art cries out for iconoclasm to break down and root out some of the things that are holding it back and keeping it from the position it deserves to occupy in this country.

In the first place, opera has offended against the simplest, the very fundamental laws of the theater. There are certain aesthetes who say that opera has no connection with the theater, that the best way to hear it is to keep the eyes shut and to listen to the orchestra and the singers. If that is true, then all opera houses should be closed immediately. A group of singers and an orchestra are enough, they say. What need for scenery, costumes, lighting, and action?

But this view is not a complete one; it is narrow, reactionary, and not founded on the facts. For opera is rooted in the theater as deeply as it is in music. It is a synthesis of both arts; it is a search for an almost impossible perfection. If opera, then, has offended against the laws of the theater, and I maintain that it has, it has committed cardinal sins. Three things fundamental to its life have not prevailed. A performance should be seen. A performance should be heard. A performance should be understood.

But opera houses here are too large. The Metropolitan and the Chicago Opera Houses, to name but two, are far too spacious. The opera companies have no choice as matters stand today; they must have houses of this size if they are to meet expenses in any fashion whatever. The low-priced seats are so far away that their occupants can neither hear nor see perfectly. And the prices of even these seats are high in comparison with those of most other entertainments.

But the patron of cheaper seats—the man and woman of modest means—is the very one that we have not reached. He is the very one we must reach. Everything, however, militates against such a contact. For under present conditions opera revolves entirely around the wealthy, the well-to-do, and the socially elite. And for many of these, attendance at the opera is not a personal need; it is not an act of interest nor an act of faith; it is a bludgeoning by social exigencies. Furthermore, the operagoer must read the libretto before the curtain goes up and must memorize it to grasp what is going on. This is all wrong! Opera must be in English in this country; we should not be obliged to listen always to something not our own.

The new opera to be produced at the Metropolitan at about the time this magazine is published—Louis Gruenberg's *Emperor Jones,* based on Eugene O'Neill's play—indicates one of the courses opera may perhaps take. It is a work that emphasizes declamation with a musical, rhythmical background; there is only one truly lyrical bit in it, the chant or the prayer—"It's a-me, O Lawd, standin' in de need o' prayer." It is a work that does not flout the laws of the theater. It was created for the theater, and the musical setting seeks only to intensify and heighten the emotional impact of the drama.

I do not consider it necessary to review here entirely the story of *Emperor Jones,* but I should like to remind the reader that it is concerned chiefly with this huge Negro, Brutus Jones, fleeing through the woods pursued by his hallucinations and the maddening, almost unceasing beat of the tom-tom.

The drumbeat—the equivalent of the tom-tom—gradually is accelerated in the opera, and ceases only during the hallucinations which haunt Jones as he flees through the forest. The drums are on all sides of the stage, and at the end of the second act even in the auditorium they give the impression that Jones is being encircled.

I must confess here and now that, like many Negroes and many of the Latin temperament, I love the grand gesture in acting and in living. I believe that a definite reaction to the school of realism in acting is taking place, that that realism can be carried too far. But the grand gesture, as I chose to call it, has much to be said for it.

Certain races have this grand gesture. They love to accent their speech in a highly dramatic manner; they love to strut around, fling their arms about, and in general to express their thoughts by their gestures. And I am not so sure that it is not just as real in its way as our so-called quiet manner of saying and doing things.

An example: a man and a woman, both young, in love with each other. They are alone. This is a moment of deep emotion for them. But there is no movement. They sit quietly, nonchalantly. He, in a casual tone of voice: "Darling, I love you. Please say you'll marry me. I'm sure we'll be very happy." That is all. Where is the sweep, the overpowering rhythm of such a moment?

Another example: A deserted country road. Four somber-looking men in a car. Again a quiet voice, almost a whisper: "So you've double-crossed us, eh? You don't get away with it this time. You're going for a ride now!" That is all. A dagger thrust, silence. Even assassination needs more punch!

Before long, I am sure, we will see a change, possibly a radical change. In the realistic school of acting of today could we have an *Othello* or a *King Lear?* It cannot be done! The school of understatement is no more real than the school of overstatement. They are simply different sets of conventions.

For my part, when I get enthusiastic, I make gestures, and love to make them. What a time I have! I cannot do that in the motion pictures or on the stage. We are accustomed to a different set of conventions. And while we should be fully conscious of the conventions of the age we live in, there is no reason for thinking they are fundamental to our life, liberty, and pursuit of happiness.

I miss on stage vital, spontaneous acting. I miss it in life. There is too much restraint. I, for one, love to speed in a car. It is one way of expressing one's self, although the cop sometimes expresses himself later.

Let us be good moderns and partake of all the flavors. Rather than go too far in one direction, we shall find that we still have a place for fantasy, for music and gesture, for rhythm and sweep. We cannot say that the Italians, for instance, are any the less natural than we simply because of their gestures, their movement, their sweep. Americans have just as much volubility, if we were impelled to use it. On the other hand, the Italians could be just as calm and controlled as we try to be if their customs so dictated.

I have indicated very briefly some of the things that might stimulate interest in the operatic art in this country. More particularly, let us look at the Metropolitan.

There must be unity in purpose and production, there must be a high *esprit de corps* in an operatic organization—an interest in opera for its beauty's sake. I am fully aware that to arrive at the just balance we should have to cut out the singer's vanity. To suggest how that could be accomplished would require the omniscience of Jehovah and the foolhardiness of a stock manipulator. At times I have felt that the artists at the Metropolitan, probably including myself, are working for their own individual glory. We work separately. We do not enter sufficiently into the spirit of the opera itself. Why? I do not know. I suspect it is because many artists have come to the Metropolitan to gain the prestige of this great institution. We think that by getting the spotlight on ourselves and keeping it focused there we shall get more from it in the end. Artistically, I do not believe so. Too often the result has been less cohesive productions.

Another static characteristic is the fear of changing the old way of doing things. Every "i" and every "t" is dotted and crossed with meticulous care. I firmly believe that it is far more important to concentrate on the spirit of the thing, even with a mistake here and there, than to sing a score letter-perfect without reaching for its inner life. A great work must be interpreted by a great individuality. Instead of doing the part precisely as it was done before, one should be permitted to do it as one sees it. I feel somehow that one is not pleading the cause of any artistic expression very profoundly unless one pleads it instinctively. It must be a combination of Wagner and the conductor and the singer, and it is not at all vanity to put it in this way.

It seems to me that a great genius and his works are not fixed things, like the stars in their courses. They are growing things, and they must be enriched by all the interpretative personalities possible. The founder of a great religion is the seed, not the roots *and* the trunk *and* the branches *and* the leaves. All that is needed is that the essential qualities be inherent in the seed.

As for myself, I do not like anything where there is nothing left for me to do, be it opera or religion or anything else.

Another factor which is militating against the popularity of opera is that the orchestra often plays too loudly and the composer has written too loudly. To hear orchestral music one should go to a concert and not to the opera. The singer gets a chance to emerge only when the orchestra is subdued. Surely it is not merely a singer's vainglory to believe people like to hear the story carried to them by beautiful voices.

No one admires the immortal genius of Wagner more than I, but I believe that he has had a corrupting influence on the lyric theater. And after Richard Strauss, Debussy, in permitting *Pelléas and Melisande* to be heard about three-quarters of the time, did something significant in the opposite direction. Mr. Gruenberg, in his opera, *Emperor Jones,* has also stipulated that the words of the singers must never be blurred or obscured by the orchestra. But these operas should be done in a more intimate theater.

What opera outside of *Aida* would not be better in a smaller theater? There is absolutely no argument about it. Of course, opera stars would have to take a smaller salary in a smaller theater, but they would be certain of receiving this salary regularly if opera were on a firm foundation; that is to say, deeply intrenched in the hearts of our people as a vital need.

Another thing worth considering is the size and shape of some of the star singers in opera. In the theater the illusion must be and is maintained. But how can a mood even be established in opera when we have Mimis and Violettas of immense girth fore and aft trying to convince the public in *La Boheme* and *Traviata* that they are breathing their last? Or a Brunnhilde in *Siegfried* who is so huge that, once awakened from her slumber on the Valkyr rock, she dare not turn to the side lest a sudden cascade of her ample proportions make the business too ridiculous? Or a dashing young Rhadames who is a head shorter than the Aida he loves, and cannot, even if he would, see his own feet when looking straight down?

Already, however, opera companies are making an effort to maintain the illusion, and at the Metropolitan today there are almost no exaggerations of this kind.

Please believe that I am not criticizing the art of opera itself. I love it too much! It is the synthesis of all musical arts. It is the most marvelous and impossible creation of man's restless imagination. I love it because of the joy of striving to attain the unattainable. But it has great and perfect moments, and these great moments are worth all the painful ones you are apt to sit through.

107

There are so many things the singer must concentrate on and do. The action must be timed precisely. You have so many bars at such a tempo in which to do a given thing. You must do it in just that way. There is no room, as on the stage, for psychological vagaries and no freedom whatever. You have to think, moreover, of the instrument itself, the voice. It must be economized. As I indicated, there are a dozen and one things to think of, but when you do reach a height, you have reached a real one.

The first time I heard *Tristan und Isolde* I sat very coldly, not clearly understanding German. I had a few theories on Wagner and had read Nietzsche's ideas on the subject. But when they came to the "Liebestod" at the end of the opera I said, "To hell with Nietzsche, this is marvelous!" And I sat there weeping.

And *Die Meistersinger!* It is my favorite opera. It causes one to weep from joy—the purity, the mellowness, and the beauty of this masterpiece!

I for one should like to partake of all the flavors. I would love to do light things, like roles in good operettas. But having established a reputation for one thing, the public is most cruel in controlling you. There you are and there they hold you. One does not make a meal of meat and bread alone; there are also salad and dessert.

I should like to try operetta, but I cannot. I am told that I am above and beyond it. That is nonsense. I am not above and beyond anything so long as it is good. I should love a role in something like *Show Boat*. It is finer and more interesting than many of the operas that I know. But my managers, knowing the temper and the feelings of the public, say "No."

What a howl arose, for example, when I went into motion pictures! Articles appeared saying that Tibbett had gone to the dogs artistically. But after my appearances in the title role of *Simone Boccanegra* at the Metropolitan last year, the tone of my critics had changed. It was said that the great god Movies didn't "get" me. The adventure had not meant retrogression. I gained from the movies and gave them what I could. I know very little about the technique of the movies or the radio, but I have always felt that if I had one fundamental quality, it was artistic sincerity. I have held fast to it. It has always been the basis of my work, and I feel it will always carry me through in any medium of expression in which I happen to find myself engaged. And it was held true for the movies.

The quality of sincere, simple concentration on the particular thing you are doing will carry you through. The concentration on one idea at a time—Garbo knows it better than any one on the screen. To be sure, there will be technical errors, but it takes a long time to learn technique.

My contact with the motion pictures began some time before I made my first picture, *The Rogue Song*. I was not interested in making shorts; the one or two operatic shorts I had seen were very bad. I was approached by one of the officials.

"We are considering doing *Pagliacci*." he said. "It has a good story and we thought you were just the man to do it. What is that aria you sing in it? You know; I forget the name."

"You mean the 'Prologue'?"

"No," he replied, "you know, the aria the leading man sings. The sob song."

"But that is a tenor part and not in my range."

"Who could sing it, then?"

I named several tenors for him. Then I suggested that the part could perhaps be transposed to a lower key so that I could sing the role. But nothing came of it.

Some time later an important moving-picture concern got in touch with me. The producers had secured the right to an operetta by Franz Lehár, *Gypsy Love,* and wanted me to do it.

I had made some screen tests the year before in a silent picture. They were terrible. They were the kind of tests in which the director gives you a telephone and tells you to express sadness, you have just heard that your grandmother has died. You make a funny face. Or you have just heard good news. Prosperity has turned the corner, express gladness. Another funny face. The results of these tests were terrible. Later I was called for some new tests in sound pictures.

"Sing 'Kiss and Again.' " they said.

"But I can't. That's a song for soprano."

"Well, what *can* you sing?"

"I can sing an opera aria, or some of the songs I sing in concert," I said.

The tests were made. I sang Iago's aria from *Otello* and "The Song of the Flea," and wore various make-ups and costumes and lots of beard. I sang also "Drink to Me Only with Thine Eyes," "The Road to Mandalay," and "Cloe," one of my favorites, by the way, among the popular songs. The aria from *Otello* was really good. They were impressed. They said I had screen personality. I did not, and still do not, know exactly what that means.

I hope I have indicated, in a meandering way, some of the germs that infect opera. I am fully aware that the depression has aggravated conditions in all affairs and in this case has brought on a crisis. But is the theater threatened with a complete cessation of activity? Are the motion pictures in danger of extinction?

The answer is obvious. Both the theater and the movies will always have audiences of some sort. So long as the human being will love a story, so long as he will seek emotional catharsis in the figures and passions of created art, so long will the stage and screen endure. But surely opera also should be *vital* to complete living. For instance it contains within itself the drama that is the foundation of the stage and screen. And music can reach corners of the heart and the soul that are too deep for words. Music expresses what is inexpressible; it articulates what is beyond the reach and the grasp of these other arts.

Some of the solutions I have in mind have already been indicated either directly or by inference. To summarize them. If the opera is a drama, then the action, the figures, the conversation should be easily seen, heard, and understood. There should be no overemphasis of either the drama or the music. The two should be merged into an orderly, coordinated whole.

Of great importance would be the writing of indigenous operas by native composers, perhaps even founded on the problems of our own environment and our own day. And finally, a deflation of the prevailing "star" system of presenting opera, thus making it possible to produce opera peopled by singers who look like the character, and, more important, to produce a well-balanced presentation at much lower cost.

If opera is to have wide-spread popularity in America, why should not the movies be a logical medium for it? They can afford to pay the leading artists the tremendous salaries demanded. They need make only one production, and then hundreds of copies of the film can be circulated throughout the country. They can guarantee to all an unobstructed view and thorough audibility. They can, by their precise mechanical controls, develop a proper balance between voice and orchestra. They can, by their close-ups, bring home the nuances of facial expression. And by bringing the audience close up of the voice, they can convey to the hearers many of the vocal subtleties often lost in the large opera house. They can do all this for a very small price to modern mass production; let us not scoff at them.

When I say opera by the motion pictures I do not mean a mere filming and recording of an opera as it is presented in the opera house. I have in mind the adapting of many operas in the repertoire to this different medium and technique. I have in mind, particularly, an original movie opera. I am firmly convinced it can be done.

I know, of course, that there might be tough sledding for opera in the movies at first. My own experience with the motion pictures has shown me that. When I started my first picture, for instance, I was told that the recording machines were so marvelous that if I could just sing lightly into them, sort of croon into them, they could take care of the rest.

"Just sing softly," they told me, "and we can blow up your voice to any volume."

"Why sing softly?" I cried. "There is less vitality in the voice if a song which is not meant to be sung softly is crooned. It isn't just volume or noise; it's the quality of the voice."

That seemed difficult for them to understand. "Tone is tone. What is the difference?" they demanded.

"You engaged a singer, not a crooner," I said, "and since you engaged me for the qualities that made me outstanding in my particular field, why not accommodate the instrument to the individual instead of trying to make the individual fit the instrument?"

I suggested that they place the microphone a little farther away for me, which they did. It was moved several feet farther than the usual three or four, and we achieved a far better effect. The very name of "opera singer" provided a difficulty. People are frightened of the breed, especially for the movies, they told me. Opera singers are expected to be fat, to gesticulate like semaphores, and to sing high notes and hold them eternally, I was told. Opera, they added, is something highbrow, and the singers are generally forbidding. All these arguments were set before me. I agreed partially, but not that opera or opera singers *should* be forbidding.

"Advertise me," I suggested. "as Lawrence Tibbett, the new singing motion picture star, instead of Lawrence Tibbett, Metropolitan Opera star." This was done except in New York. From the response by fan mail, I found that people all over knew that I was in the Metropolitan. My being an "opera singer" was not in itself enough to repel them.

I am assuming, of course, that comparative trifles like these will be taken in stride in the future. At any rate, the taking in hand of the opera by the motion pictures might have another beneficial effect. It would lead to the development of a taste for it among a large public.

Enough of these people might be stimulated to desire to see and hear performances in the theater, creating a new and large audience for flesh-and-blood performances. For, in the last analysis, nothing the art of the screen can do can replace that highly significant personal contact both for singers and audience.

I cannot pass on without saying a word about the fetish of the "golden age of singing." Often we enjoy an experience most either before or after it happens. That is true of those who wail that the "golden age of singing" is no more. It seems to me to be just a case of mother's biscuits. Half the people who talk about the "golden age" are merely confessing that they have lost their enthusiasm.

I feel that there is no comparison between two beautiful or thrilling things. Why compare Debussy with Beethoven? Why try to discuss which is the greater composer? Why try to decide whether the moonlight or the sunlight is the more beautiful? They both are; they both exist.

Why must we baritones, for example, continually be compared with Battistini, Campanari, Maurel, Navarini? First of all, music has become much more difficult. Our repertories are larger and broader. We have to act and sing in more and various schools. But what does all that matter? We are. They were. Is not that enough?

My musical education was followed entirely in this country. I have been asked to sing in Europe, but refused, feeling I would retain my individuality more effectively here. I should like to feel that my quality of voice is an essential American quality.

What is the essentially American thing about a genuine American singer? I think, on the whole, it is greater directness and simplicity. I think it is honesty and sincerity of purpose. These qualities are not necessarily American. Any genuine artist may have them. But to the American artist I say emphatically: "Be yourself! Stop posing! Appreciate the things that lie at your doorstep!"

Nothing seems more reprehensible to me than this practice of not being able to tell what you like yourself unless it has a label on it; unless, in music, for instance, the work has been composed by Bach, Beethoven, Brahms.

I had a talk recently with a musician, a very fine musician from a technical point of view. He told me it was awful to cheapen myself by singing Nevin's "Oh, That We Two Were Maying."

"I like it." I said. "Every time I hear that song I feel weepy. Maybe I am sentimental, soft, but I like it."

"Good Lord, can't you see that it's cheap?" he said.

"No." I returned. "You are one of those musicians who have no taste of his own. All of your taste in music is what you have been told you ought to have. When you hear a piece of music you don't ask your heart whether you like it or not. You either look to see who composed it, or you say, 'Is it like something else by some good or recognized composer?' Your standards are absolutely fixed for you. You cannot see the beauty that is under your very nose. I shall go even further. I even like 'The Perfect Day.' It's blame good melody."

"It's intrinsically a bad melody," he said.

Sometime later he was playing a Schumann sonata—I don't recall which one—and out popped this melody. The same harmonization, although it was a little faster. I do not mean that the melody is good because Schumann wrote it. I mean that I like it, whether it is Schumann or Carrie Jacobs Bond.

The suggestions made in this article offer only a few possible courses that might be followed. I am more concerned at the moment with the future of opera. To overcome the peril that encircles it opera must get off its artistic high horse. It must begin to put its house in order. It must obey the rules of the theater. It must examine itself and find a solution. Its present estate is not inevitable.

The growth of opera can be stimulated in this country so that it will become part of the national cultural life. But first there must be concern for its present and future. And as a beginning we can at least analyze the situation honestly and seek to find where the trouble lies.

111

Lawrence Tibbett;
A Temperament-Silhouette

by

P. K. Thomajan

FROM *THE MUSICIAN*, FOR JANUARY, 1934, P. 3

What combination of elements is this man compounded of! This American boy from the fields of Bakersfield, who invaded with such success the most formidable citadel of music, without European credentials. This Titan of tone, this Thor of thunderous power, charges one's being with volts and revolts. In his presence, one feels in the midst of precipitous Tibetian peaks and atop Himalayas of lofty song.

Lawrence Tibbett is a gale-fellow-well-met, a lithe, blithe figure, a six-footer with seven-leagued boots that reach from the Bahamas to Bohemia. His are tremendous appetites.

He believes in traveling wide open to all that life has to offer. There is a surging, splurging, lunging, plunging vehemence to his spiritedness. Life absorbs him and he absorbs life. There is wine in the blood of this adventurous troubador. His nature burns at white heat with a hard gem-like flame. He loves straightaways and breakaways. He craves the lash of the frenzied sea, the travel over highways at 96 per, to thrust himself forward against hostile resistance and let fury meet fury. Fighting and whipping a steel-head trout out of a stream, gives him a sensation that he can subtly transpose to a role. He has zest for fierce contacts and impacts, a passion for contours and a disdain for detours.

Lawrence Tibbett lives in the moment and the moment lives in him. He followed the course of the bent that wound through him, which led him to an ocean of sublime realization. Tibbett takes life as it hums. He has no specific design for living, except to beautify with his lavish resources the pattern and texture of the second. Tibbett feels that those who skimp err most dangerously; that those who give to overflowing

112

91. Lawrence Tibbett, Artistic Director of the Opera Television Theater, congratulates the soloists after the premiere of *Carmen,* the organization's first production on CBS, 1 January 1950. L. to r.: Tibbett, Robert Merrill, Gladys Swarthout, and Robert Rounseville. Photo: CBS. From the Editor's collection.

92. Tibbett's last new role at the Metropolitan: Ivan Khovansky in Mussorgskii's
Khovanshchina, on 16 February 1950. Courtesy of Metropolitan Opera Archives.

93. Elain Malbin as Violetta, Tibbett as Giorgio Germont, and tenor Brooks McCormack as Alfredo Germont in the CBS-TV Opera Television Theatre presentation of *La Traviata,* 12 March 1950. Photo: International News Photos. From the Editor's collection.

94. Music commentator Tibbett hosting the NBC radio series "Golden Voices," 2 October 1952. Photo: NBC. From the Editor's collection.

pursue the safer course. Thus thinks this avid epicurean.

Behind that supple voice which rings out so free and clear, is an entity kinetically adjusted to the potent things in and about him. That healthy vibrancy emanates from one who strives his utmost to make life an experience in elation and relevation, to be in tune with both the finite and the infinite. Tibbett has the desire to live freshly, to make living a series of inspiring surprises, to originalize the minutest matters. To rise up in the morning and discover the sunrise for the first time. To be as much as possible—the victim of one's verves. To have everything come clean with a gleam. Every fibre must twang to the tang of things. He rules out second-hand interceptions from his conceptions. Thus, his personality acquires a precious integrity equipped to communicate rare and authentic interpertations.

This Metropolitan meteor worships Walt Whitman as an American god, that bard who bombarded our land with his Pan-erotic messages of an exultant freedom for a starved and parched humanity. Whitman's lusty wholesomeness strikes a bold note in Tibbett's fervent makeup. Frank Lloyd Wright, the noted modernist architect, also occupies a high place in the realm of his ideals. The virility of a Bellows painting, the fine line of a Zorn etching, the bite of a Bierce epigram, the gaunt haunting quality of a Jeffers poem, the primitive hues of a Gaugin, the torrid tempos of Duke Ellington are a few of the things that Lawrence Tibbett throbs to and keep him pulsating. These with other intangible factors, balance, complete and shape those rounded notes that roll forth from his opened lips, almost of their own accord.

The composition of a character like Emperor Jones, Tibbett's triumph of triumphs, calls for the application of superhuman effort. First of all, it requires a completely plastic approach, to let the words and music of a new role take hold of him, instead of submitting it to rigid reasonings. This abstract abandon enables him to secure the instinctive responsiveness that the part must evoke on the part of his audience. Tibbett believes that the instincts are surer than the mind in interpreting emotional values. Furthermore, he senses that there is more to a character than the mere sight and sound of it, that there must be a certain something in its mien and manner that touches untouchable phases of himself and others. An alert intellectual perspective finishes off effects with studied modulations. After the rendition of a role, Tibbett feels himself purged, a mass of illuminated consciousness that glows gloriously. But the going through with the part—perfectly—that is the tortuous thing. Tibbett's ever-present task is to keep his nature close to the fundamental molding forces of life, to avoid lapsing into systems and formulas that freeze the inner flow, which waters the garden of one's heart.

The sonorous sound of Tibbett singing scourges courage to strut out of ruts. The unleashing of his voice unchains one's sense of bondage and challenges one to rise up to his true stature and status. Then he can shade off into a seraphic serenity, become an egoless melody-medium of compassionate magnitude, care-caressing and deeply assuaging.

Lawrence Tibbett—may you go unfettered and unfaltering . . . farther and farther . . . on De Glory Road!

Should I Change Teachers?
An interview with the eminent baritone Lawrence Tibbett

by

Juliette Laine

FROM *THE ETUDE*, VOL. 53, 458–9, AUGUST 1935

The average student seems to spend a lot of time trying to make up his mind whether or not to change teachers. Many never remain long enough with any one teacher to find out really whether he is good for them or not; while others, through a misguided sense of loyalty, remain too long with the wrong teacher. Some spend their days going from one studio to another, vainly trying to get an honest, unbiased opinion; while others try just as carefully—or so it would seem—to avoid those teachers who give too honest and unflattering an opinion.

It is sometimes very difficult to convince a student that he is on the right road and that he is progressing as rapidly as could be expected; and it is usually just as difficult to convince another that he is all wrong and cannot expect to get anywhere unless he makes drastic changes in his method or his teacher.

What to do? Ah, there's the rub!

It is impossible to lay any hard and fast rules about the matter, for the simple reason that no two voices respond to cultivation in quite the same way or in the same space of time. Some voices develop with amazing rapidity, while others seem to require an interminable length of time to show any progress. Therefore it is sometimes difficult to determine whether the fault lies in the teacher and his method, whether in the pupil and his lack of application, or whether the difficulty is largely physiological. And, until one knows the cause, there is little that can be done toward rectifying it.

There are today a number of fearful and wonderful methods being taught; and though most of us are pretty quick at detecting fraud and bunkum in other matters, what we swallow in the way of fake vocal teachers passes understanding. However, be his teacher's method sane or silly, any pupil of moderate intelligence should be capable of determining whether he is making any headway or not. No one can expect to acquire a fine technic in a few months, but he should be able to do a few things well enough to know whether he is on the right road or whether he is just groping in the dark.

Most of the singers who are on the wrong road discover that fact by the difficulty they begin to have with the tones at the extremes of their compass. Tenors and sopranos find their top C's and B-flats are not so free and clear as before. Bassos begin to lose their lower tones without any increase in the number of upper tones. Sometimes they quiet their fears with the thought that their voice is changing; but that is rarely the case. Moreover, they now begin to have difficulty with the *messa di voce*. They find they must sing everything at the same degree of power; *crescendo* or *decrescendo* becomes first difficult and presently impossible. These things are danger signals of the utmost importance and must not be ignored if the voice is to be saved.

There is one way that every student can test his voice, and it is as infallible as it is simple. When in doubt, repeat the note or phrase just sung, but very softly. In the lightest *pianissimo*—not just a thin, pinched tone, but a true *pianissimo*—sing that note or phrase at the pitch at which you had been singing, and then work up and down the scale, throughout the entire compass of the voice. If this is found to be impossible and it is discovered that there must be an entirely different adjustment, going into half or full voice at certain points, then you may be sure that your tones are being produced incorrectly. A voice that can sing only in full voice is not being correctly produced; and, unless this tension or muscular interference is eliminated, it is actually dangerous, as well as useless, to continue practicing. A good tone never will be obtained by merely strengthening a bad one!

Any teacher, who allows a pupil to sing in full voice before he has acquired a fairly good management of his *pianissimo* and half voice, is working along the wrong lines— to put it mildly! It is only in the beginning, before he has been permitted to strain or tighten his throat, that he is able to abandon the faulty mannerisms. After these habits have been allowed to continue for a year or two, it is almost impossible to get back on the right track again. It is difficult to unlearn things and to begin again at the beginning; it takes time and endless patience.

Another acid test for the voice is the *messa di voce*. This exercise consists of taking a single sustained tone, beginning very softly, and then, without any apparent change in the vocal mechanism, gradually increasing to full voice, and then again diminishing, very gradually, and letting the tone fade out into a finely spun *pianissimo*. A singer who cannot do this cannot be said to have control of his voice. Of course, no one can do it beautifully at first; that is not to be expected. Nevertheless, one should be able to do it well enough to rest assured that it lies within his possibilities. Careful practice will eventually bring it to perfection.

Will Modern Music Last?

by

Lawrence Tibbett

FROM *MELODY*; UNDATED CLIPPING

One of the greatest thrills of an artistic career comes from the recognition which one's work wins from the public. In other words, having lived up to his ideal as best as he can and perfected his techniques insofar as his natural endowments permit, the sincere artist turns with a clear conscience to that most pleasant of modern indoor sports—the perusal of his "fan mail."

Until recent years, the operatic artist had very little fan mail. A decade ago the physical concentration of opera in a few large cities, no less than the nature of opera itself, acted strictly to limit his audience to that small fraction of the public which buys dress circle seats at the Metropolitan. Although at the top of his profession, he could have no hope of projecting his personality and influence beyond this tiny group. The successful novelist of that period might make himself known and loved in the most remote hamlet in the land. The famous actor found the road open to him and theaters crammed in every state in the Union. But the operatic singer remained tied to New York and Chicago. The means whereby he could reach the great mass of Americans had not yet been invented. There was no form of musical entertainment which reached the entire public from coast to coast. It was physically impossible to carry great music to all the people, those of low and high degree alike.

Today that situation has been completely changed. The advent of the radio has effected this change, and done it so suddenly that many people are not yet aware of the consequences. I am glad to believe that I am one of those who recognized this altering state of affairs from the first and adapted myself to it.

From my youth I have felt that there was much justice in the often heard criticism that American music, in trying to be "classical" merely succeeded in being foreign. American artists were under the necessity of studying abroad before they dared claim any recognition of their talents. The bills offered to the public consist almost entirely of foreign operas sung exclusively in foreign languages. No music native to our soil was given any consideration, and quite naturally therefore, opera remained a thing apart from the current of real life, a hot-house flower, a cloistered art reserved for the few, drawing nothing from the genius of our own people and adding very little to their pleasure.

As I said a moment ago, the radio has happily ended that condition. Today, a great chorus being sung in a New York studio is heard at the same moment by the President in Washington and by a lonely rancher in his Texas cabin. The public to which the operatic artist now addresses himself embraces the entire population of the country; his "fan mail," if you please, pours in from all strata of society and from every corner of the nation, and this fact has had a tremendous effect—and I believe a healthy effect—upon the music which is presented no less than upon the attitude of the singer toward his art.

I speak of this as a happy condition because I firmly believe that there is in American life all the necessary material for the production of great dramatic music. There are some people still inclined to look askance at so called "popular" music and to infer that between it and what they are pleased to call "the classics" there is a great gulf fixed. Personally I think the dividing line is quite shadowy; what is "classic" today was "popular" once, and it is easily possible that many of our current popular hits become the classics of tomorrow.

I have given proof of this opinion by my part in the rendition of Charles Ridgeway's *Traffic*, a work whose inspiration is modern life in a great city, with its turmoil and confusion. Moreover in my programs on the air I make increasing use of the music of contemporary writers—music which speaks the emotion of our present life—such songs as *Ol' Man River, De Glory Road, Dreams in My Heart,* and *The American Lullaby.* Twenty years ago, had I been singing professionally, I should not have dared use these numbers in any concert meant to be taken seriously. The limited audience to which they were offered would have been embarrassed by them. I am able to use such songs today because the national audience which is now "the public" recognizes in them something vital and attuned to the tempo of the time.

Just what will be the nature of American opera when it comes? I doubt if any man living whose opinion is worth would dare answer that question precisely. Certainly four such works as *The King's Henchman, Peter Ibbetson, The Emperor Jones* and *Merry Mount* constitute a very respectable nucleus for a native opera. But this America of ours is too vast and the forces which create and solve its problems are too complicated for anyone safely to predict in what artistic form it may decide to express itself. Will jazz leave a permanent impression upon it?

I am no prophet; therefore I ask these questions, but I do not presume to answer them. However, I am glad that I have seen the birth of American music. I am proud to be an American singer now because no longer is an American singer a worker in an alien art.

117

Lawrence Tibbett

by

W. S. Meadows

FROM *THE GRAMOPHONE,* JULY 1938, p. 49–50

Splendidly proportioned for all his height, Lawrence Tibbett immediately impresses with his immense vitality and personality which is fantastic, charming and overwhelming. He talks as well as he sings and you would never guess his age from his unlined, youthful face. And there is a great deal in him of the optimism, courage and high spirits of youth.

I had the queerest interview with him when he was recently in this country and staying at the Savoy. I had not intended to stay for longer than an hour, actually we talked for over four. It was a singular conversation; Lawrence Tibbett should have been the theme, but the theme became so hidden in the ensuing variations that it was almost lost in the secondary themes of other personalities. And these delightful variations were always being interrupted by discreet rappings at the door and a too heavily scored part for the telephone.

Chaliapin, Caruso: we discussed their art, and Tibbett told me of the immense influence these two singers had had upon him. Always I tried to get him back to the theme of Tibbett, always he was reticent, reluctant to develop this theme, willing at any opportunity to go off at a tangent. In this article I have endeavored to keep to the theme!

When I first entered his apartment a voice was saying into the telephone: "Who's giving the concert—the girl or me?" Any egoism that might have been expressed in that sentence was negatived by a roar of laughter. The voice and the laugh belonged to Lawrence Tibbett. I explained to him the object of my visit, that I thought readers of THE GRAMOPHONE would be interested in some account of his career.

"Well," he said, "I guess mine is the usual sort of story. One starts with an objective, but it isn't all so easy as that. One also begins with certain inferiorities and inhibi-

118

tions which have to be overcome. People born strong are in a serious way of becoming weak, those who are uncertain of themselves at the start have the best chance of eventually winning through. I think this formula applies to people of the theatre. Most of the prominent, if not the really great musicians, have been born in humble circumstances, and had to overcome many obstacles."

"That's a grand opening," I remarked. "Go on." He didn't. He went off at a tangent.

"I had an argument at lunch today with Lady Oxford about Toscanini," he inconsequentially continued. "I admire him profoundly, to the limit of his publicity. He has been put on a pedestal, and succeeds in living there. My wife and I have a farm in Connecticut, two hours journey from New York. It's an old farm house built about 150 years ago, with 72 acres of woodland and orchards and meadows, and a lake. It's called Honey Hill Farm. We go there week-ends to rest and be quiet. Toscanini is coming to stay with us. When he comes there is a question I must ask him and that is whether he considers a conductor can get the greatest results by fear, by intimidating those who are collaborating with him, or by love."

I begged him not to drag red herrings across the path of his career. He laughed, and talked of his reception in this country, and said that the praise which had pleased him most was the verdict of one critic that he had "sung a simple song well."

"I was born in a wild and wooly town. Bakersfield, California—the centre of the oil industry of the U.S.A. Father was an old-fashioned silent-film sheriff who shot people. He was shot by the most famous bandit in California.

"The American *Who's Who* states that I made my operatic debut with the Metropolitan Opera Company as Valentine, in *Faust*. I did nothing of the kind. My first appearance was in the smallest part of any opera. It was not even a solo. It was the part of the monk, Tchelkalov, in *Boris Godunov*. All I had to do was to sing a duet with another monk in the wings and then walk silently across the stage.

"That was typical of my career, a 'cock-eyed' one if you like. I studied to be an orchestral conductor, wanted to be an actor, and turn out to be an operatic singer. I only started to study singing when I found myself in an operatic company.

"It was on the first day of the year 1925 that I emerged from obscurity. Then I was a mass of complexes; ashamed of my too humble beginnings, and trying to invest my life with an absurd glamour. It was then that I gave out that I had made my debut in *Faust*. Ridiculous, I know, but then my life has been full of ridiculous things.

"My singing teacher was Frank La Forge, now the best known accompanist in the States and the most expensive teacher in New York. Frank got me a job in the Metropolitan Opera Company by suggesting that I could learn quickly. They didn't want me, at the most they thought I had a pretty voice. I was asked if I knew anything about opera. I said, 'Absolutely nothing.' I didn't know one role.

"Father was killed when I was seven years old. Shot by a famous bandit who held up stage coaches in the finest tradition of the old days of the wild west, father and he shot it off and father got the worst of it. Then father's brother stepped in, took a pot shot at the bandit, and killed him. It is a famous episode in the history of Bakersfield, if not to the rest of the world.

"Four days before this, father had given me the hell of a spanking for running home from school. I'd had a fight and got badly licked. I went home, sobbing my heart out, thinking I'd get some sympathy. Did I? I got another thrashing and was sent straight back to school. I received all my meagre education in a public—what you would call an elementary—school.

"That incident is like a theme running through my life. Someone always spanks me and sends me back to something I've been trying to run away from.

"My family were pioneers both on my mother's and father's side, came from Celtic stock—Welsh, Scotch and Irish ancestors. That explains a lot to me. I don't think British people realise as much as they should that it was their adventurous spirit which created America, and America is really their offspring."

"Red herring," I interrupted. "Sorry, please."

"Sorry," said Tibbett. "I was the youngest of four children. Mother soon spent what little money father had left. She had to work, and now she worked for us.

"My eldest brother had a beautiful voice. He was the only one of the family who received a really good musical education. He became a singer and made a name for himself in musical comedy. Now he's a miner in the Mojave Desert, California.

"When father died the scene moves to Los Angeles. Mother managed to buy a boarding-house. For a while she ran it very successfully, then more and more unsuccessfully. For a few years, however, she kept us together and put me through a co-educational school. I never managed to get into college. I wanted to, but the War came along. I joined up when I was nineteen, in 1917.

"My voice wasn't a great asset to me in the navy. Most times I was told to 'Stop that noise.' It rattled me. I had a fight with one fellow who couldn't bear the sound of my voice. I won. After that I was allowed to sing. My fists alone had established that right.

"I had begun to earn my way when I was sixteen, working in a newspaper office at week-ends. During school vacations I got jobs on the California fruit farms, picking fruit. I ate more than I picked. I still eat fruit occasionally.

"It all ends up in a simple man standing on a stage singing a simple song."

"Not yet," I said. "Red herring. We're only halfway through the story."

"All right," said Tibbett. "Well, I managed somehow to get through high school, heaven knows how. It lasted five years. Trigonometry, philosophy, economics, geography, history, it has taken me half my life to forget most of it. Now, fortunately, I couldn't imagine myself solving the simplest algebraic problem. Only thing of value to me that I learnt at school was acting. The school had an excellent dramatic department where I picked up something of acting, singing and music.

"Finally, after all this I emerged some time as Pish-Tush in Gilbert and Sullivan's *The Mikado*.

"But between school and this I had to make a living, then and for many years to come the chief factor in life was the economic urge. There were times when rent was a weekly problem; once I was precious near evicted. More crucial still was when I had to raise money on a life insurance to get to New York and have more lessons.

"My early years were little else but doing things I didn't want to do, because I had to, and wanting and working for something that I never could possibly be. At this time I got to know almost by heart Berlioz's manual of orchestration and attended all the rehearsals of the Los Angeles symphony orchestra. I was crazy to be a conductor. I used to try and forget about music by studying tonal balance—English audiences are full of people who, throughout a performance, keep their eyes glued to a score, as if music was something for the eyes and not for the ears. Music should be something to throw you back on yourself, and make you forget your English. Don't you feel that?"

"I feel nothing about it," I said. "It's a red herring."

"Perhaps you're right," said Tibbett. "Mike Newman, the showman, gave me my first real chance to sing in public, at Grauman's old Million Dollar Theatre. Years after, he came to see me when I was making a film on the Twentieth Century Studios, Hollywood. 'Hello, Mike,' I said, 'glad to see you, you owe me some money.' 'How's that?' he said, astonished 'Why,' I said, 'you been telling everybody that you found me and paid me fifteen dollars every time I sang. I only got ten. Where's the back pay?'

"When my good times came, I began to receive offers to go abroad. For years I put off accepting these offers until such time when I had gained more confidence in myself and had more to offer—something of myself, my time, my country. Then I came to Europe, and one of your prominent critics said, 'This promising young man bills himself as a baritone. Not at all. He's a bass.' There's still something of the cowboy in me: that put me back on my haunches. That was after my first appearance in this country at the Queen's Hall. I'd already appeared in *Tosca,* and given what I considered a fair performance. Very nervous, I did not give of my best, but it was not awfully bad. Then I gave a song recital. I thought I sang pretty well as singing goes, and was sure that I had made a tremendous success. I never had met such enthusiasm elsewhere. All these strange people yelling and shouting made me think that I was better than I thought I was! Next morning, I read about myself in the newspapers. I'd been right about myself after all.

"I don't claim to know a lot about German Lieder. I went to the Continent and sang Lieder. I sang some of Mr. Brahms' and Mr. Strauss' songs in cities where they were written. It pleased me that the critics seemed to think it was good. At least they said I presented a fresh approach to them. I hope that was meant well.

"If my self-conceit ever begins to get the better of me I put one of my own records on the gramophone. Listening to my own voice sobers me. Until I heard my first record I thought I was a good singer. The gramophone is my severest critic and my greatest surprise. I find it far more nerve-racking to make a record of one song than to give a concert of twenty. I don't like making records, and when I have made them I infinitely prefer listening to other people's!

"All my recording has been done in America, and I imagine that I have now made about forty-five records."

I think if I had stayed another four hours he might have told me something about himself. But it was an experience meeting him. We've arranged to meet again in 1939. That's when he next comes again to this country.

Opera in English?

by

Lawrence Tibbett

FROM *THE ROTARIAN*, DECEMBER 1938, P. 12–2, 59–62

I believe opera has a good chance of becoming popular with the rank and file of America under certain conditions, one of the first being that it shall be opera in English. Furthermore, I believe the development of opera has been retarded to a considerable extent because it has been unintelligible to the people. There are, of course, other reasons, but that is the chief one. Don't misunderstand me—I have a strong devotion for opera, since it is largely my life. But I do not see great hope for it until some of the deadwood is cleared away. It is because of my desire to have opera become a real factor in American life that I feel the need of speaking frankly.

In the first place, what is opera? It is a fusion of two arts—music and drama. Music has been called the language of the emotions; speech is a medium for expressing thought. In its searching after the unattainable, it is an ideal and I love it for that.

Now, Americans like drama, as evidenced by their support of stage productions, and they like music, since they have spent more for it than any other country in the world. Then why hasn't opera taken root in the United States as it has in Italy, France, and Germany?

As I see it, traditional opera has been transplanted here without being adapted to our peculiar needs and therefore does not find a soil favorable to its growth. The art has no national history here. We do not have a background that would make us sympathetic to opera as now produced. As a result, we stand somewhat in awe, and are told that it is good for us culturally, which, to my mind, is a faulty psychological approach. While this can also be said of England, with most other countries it is different. In Italy, France, Germany, opera thrives naturally because if not created by native writers, it has been adapted by translation into the mother tongue.

Talk opera to an Italian, for instance, and you are talking a language he understands. On occasion I have an Italian barber who will regale me with opera by the hour, reeling off names of singers who have sung sundry roles and passing judgment on them as an American barber does on baseball players. And this man is fairly typical of the average person in Italy.

The Italian takes his opera as we do our baseball. He lives it and speaks its lingo. Italians whistle operatic arias on the streets as we do popular songs. To the Italian, *La donna è mobile* has associations and meaning. To the American it sounds vaguely like the name of a lubricating oil. In the opera houses in Italy, audiences are very demonstrative, and the singer soon knows whether he is pleasing them or not. They will yell, whistle, hiss, stamp their feet, and otherwise vent their feelings. If greatly pleased, they may carry the singer off on their shoulders after the performance. If displeased, they may throw overripe vegetables.

The story is told of the tenor who aroused the ire of one audience to such an extent that a crowd gathered at the stage door after the performance. The management succeeded in smuggling him out through a secret passage or he might have resembled a prize fighter after the "K.O." However, usually when a singer does not please, the audience demands that another be substituted. In France, audiences are also quick to praise or censure.

Such audience reception can be duplicated in America at a big-league baseball game, indicating that we do take seriously something we understand, but not at the opera. Some Americans go to the opera because they like it genuinely, others because it is the thing to do. American audiences are more polite and restrained. If the people in an American audience do not like the singer, they may walk out, but the provocation must be extreme. In other countries the singer does the walking. Audiences in Latin countries generally bestow the bouquets and brickbats. In Nordic countries the task is assigned to the critics.

Another important difference is that opera in other countries is not a luxury, but within the reach of the rank and file. In Italy a seat may be secured in the gallery for as little as 25 cents in American money. But in the most important respect, continental countries, excepting England, demand that opera be sung in the native tongue. They would not listen to it otherwise.

Now how can Americans expect opera to take much of a foothold here until the people understand what is being sung on the stage as is done in other countries? And in its present form it has had a pretty fair chance and press that has gone to exceptional pains to glorify it.

For some years prior to the debacle of 1929, opera seemed to be going places in the United States. But the depression almost wiped it out. In 1933, that redoubtable last stronghold, the Metropolitan, in New York City, went to the people with its save-the-opera campaign in an attempt to raise $300,000. As the situation now stands, the Metropolitan has a season of 16 weeks cut down from 24, Chicago has eight weeks, San Francisco six, St. Louis and other cities proportionately, with a few traveling companies thrown in.

Notwithstanding, radio has been bringing Metropolitan opera to the masses for several years and has undoubtedly quickened interest. What were your reactions to these broadcasts? Did you by any chance wonder about what the performers might be singing? If opera has taken a real hold in America, there should be some evidence of it by now. Or will it ever take hold with the masses? I think this can only be accomplished when it is brought more in conformity with our temperament, our times, and our tempo.

There are three fundamental laws of the theater against which opera chiefly offends. These are that patrons should be able to see, to hear, and to understand. If you have the price to sit down front at the Metropolitan, you will be able to see and hear. You will not understand unless you are thoroughly familiar with the opera or able to speak Italian, French or German chiefly. Even though you are a skilled linguist in several languages, you will still be handicapped, since it is difficult for mere words to be heard above the orchestra. This condition may be justified to some extent, since the Metropolitan is a large house and the sound must be projected to the farthest corners. Just for fun, Caruso used to *ad lib* some of his lines in any language that came to mind and no one seemed to be the wiser. While singing a role, the late Chaliapin, the great Russian basso, once told his valet in the wings to go home and get him a change of underwear. If the singer forgets the words, most any stock phrases can be used to fill the breach, since they will be rarely understood by the audience anyway.

Another thing is not to be overlooked in discussing the question of why opera has not taken a firmer grip in the United States. That is Anglo-Saxon psychology. Neither Americans nor Englishmen have ever accepted the traditional form of opera—that characters on the stage should sing instead of speak their lines. This strikes Americans and Englishmen as humorous at times; other times as irritating. The more common-place the lines, the more humorous it seems to sing instead of speak them. If the situation is deliberately funny, the proprieties are not offended. With humor and satire Gilbert and Sullivan operas have been hugely successful. But to ennoble a platitude with song strikes the average Anglo-Saxon as overdoing it. Which is only another argument for the need of adaptation. Not only do we require translations, but also there is a strong possibility that we need more spoken dialogue.

In the theater we demand realism, pace, and action reflective of modern living. And opera will have to conform to these requirements if it ever hopes to reach the average man. Victor Herbert once wrote a grand-opera sketch for the Lambs in which the singers took half an hour to announce "The house is afire." By the time this timely notice had been circulated among the entire ensemble, the house had burned down.

One compensation for the tired businessman is that he finds ample opportunity to relax at the opera. The story is told of one such who went on a "Wagner night," ensconced himself comfortably, fell asleep, and began to snore. Awakened by the usher who was shaking him, he remonstrated, "But this is Wagner." "That's just it," replied the usher. "You're keeping the others awake."

But when one considers the points I have raised—that opera is not a natural growth in the United States, that it is not in step with American tastes and temperament—the need for adaptation would seem apparent. And, above all, we should have opera in English. Otherwise it's a handicap not only to patrons, but also to native American singers. The latter find little use for the one tongue they know thoroughly, but must prepare themselves extensively in a number of others. At present there are only a few opportunities for Americans who would become opera singers. Those few must decide to put in endless study and preparation. On the other hand, why should patrons have to race through librettos before the performance in order to know what it is all about?

Some stock objections to opera in the vernacular have been that the majority of translations so far have been too literal, unsingable, and generally unsatisfactory, and that the subleties of the original are lost in translation anyway. The answer is that we have satisfactory translations which indicate that it can be done. Sufficient English has been sung in opera houses to make ridiculous the claim that English is not a singable language. Beautiful use of English has been made in songs and oratorios. The theatrical effectiveness of the English language has been demonstrated time and again in a number of operettas which have much in common with opera. Opera in English is not only possible, but it is also necessary.

It will come, of course, with the creation of native opera, and that is something in which we are beginning to feel our way. A genuine American style will, I believe, stem from the theater as has the traditional opera. Such productions as *The King's Henchman, Peter Ibbetson, Emperor Jones, Merry Mount, Show Boat, Porgy and Bess,* are forerunners of what's to come. They reflect life in the American manner—spontaneity—some providing an intermingling of dialogue and singing, all giving entertainment that is generally acceptable. It is illuminating to note that in the past ten years no important opera by a contemporary composer has held the boards so long at the Metropolitan as have the first four productions I have mentioned.

But the real hope of opera in America is the motion picture film. Since the film found its tongue, there has been an epidemic of musical productions, with an increasing number of opera singers casting eyes toward Hollywood. While the attempts at serious music were at first very sporadic and musical numbers were spotted sparingly in the film, producers are giving more and more attention to masterpieces.

The screen offers many advantages as a medium for opera in English, and such productions will no doubt come in time. They will not be confined to the stage limitations regarding locations, sets, and scenery. Nor will patrons be confronted with such discrepancies as a Radames who is a head shorter than his beloved Aida who is twice as large in girth as he. In this respect the movies have already had a pronounced effect in streamlining the appearance of singers. Movie audiences will demand singers pleasing to the eye as well as the ear, swifter action, more realism. Accompanimental music to heighten the action now forms a part of almost every film and is sometimes used effectively in lieu of dialogue. In all this we are feeling our way toward a real American opera.

In motion pictures it is possible to have a close-up not only of the singer, but also of the voice, and a degree of perfection is achieved impossible on the stage. In action scenes—as, for instance, a singer riding across country—the photographic close-ups are made first and the rider's singing reproduced in the studio, the voice being "dubbed in." The singer merely repeats the horseback song while watching the lip action on the screen, and the "dubbing in" is done to a split second, as you may have noticed. The mixer in the studio can also blend his orchestral instruments and voice for almost any effect desired. Each group of instruments has its own microphone that feeds into the monitor cabinet. The singer's voice arrives via its own microphone, and by tuning down or up on the various receptions, the desired blend can be produced.

It will not come overnight, but I believe we are on our way to an American form of music drama and the screen will be its medium. Up to comparatively recent years we have had to depend on the other countries for our art, but we are beginning to stand

125

on our own feet musically. We have already become the music center of the world and will eventually give to the world a characteristic form of music drama. In English, of course.

APPENDIX

Lawrence Tibbett (1896–1960)
A Discography

by

W. R. Moran

HONORARY CURATOR, ARCHIVE OF RECORDED SOUND, STANFORD UNIVERSITY

I. THE VICTOR RECORDINGS

Discog. No.	Matrix-Take	Date	Victor Cat. No.	HMV Cat. No.	Other	LP Recordings	Speed (rpm)
1.	Die Allmacht (Pyrker, trans. Baker-Schubert, D.852) (E) (Pf. Stewart Wille)						
	CS-046070-1,-2	4 Jan. '40	15891	(DB 5762)	-------	VIC 1340	78.26
*2.	The Bailiff's Daughter (Old English Ballad) (E) (Pf. Stewart Wille)						
	CS-75708-1,-2	28 Mar. '33	-------	-------	-------	-------	
3.	The Bailiff's Daughter (Old English Ballad) (E) (Pf. Stewart Wille)						
	CS-046067-1,-2	4 Jan. '40	15549	-------	-------	CAL 168	78.26
*4.	UN BALLO IN MASCHERA: Eri tu che macchiavi (Verdi) (I) (Or. Nathaniel Shilkret)						
	CVE-53454-1	31 May '29				-------	
	-2	15 April '30	7353	-------	-------	LM 6705-4	76.60
			11-8861			VIC 1340	
						CAL 171	
	-3,-4	15 April '30	7353	DB 1478	-------	-------	76.60
			15819				
*5.	IL BARBIERE DI SIVIGLIA: Largo al factotum (Rossini) (I) (Or. Nathaniel Shilkret)						
	CVE-59753-1	15 April '30	7353	-------	-------	LM 6705-4	76.60
						VIC 1340	
						CAL 171	
						LM 21034	
	-2,-3,-4	15 April '30	7353	DB 1478	-------	-------	76.60
			14202				
6.	IL BARBIERE DI SIVIGLIA: Senti, ma Lindoro . . . Dunque io son (Rossini) (w. Amelita Galli-Curci) (I) (Or. Bourdon)						
	BVE-35446-1,-2,-3,-4	7 May '26	-------	-------	-------	-------	
7.	Battle Hymn of the Republic (Julia Ward Howe–William Steffe, Orch. by Bruno Reibold) (Or. dir. by Wilfred Pelletier)						
	BS-036848-1,-1A	3 May '39	4433	-------	-------	OASI 5865	78.26
8.	Believe Me, If All Those Endearing Young Charms (Thomas Moore) (Hp. Lapitino; Or. Rosario Bourdon)						
	BVE-37879-1,-2,-3	30 Mar. '27	1238	DA 886	-------	CAE 158	76.60
						CAL 168	
9.	Calm as the Night (Carl Goetz) (w. Lucrezia Bori) (Or. Bourdon)						
	BVE-38854-1,-2,-3	1 June '27	3043	DA 912	-------	OASI 5864	77.43
			1747				

*10. CARMEN: Votre toast! (Chanson du Toréador) (Bizet) (F) (w. Metropolitan Opera Chorus and Orchestra, conducted by Giulio Setti)

CVE-51117-1,-2,-3   3 April '29   ------   ------   LM 7605-4   76.00
      -4   8 April '29   8124   CAL 171
                                    CAL 346
                                    VIC 1340
                                    V-Disc 208-A

D4-TC-85 (Dubbing of take 4, above)
      -5   8 April '29   8124   DB 1298   ------   OASI 5861   76.00
                                 14202

CONTES D'HOFFMANN see "Tales of Hoffmann"

11. The Crucifix (Faure) (E) (w. Richard Crooks) (Organ: Mark Andrews)

BVE-43720-1,-2,-3   10 April '28   ------   ------   ------   76.60
CVE-43720-1,-2,-3   30 Jan. '29   ------   ------   ------

12. THE CRUCIFIXION: So thou liftest Thy petition (Sir John Stainer) (w. Richard Crooks) (Organ: Mark Andrews)

BVE-43721-1,-2,-3   10 April '28   ------   ------   ------
CVE-43721-1,-2,-3   30 Jan. '29   ------   ------   ------

NOTE: [ ] = side numbers within sets

*THE CRUCIFIXION (Oratorio in 12 parts by Sir John Stainer) (w. Richard Crooks, Wilfred Glenn, Frank Croxton & Trinity Choir, dir. Clifford Cairns. Organ: Mark Andrews) (Album M-64)

13.[1]. (a) And they came to a place called Gethsemane (Crooks); (b) Could ye not watch with me one brief hour? (Tibbett)

CVE-53735-1,-2   27 May '29   9424   D 1817   ------   CAL 235   77.43
                             9430   D 7770   VIC 1403
                             13262

14.[2]. (a) And they laid their hands on Him (Crooks, Tibbett, Glenn); (b) Processional to Calvary (Andrews)

CVE-53736-1,-2   27 May '29   9424   D 1817   ------   CAL 235   77.43
                             9431   D 7771   VIC 1403
                             13262

[3]. Processional to Calvary, pt. 2: Fling wide the Gates (Trinity Choir & Andrews)

CVE-53737-1   27 May '29   9425   D 1818   ------   CAL 235   77.43
                         9432   D 7772   VIC 1403
                         13263

*see NOTES at end

Discog. No.	Matrix-Take	Date	Victor Cat. No.	HMV Cat. No.	Other	LP Recordings	Speed (rpm)
[4].	Processional to Calvary, pt. 3: How sweet is the Grace (Crooks)						
	CVE-53738-<u>1</u>,-2	27 May '29	9425 9433 13264	D 1818 D 7773	-------	CAL 235 VIC 1403	77.43
15.[5].	(a) And when they were come (Tibbett); (b) Cross of Jesus (Choir); (c) He made Himself no reputation (Tibbett)						
	CVE-53739-1,-<u>2</u>	27 May '29	9426 9434 13265	D 1819 D 7774	-------	CAL 235 VIC 1403	77.43
[6].	King ever Glorious (Crooks)						
	CVE-53740-1,-<u>2</u>	27 May '29	9426 9435 13266	D 1819 D 7775	-------	CAL 235 VIC 1403	77.43
16.[7].	(a) And as Moses lifted up the serpent (Tibbett); (b) God so loved the world (Choir)						
	CVE-53741-1,-<u>2</u>	28 May '29	9427 9430 13266	D 1820 D 7775	-------	CAL 235 VIC 1403	77.43
17.[8].	(a) Jesus said, "Father forgive them" (Crooks); (b) So Thou liftest Thy petition (Crooks & Tibbett)						
	CVE-53742-1	28 May '29	9427 9431 13265	D 1820 D 7774	-------	CAL 235 VIC 1403	77.43
18.[9].	(a) Jesus, the crucified (Choir); (b) And one of the Malefactors (Tibbett, Glenn, Croxton); (c) I adore Thee (Choir)						
	CVE-53743-<u>1</u>,-2	28 May '29	9428 9432 13264	D 1821 D 7773	-------	CAL 235 VIC 1403	77.43
19.[10].	(a) When Jesus therefore saw his mother (Crooks, Tibbett); (b) Is it nothing to you? (Tibbett)						
	CVE-53744-1,-<u>2</u>	28 May '29	9428 9433 13263	D 1821 D 7772	-------	CAL 235 VIC 1403	77.43
[11].	From the throne of His cross, pt. 1 (Choir)						
	CVE-53745-<u>1</u>,-2	28 May '29	9429 9434 13262	D 1822 D 7771	-------	CAL 235 VIC 1403	77.43

[12]. (a) From the throne of His cross, pt. 2 (Choir); (b) After this (Crooks); (c) All for Jesus (Choir)

CVE-53746-1,-2	28 May '29	9429	D 1822	CAL 235	77.43
		9435	D 7770	VIC 1403	
		13261	———		

*20. THE CUBAN LOVE SONG: Cuban Love Song (from M-G-M film) (Herbert Stothart-Dorothy Fields-Jimmy McHugh) (Pf. Stewart Wille)

| PBVE-68328-1,-2 | 28 Oct. '31 | 1550 | DA 1251 | | 78.26 |

*21. THE CUBAN LOVE SONG: Cuban Love Song (from M-G-M film) (Herbert Stothart-Dorothy Fields-Jimmy McHugh) (Or. Nathaniel Shilkret)

| BVE-69068-1,-2,-3,-4 | 10 Dec. '31 | (1550: see NOTE) | ——— | | 77.43 |

*22. THE CUBAN LOVE SONG: Cuban Love Song (from M-G-M film) (Herbert Stothart-Dorothy Fields-Jimmy McHugh) (Tenor part only. No accompaniment)

| BVE-69071-1,-2 | 12 Dec. '31 | 1550 | ——— | CAE 160 | 77.43 |
| | | | | CAL 168 | 77.43 |

23. THE CUBAN LOVE SONG: Tramps at Sea (from M-G-M film) (Herbert Stothart-Dorothy Fields-Jimmy McHugh) (Pf. Stewart Wille)

| PBVE-68327-1,-2,-3 | 26 Oct. '31 | 1550 | DA 1251 | CAL 171 | 78.26 |
| | | | | OASI 5866 | |

*24. Drink To Me Only With Thine Eyes (Ben Jonson) (Pf. Roy Shields) —(Test recording)

| | 13 Apr. '25 | ——— | ——— | | |

25. Drink To Me Only With Thine Eyes (Ben Jonson) Or. Bourdon

| BVE-37878-1,-2,-3 | 30 Mar. '27 | 1238 | DA 886 | CAE 160 | 76.60 |
| | | | | OASI 5864 | |

*26. Edward (Herder—Karl Loewe, Op. 1 No. 1) (E) (Pf. Stewart Wille)

| PCVE-68333-1,-2 | 29 Oct. '31 | 7486 | ——— | VIC 1340 | 78.26 |
| CVE-68333-3,-4 | 12 Dec. '31 | 7486 | DB 1684 | ——— | 77.43 |

27. EMPEROR JONES: Oh Lord! . . . Standin' in the need of prayer (Louis Gruenberg, Op. 36) (w. Metropolitan Opera House Orch., cond. by Wilfred Pelletier)

CS-81087-1	19 Jan. '34	———	———	LM 6705-4	78.26
-1A,-2,-2A	19 Jan. '34	7959	ED 24	OASI 5863	77.43
				MET 403	

28. FALSTAFF: È sogno o realtà? (Ford's Monologue) (Verdi) (I) (Or. Rosario Bourdon)

| CVE-34930-1,-2,-3,-4,-5 | 3 Mar. '26 | ——— | ——— | MET 403 | |
| | | | | EMI EX 2901693 | |

Discog. No.	Matrix-Take	Date	Victor Cat. No.	HMV Cat. No.	Other	LP Recordings	Speed (rpm)
*29.	FAUST: O sainte medaille . . . Avant de quitter ces lieux (Gounod) (F) (Or. Nathaniel Shilkret)						
	CS-82331-1,-1A	20 April '34	8452	DB 2262	-------	LM 6705-4 VIC 1340 CAL 171	77.43
*30.	THE FORTUNE TELLER: Gypsy Love Song (Harry B. Smith-Victor Herbert) (Pf. Roy Shields)						
	—(Test recording)	13 Apr. '25				-------	
31.	De Glory Road (Clement Wood-Jacques Wolfe) (Pf. Stewart Wille)						
	PCVE-68331-1,-2	29 Oct. '31		-------	-------		
	CVE-68331-3,-4,-5	10 Dec. '31	7486	DB 1684	-------	CAL 168	77.43
*32.	Goin' Home (Williams Arms Fisher, adapted from Largo movement, Dvorak's Symphony "From the New World") (E) (Or. Alexander Smallens)						
	CS-02176-1	19 Oct. '36	15549 11-8860	DB 3036	-------	CAL 168 CAE 217	77.43
33.	Hallelujah Rhythm (Jacques Wolf) (Or. Alexander Smallens)						
	CS-02175-1,-1A	19 Oct. '36	-------	-------	-------	EJS 397	77.43
*34.	If Love Hath Entered Thy Heart (Marz) (Pf. Stewart Wille)						
	BS-75709-1	28 Mar. '33	-------	-------	-------	-------	
35.	IN A PERSIAN GARDEN: Myself when young (Omar Khayyam, trans. Fitzgerald-Liza Lehmann) (Or. dir. by Nathaniel Shilkret)						
	BS-82332-1,-1A,-2	20 April '34	1706	DA 1383	-------	CAE 158	77.43
*36.	A Kingdom by the Sea (Fee-Somervel) (Pf. Stewart Wille)						
	CS-74704-1,-2,-3	16 Dec. '32	-------	-------	-------	OASI 5865	
37.	A Kingdom by the Sea (Fee-Somervell) (Pf. Stewart Wille)						
	CS-046068-1,-1A	4 Jan. '40	-------	-------	-------	-------	
*38.	THE KING'S HENCHMAN: Oh, Caesar, great wert thou! (Finale, Act 1) (Edna St. Vincent Millay-Deems Taylor) (E) (w. Metropolitan Opera Chor. & Orch. dir. by Giulio Setti)						
	CVE-43613-1,-2,-3	5 April '28	(6845) 8103	-------	-------	OASI 5863	76.00

*39. THE KING'S HENCHMAN: Nay, Maccus, lay him down (Finale, Act 3) (Edna St. Vincent Millay-Deems Taylor) (E) (w. Metropolitan Opera Chor. & Orch. dir. by Giulio Setti) (CR)
CVE-43614-1,-2,-3   5 April '28   (6845)   ------   ------   CAL 171   76.00
8103
11-8932   CRM 8-5177

*40. Last Night When We Were Young (E. Y. Harburg-Harold Arlen) (Or. Nathaniel Shilkret)
CS-95370-1,-1A   10 Oct. '35   11877   ------   ------   ------   77.43

41. Life is a Dream (Used in M-G-M film "The Prodigal" — "The Southerner") (Arthur Freed-Oskar Straus) (Or. Nathaniel Shilkret)
BVE-67493-1,-2   6 Mar. '31   1507   DA 1206   ------   CAE 158   77.43
OASI 5865

*42. Love's Old Sweet Song (G. Clifton Bingham-J. L. Molloy) (Pf. Roy Shields)
—(Test recording)   13 April '25   ------   ------   ------   ------

*43. Love Went A-Riding (Frank Bridge) (Pf. accompaniment)
—(Test recording)   18 Mar. '25   ------   ------   ------

44. THE MERRY MOUNT: Oh, 'tis an Earth Defiled (Howard Hanson) (w. Metropolitan Opera House Orch. cond. by Wilfred Pelletier) (CR)
CS-81086-1,-1A,-2,-2A   19 Jan. '34   7959   ------   ED 24   CAL 171   77.43
11-8932
V-Disc CL-5B (JDB-264)

45. MUSIC IN THE AIR: And Love Was Born (Hammerstein II-Kern) (Or. Nathaniel Shilkret)
BS-74656-1,-2   8 Dec. '32   1612   DA 1313   ------   ERAT-24   77.43
OASI 5864

46. MUSIC IN THE AIR: The Song Is You (Oscar Hammerstein II-Jerome Kern) (Or. Nathaniel Shilkret)
BS-74653-1,-2   8 Dec. '32   1612   DA 1313   ------   OASI 5864   77.43

*47. My Own United States (Stanislaus Stangé-Julian Edwards, Orch. Reibold) (Or. Wilfred Pelletier)
BS-036852-1,-1A,-2,-2A   3 May '39   4433   ------   ------   OASI 5865   78.26

*48. THE NEW MOON: Lover Come Back To Me (Oscar Hammerstein II-Sigmund Romberg) (Pf. Stewart Wille)
BVE-67495-1   6 Mar. '31   1506   DA 1200   ------   CAE 160   77.43
CAL 168

*49. THE NEW MOON: Wanting You (Oscar Hammerstein II-Sigmund Romberg) (Pf. Stewart Wille)
BVE-67494-1   6 Mar. '31   1506   DA 1200   ------   CAE 217   77.43

Discog. No.	Matrix-Take	Date	Victor Cat. No.	HMV Cat. No.	Other	LP Recordings	Speed (rpm)
50.	None But the Lonely Heart (Goethe, trans. Mey-Tchaikovsky, Op. 6, No. 6) (E) (Or. N. Shilkret)						
	BS-82333-1,-2	20 April '34	1706	DA 1383	————	CAE 158 CAL 168 VIC 1340 CAE 217	77.43
51.	Oh That We Two Were Maying (Charles Kingsley-Ethelbert Nevin, Op. 2, No. 8) (Or. Bourdon)						
	BVE-35474-1,-2,-3,-4,-5,-6	24 May '26	1172	DA 829	————	OASI 5866	76.60
*52.	Old Black Joe (Stephen C. Foster, arr. Bourdon) (w. Shannon Qt.) (Hp. Lapitino; Or. Bourdon)						
	BVE-37880-1,-2,-3	31 Mar. '27	1265	DA 909	————	CAL 168 CAE 217	76.60
*53.	On the Road to Mandalay (Rudyard Kipling-Oley Speaks) (E) (Pf. Stewart Wille)						
	CVE-45190-1	29 May '28			————	————	
54.	On the Road to Mandalay (Rudyard Kipling-Oley Speaks) (E) (Or. Nathaniel Shilkret)						
	CS-95371-1,-1A	10 Oct. '35	11877 11-8862	DB 3036	————	CAL 168 CAE 160	77.43
55.	OTELLO: Credo in un Dio crudel (Verdi) (I) (Or. Alexander Smallens)						
	CS-02174-1,-1A	19 Oct. '36	(14182)	————	————	————	77.43
	OTELLO: Abridged version in 12 parts (w. Giovanni Martinelli, Helen Jepson, Nicolas Massue, Herman Dreeben, with members of the Metropolitan Opera House Chorus and Orchestra, cond. by Wilfred Pelletier) (Sung in Italian) (Album M-620)						
56.[1].	Inaffia l'ugola! (Brindisi) (Tibbett, Massue, Dreeben & Chorus)						
	CS-036849-1,-1A	3 May '39	15801 15807 15989	DB 5716 DB 5788	————	VIC 1185 VIC 1365	78.26
57.[4].	Vanne! La tua meta . . . Credo in un Dio crudel (Tibbett)						
	CS-036855-1,-1A	3 May '39	15802	DB 5717	————	LM 6705-4 VIC 1185 VIC 1365 ERAT 24	78.26
	-2,-2A	9 May '39	15810 15992	DB 5789	————		

No.	Title / Matrix	Date					
58.[5].	Non pensateci più . . . Tu? Indietro! . . . Ora e per sempre addio (Tibbett, Martinelli)						
	CS-036869-1	9 May '39	15803	DB 5718	------		78.26
			15811&15993	DB 5790			
	-2,-2A	9 May '39	15803		------	VIC 1185	78.26
			15811			VIC 1365	
			15993			LM 6174-4	
59.[6].	E qual certezza sognate . . . Era la notte (Tibbett)						
	CS-036854-1,-1A	3 May '39	15803	DB 5718	------	VIC 1185	78.26
			15812	DB 5790		VIC 1365	
			15994			LM 21035	
60.[7].	Oh! mostruosa colpa! . . . Ah! mille vite . . . Sì, pel ciel (Tibbett, Martinelli)						
	CS-036870-1,-1A,-2,-2A	9 May '39	15804	DB 5719	------	VIC 1185	78.26
			15807	DB 5791		VIC 1365	
			15994				
61.[8].	Dio! mi potevi scagliar tutti i mali . . . Cassio è la! (Tibbett, Martinelli)						
	CS-036871-1,-1A	9 May '39	15804	DB 5720	------	VIC 1185	78.26
			15808	DB 5792		VIC 1365	
			15993			MET 404	
62.[9].	Vieni; l'aula è deserta . . . Questo è una ragna (Tibbett, Martinelli, Massue)						
	CS-036851-1,-1A,-2,-2A	3 May '39	15805	DB 5720	------	VIC 1185	78.26
			15809	DB 5792		VIC 1365	
			15992				
63.	THE PACKET BOAT: Roustabout (Braley-Hughes) (E) (Pf. Stewart Wille)						
	BVE-45188-1,-2,-3	29 May '28			------		76.60
64.	I PAGLIACCI: Si può? . . . Si può? (Prologo, pt. 1) (Leoncavallo) (I) (Or. Bourdon)						
	CVE-35481-1,-2	7 June '26	6587		------	CAL 171	77.43
						VIC 1340	
						LM 20124	
	-3	7 June '26	6587	DB 975			77.43
65.	I PAGLIACCI: Un nido di memorie (Prologo, pt. 2) (Leoncavallo) (I) (Or. Bourdon)						
	CVE-35482-1,-2,-3	7 June '26	6587	DB 975	------	CAL 171	77.43
						VIC 1340	
						LM 20124	

Discog. No.	Matrix-Take	Date	Victor Cat. No.	HMV Cat. No.	Other	LP Recordings	Speed (rpm)
66.	Pilgrim's Song (Tolstoi, trans. England—Tchaikovsky, Op. 47, No. 5) (E) (Or. Nathaniel Shilkret)						
	CS-74654-1,-2	8 Dec. '32	7779	DB 1945	-------	VIC 1340 / LM 20124	77.43
	*PORGY AND BESS: Selections from the DuBose Heyward-George Gershwin opera (w. Helen Jepson and the orchestra and chorus of the original New York production, cond. by Alexander Smallens) (Recorded under the personal supervision of the composer) (Album C-25)						
67.[1].	It Ain't Necessarily So (Tibbett & Chorus)						
	CS-95466-1,-2	23 Oct. '35	11878	DB 2735 / DB 3395	ED 44	ERAT 23 / CAL 500 / CAM 6	77.43
68.[2].	The Buzzard Song (Tibbett & Chorus)						
	CS-95389-1,-2,-2A	14 Oct. '35	11878	-------	-------	-------	77.43
	-3	23 Oct. '35	11878	DB 2735	-------	CAL 500 / CAM 6 / AVM 1-1742	77.43
69.[3].	(a) Summertime & Crap Game (Tibbett & Jepson); (b) A Woman is a Sometime Thing (Tibbett)						
	CS-95387-1	23 Oct. '35	11879	DB 2736	-------	CAL 500 / CAM 6	77.43
70.[4].	Bess, You Is My Woman Now (Tibbett & Jepson)						
	CS-95388-1	14 Oct. '35	11879	DB 2736 / DB 3396	-------	CAL 500 / CAM 6 / AVM 1-1742	77.43
71.[5].	I Got Plenty o' Nuttin' (Tibbett)						
	CS-95390-1,-1A	14 Oct. '35	-------	-------	-------	-------	
	-2,-3	23 Oct. '35	11880 / 11-8860	DB 2737 / DB 3395	ED 44	CAL 500 / CAM 6 / AVM 1-1742	77.43
72.[6].	Where Is My Bess? (Tibbett)						
	CS-95467-1,-2	23 Oct. '35	11880	DB 2737	-------	CAL 500 / CAM 6	77.43
*73.	Retreat (Frank La Forge) (Pf. accompaniment)						
	—(Test recording)	18 Mar. '25	-------	-------	-------	-------	

74. RIGOLETTO: Cortigiani, vil razza, dannata (Verdi) (Or. Alexander Smallens)
CS-02173-1,-2,-3   19 Oct. '36   (14182)   ——   ——   OASI 5861
MET 404

75. RIGOLETTO: Sì, vendetta, tremenda vendetta (Verdi) (w. Amelita Galli-Curci) (I) (Or. Bourdon)
BVE-35447-1,-2,-3,-4   7 May '26   ——   ——

76. THE ROGUE SONG: The Narrative (from the M-G-M film) (Clifford Grey-Herbert Stothart) (Or. cond. by Nathaniel Shilkret)
BVE-58188-1,-2,-3   13 Jan. '30   1446   DA 1101   CAL 168   76.60
OASI 5866

77. THE ROGUE SONG: The Rogue Song (from the M-G-M film) (Clifford Grey, Herbert Stothart) (Or. cond. by Nathaniel Shilkret)
BVE-58187-1,-2,-3   13 Jan. '30   1446   DA 1101   CAE 160   76.60

78. THE ROGUE SONG: When I'm Looking At You (from the M-G-M film) (Clifford Grey-Herbert Stothart) (Or. cond. by Nathaniel Shilkret)
BVE-58195-1,-2,-3,-4   15 Jan. '30   1447   DA 1102   OASI 5866   76.60

*79. THE ROGUE SONG: The White Dove (from the M-G-M film) (Clifford Grey—arr. from Franz Lehár by Herbert Stothart) (Or. cond. by Nathaniel Shilkret)
BVE-58196-1,-2,-3   15 Jan. '30   1447   DA 1102   OASI 5866   76.60

80. SEMELE: Where'er You Walk (G. F. Handel) (E) (Pf. Stewart Wille)
CS-046065-1,-2,-2A   4 Jan. '40   17456   (DB 5849) ED 59   LCT 1158   78.26
LCT 1115

81. Shake Your Brown Feet, Honey (Langston Hughes-Carpenter) (E) (Pf. Stewart Wille)
BVE-45187-1,-2,-3   29 May '28   ——   ——   76.60

82. Short'nin' Bread (Clement Wood-Jacques Wolfe) (Pf. Stewart Wille)
PBVE-68332-1,-2   29 Oct. '31   ——   ——

*83. SHOW BOAT: Ol' Man River (Oscar Hammerstein II—Jerome Kern) (Pf. Stewart Wille)
CS-74705-1,-2   16 Dec. '32   ——   ——   OASI 5864

84. SIMON BOCCANEGRA: Dinne . . . alcun là non vedesti? . . . Figlia! tal nome palpito (Verdi) (I) (w. Rose Bampton & Members of the Metropolitan Opera House Orchestra, cond. by Wilfred Pelletier)
CS-036853-1,-1A   3 May '39   15642   DB 3950   ERAT 24   78.26
DB 6018   COLH 127
OASI 5863

Discog. No.	Matrix-Take	Date	Victor Cat. No.	HMV Cat. No.	Other	LP Recordings	Speed (rpm)
85.	SIMON BOCCANEGRA: Plebe! Patrizi! Popolo . . . Piango su voi, sul placido (Verdi) (I) (w. Rose Bampton, Giovanni Martinelli, Leonard Warren, Robert Nicholson, & Members of the Metropolitan Opera House Chorus and Orchestra, cond. by Wilfred Pelletier)						
	CS-036850-1,-1A	3 May '39	15642	DB 3950 / DB 6018	———	LM 6171-3 / LCT 6701 / OASI 5863	78.26
86.	Song of the Flea (Goethe, trans. Newmarch—Moussorgsky) (E) (Or. Rosario Bourdon)						
	CVE-34931-1,-2,-3,-4	3 Mar. '26	———			———	
*87.	Song of the Flea (Goethe, trans. Newmarch—Moussorgsky) (E) (Or. Nathaniel Shilkret)						
	CS-74655-1	8 Dec. '32	7779			VIC 1340 / CAL 168 / OASI 5863	77.43
	-2	8 Dec. '32	7779	DB 1945		———	77.43
88.	Song of the Flea (Goethe, trans. Newmarch—Moussorgsky) (E) (Pf. Stewart Wille)						
	CS-75707-1,-2	28 Mar. '33					
*89.	A Star Was His Candle (Hoare—del Riego) (E) (Pf. Stewart Wille)						
	BS-045764-1,-2	15 Dec. '39				———	78.26
	BS-045765-1	15 Dec. '39				———	
90.	TALES OF HOFFMANN: Barcarolle ("Belle nuit, o nuit d'amour") (Offenbach) (E) (w. Lucrezia Bori) (Harp: Lapitino; Or. Bourdon)						
	BVE-38855-1,-2,-3	1 June '27	3043 / 1747	DA 912	———	OASI 5864	77.43
91.	TANNHÄUSER: Wie Todesahnung Dämmrung deckt die Lande . . . O du, mein holder Abendstern (Wagner) (G) (Or. Nathaniel Shilkret)						
	CS-82330-1,-1A	20 April '34	8452 / 11-8862	DB 2262	———	CAL 171 / LM 20135	77.43
92.	THEODORA: Defend Her! Heaven (G. F. Handel) (E) (Pf. Stewart Wille)						
	CS-046066-1,-2,-3,-3A	4 Jan. '40	17456	(DB 5849)	ED 59	CAL 168	78.26
93.	Thy Beaming Eyes (W. H. Gardner—Edward A. MacDowell) (Or. Bourdon)						
	BVE-35475-1,-2,-3,-4	24 May '26	———			———	
	-5,-6,-7,-8	7 June '26	1172	DA 829	———	OASI 5866	77.43

*94. TOSCA: Tre sbirri, una carrozza (Te Deum) (Puccini) (I) (w. Metropolitan Opera House Chor. and Orch., cond. by Giulio Setti)
CVE-51116-1,-2,-3   3 April '29   8124   DB 1298   ------   76.00
         -4   10 April '29   8124   ------   VIC 1340   76.00
                                      11-8861   CAL 171

95. Travelin' to de Grave (Spiritual, arr. Reddick) (E) (Pf. Stewart Wille)
BVE-45189-1,-2,-3   29 May '28   ------   ------   ------   76.60

*96. Uncle Ned (Stephen C. Foster, arr. Bourdon) (w. Shannon Qt.) (Or. Bourdon)
BVE-37881-1,-2,-3,-4   31 Mar. '27   ------   ------   ------
          -5,-6,-7   31 May '27   1265   DA 909   OASI 5864   77.43

DIE WALKÜRE: Wotan's Farewell (Wagner) (G) (w. Philadelphia Symphony Orch., cond. by Leopold Stokowski) (included in Album M-248, "Excerpts from Act III", arr. by Stokowski)

97.[4]. Leb' wohl du kühnes, herrliches Kind!
CS-83105-1,-1A   30 April '34   8543   DB 2471   ------   OASI 5861   77.43
                                8549   DB 7958
                                16643

98.[5]. Denn Einer nur freie die Braut . . . Der Augen leuchtendes Paar
CS-83106-1,-1A   30 April '34   8544   DB 2472   ------   OASI 5862   77.43
                                8546   DB 7958
                                16643

99.[6]. Zum letzten Mal letz' es mich heut' mit des Lebewohles
CS-83107-1,-1A   30 April '34   8544   DB 2472   ------   OASI 5862   77.43
                                8547   DB 7957
                                16642

100.[7]. Loge hör'! Lausche hieher!
CS-83108-1,-1A   30 April '34   8545   DB 2473   ------   OASI 5862   77.43
                                8548   DB 7956
                                16641

101.[8]. Wer meines Speeres Spitze fürchtet
CS-83109-1,-1A   30 April '34   8545   DB 2473   ------   OASI 5862   77.43
                                8549   DB 7955
                                16640

Discog. No.	Matrix-Take	Date	Victor Cat. No.	HMV Cat. No.	Other	LP Recordings	Speed (rpm)
102.	Der Wanderer (Schmidt von Lübeck—Schubert, D. 439) (E) (Pf. Stewart Wille)						
	CS-046069-1,-1A	4 Jan. '40	15891	(DB 5762)	———	VIC 1340	78.26
103.	Without a Song (from "Great Day"; used in the M-G-M film "The Prodigal" — "The Southerner") (Rose Eliscu-Vincent Youmans) (Or. Nathaniel Shilkret)						
	BVE-67492-1,-2	6 Mar. '31	1507	DA 1206	———	CAE 158 OASI 5865	77.43

140

NOTES ON THE RECORDINGS

Underlined takes are those used on published recordings on catalog numbers shown. Where no catalog numbers are given, the recording was unpublished; takes underlined for unpublished recordings indicate those which are known to have survived as test pressings. Catalog numbers shown in parentheses were assigned but not issued.

2. "Recorded at the request of The Gramophone Co."

4. Take 2 issued on post-war pressings only.

5. Take 1 issued on post-war pressings only.

10. Take 4 issued on post-war pressings only; re-cut 17 September 1942 on CS 51117-2R.

13/19. The "Trinity Choir" was the name given to the Victor "house" chorus when singing religious music. On this occasion it was made up as follows:
Sopranos: L. I. Marsh, O. Kline, D. Baker, R. Rogers, E. S. Hager
Altos: E. Baker, H. Clark, R. Bryant, E. Indemauer
Basses: F. Croxton, W. Glenn, E. Shaw, J. Stanley, S. Baughman

20. Recorded in Hollywood. Pre-war issues only.

21. Sung ½ tone lower than No. 20. BVE-69068-3 is a solo. It was played during the recording of BVE-69071-2, at which time Tibbett added the tenor part to the refrain. This dual recording replaced No. 20 in the American catalogs. The dual recording stunt was used in the last scene of the film.

22. Both pre- and post-war pressings of 1550 used this same recording.

24. A second trial session for Victor (see note under 43.) took place on 13 April '25. Both electrical and acoustical recordings were made that day and it is the author's assumption that these were electrical recordings. Like other tests, they bear no numbers. (See also notes under 30. and 42.)

26. Take 2 was made in Hollywood and issued on post-war pressings only. Note words: ". . . and why so sad *gang* ye?" Take 4 was made in Camden, N.J. and issued on pre-war pressings. Note: ". . . and why so sad *go* ye?"

29. Post-war pressings are of the same performance, either re-cut masters or possibly Take 1A.

30. See note under 24.

32. Post-war pressings were from re-cut master with finer grooves, thus leaving a larger center, but the performance is the same.

34. Marked "Personal Recording".

36. Marked "Personal Recording".

38. Tibbett created the role of Eadgar at the Metropolitan Opera House world premiere on 17 February 1927. The music here recorded from Act 1 is sung in the opera by Maccus, a minor role, created by William Gustafson.

39. The music here recorded is from the role Tibbett created.

40. This song was composed for the 20th Century-Fox film "Metropolitan," but for some reason was not used in the final release.

42. See note under 24.

43. This selection (and also No. 73) were Tibbett's "trial" or audition recordings for Victor. Although a few experimental electrical recordings had been made in February, 1925, and one studio was used for electrical recording from March 11 onwards, the two Tibbett tests were probably acoustical recordings.

47. This song is from a long-forgotten musical comedy called *When Johnny Comes Marching Home*. The author of the lyrics, Stangé, is remembered today for his adaptation of *The Chocolate Soldier* from Shaw's *Arms and the Man*. The composer, Julian Edwards, (1855–1910) was an operatic conductor before he came to the United States in 1888. He com-

posed a number of light operas, including *Brain Boru* and *Dolly Varden*.

48/49. These were made as "Personal Recordings" for the artist, so their release was not anticipated. This probably explains why they were made with piano accompaniment. Why they were not remade with orchestra is not known.

52. On this occasion the "Shannon Quartet" consisted of Lewis James, Charles Harrison, James Shaw and Wilfred Glenn.

53. Marked "Personal Recording".

67/72. The New York premiere of *Porgy and Bess* took place on 10 October 1935. It is interesting to note that the first session of this recording series took place (in Liederkranz Hall, N.Y.) just four days later. Plans for the recording session, using two prominent Metropolitan Opera artists, must have been made well in advance of the New York opening! It is well known that Gershwin hoped to have his work produced at the Metropolitan Opera with Tibbett as Porgy.

73. See note under 43.

79. The music, originally from Lehár's *Zigeunerliebe,* was recorded by John McCormack with only slightly altered words as "Balalaika: The Magic of Your Love".

83. Marked "Personal Recording".

87. Take 1 issued on post-war pressings only.

89. BS-045764-2 opens with a spoken Christmas greeting by Tibbett on behalf of RCA and himself, and closes with a hearty "Merry Christmas to you all." BS-045765-1 is marked "For Reference" in the recording books.

94. Take 4 issued on post-war pressings only; re-cut 17 September 1942 on CS-51116-2R.

96. In this recording the "Shannon Quartet" consisted of Charles Hart, Lambert Murphy, Royal Dadmun and James Stanley. There is a note in the recording book: "Date delayed due to absence of Crooks, replaced by Hart.", but Crooks was present, along with Murphy, Dadmun and Baughman in Camden the next day to record with Louise Homer and Mark Andrews (organ) while Bori and Tibbett were recording at Liederkranz Hall in New York.

II. OTHER RECORDINGS

Lawrence Tibbett's career began just before the advent of electrical recording (see NOTE No. 39), covered the early days of American Radio and the introduction of the sound motion picture; he was very active in all these fields. Instantaneous recording from radio became more or less common by 1934, when there were a number of commercial studios established which would make "custom recordings" for artists. Initially, such recordings were cut on aluminum; later superior recordings were cut on acetate-coated aluminum discs. Many such discs have survived from programs such as "The Packard Hour", the "General Motors Hour", "The Atwater Kent Hour", "The Ford Sunday Evening Hour" and "The Telephone Hour", and many of these have appeared, unfortunately often unidentified as to date and source, on "Private Label" Lps. In addition, Tibbett took part in some 34 Saturday Afternoon Metropolitan Opera Broadcasts from 1932 through 1950; most of these performances have been preserved. Tibbett was one of the first artists of international reputation to appear in full-length motion pictures. These sound tracks have been made available through television runs to thousands with today's tape recorders. In addition, from time to time, pressings of recordings made for use in some of these films have turned up. This great mass of radio and motion picture material exists in private collections, with much of it widely available on "private" LP issues. The listings which follow undoubtedly represent only a sampling of such "non-commercial" recordings by Lawrence Tibbett.

1. METROPOLITAN OPERA BROADCASTS

CONTES D'HOFFMAN (Tibbett as Lindorf, Coppelius, Dapertutto & Dr. Miracle) (w. Bovy; Maison, & c., cond. de Abravanel) 23 Jan. '37 (UORC 206) (Highlights, HduC)

EMPEROR JONES (Brutus Jones) (World Premier) (cond. Serafin) 7 Jan. '33

FAUST (Valentin) (w. Norena, Martinelli, Pinza, cond. Hasselmans) 17 Feb. '34

FORZA DEL DESTINO (Don Carlos) (w. Roman, Jagel, Pinza, cond. Walter) 23 Jan. '43 (EJS 211)

FORZA DEL DESTINO (Don Carlos) (w. Roman, Jagel, Pinza, cond. Walter) 27 Nov. '43 (EJS 561?, inc.)

KHOVANCHINA (Ivan) (w. Stevens, Stoska, Kullman, Hines, Weede, cond. Cooper). 25 Feb. '50 (EJS 262, inc.; UORC 295)

MERRY MOUNT (Wrestling Bradford) (w. Ljungberg, Swarthout, Johnson, cond. Serafin) 10 Feb. '34 (World Première) (EJS 134)

OTELLO (Iago) (w. Rethberg, Martinelli, cond. Panizza) 12 Feb. '38 (EJS 181)

OTELLO (Iago) (w. Caniglia, Martinelli, cond. Panizza) 3 Dec. '38 (EJS 281)

OTELLO (Iago) (w. Rethberg, Martinelli, cond. Panizza) 24 Feb. '40 (EJS 106) (MET Hist. Bdcst. 4)

OTELLO (Iago) (w. Roman, Martinelli, cond. Panizza) 18 Jan. '41 (UORC 192) (EJS 264, inc.)

PAGLIACCI (Tonio) (w. Q. Mario, Martinelli, cond. Bellezza) 10 Mar. '34 (EJS 260)

PAGLIACCI (Tonio) (w. Greco, Martinelli, cond. Calusio) 1 Feb. '41 (EJS 105)

PELLÉAS ET MELISANDE (Golaud) (w. Sayão, Singher, Kipnis, cond. Cooper) 13 Jan. '45 (UORC 187)

PETER GRIMES (Capt. Balstrode) (w. Stoska, Madeira, Hines, cond. Cooper) 12 Feb. '49

PETER IBBETSON (Col. Ibbetson) (w. Bori, Swarthout, Johnson, cond. Serafin) 26 Mar. '32 (inc.)

PETER IBBETSON (Col. Ibbetson) (w. Bori, Swarthout, Johnson, cond. Serafin) 17 Mar. '34 (UORC 143)

RIGOLETTO (Rigoletto) (w. Pons, Jagel, cond. Panizza) 28 Dec. '35 (Highlights, EJS 551 & 213)

RIGOLETTO (Rigoletto) (w. Pons, Kiepura, cond. Papi) 11 Mar. '39 (EJS 131)

SIMON BOCCANEGRA (Doge) (w. Müller, Martinelli, Pinza, cond. Serafin) (First U.S. prod.) 6 Feb. '32 (inc.)

SIMON BOCCANEGRA (Doge) (w. Rethberg, Martinelli, Pinza, cond. Panizza) 16 Feb. '35 (UORC 161 + EJS 177)

SIMON BOCCANEGRA (Doge) (w. Rethberg, Martinelli, Pinza, cond. Panizza) 21 Jan. '39 (EJS 108) (MET Hist. Bdcsts. 13)

IL TABARRO (Michele) (w. Albanese, Jagel, cond. Sodero) 5 Jan. '46 (EJS 193)

TANNHÄUSER (Wolfram) (w. Rethberg, Melchior, cond. Bodanzky) 16 Apr. '32 (inc.)

TANNHÄUSER (Wolfram) (w. Flagstad, Melchior, List, cond. Bodanzky) 18 Jan. '36 (EJS 109)

TOSCA (Scarpia) (w. Moore, Peerce, cond. Sodero) 9 Feb. '46 (Met. Arch.) (Pvt. tape)

TOSCA (Scarpia) (w. Dosia, Peerce, cond. Antonicelli) 20 Nov. '47

TRAVIATA (Germont) (w. Bori, Tokatyan, cond. Serafin) 28 Jan. '33

TRAVIATA (Germont) (w. Ponselle, Jagel, cond. Panizza) 5 Jan. '35 (EJS 107) (Act 2, Scene 2 on MET 100)

TRAVIATA (Germont) (w. Jepson, Crooks, cond. Panizza) 23 Dec. '39 (Highlights, EJS 540)

TRAVIATA (Germont) (w. Novotna, Peerce, cond. Panizza) 29 Nov. '41

TRAVIATA (Germont) (w. Albanese, Kullmann, cond. Sodero) 5 Dec. '42

TRAVIATA (Germont) (w. Albanese, Peerce, cond. Sodero) 1 Jan. '44

TRAVIATA (Germont) (w. Albanese, Peerce, cond. Sodero) 17 Feb. '45 (AFRS No. 12)

2. COVENT GARDEN OPERA BROADCASTS

DON JUAN DE MAÑARA (Don Juan) (w. Andreva, Noble, Williams, cond. Goossens) 28 June '37 (Met. Arch.)

3. MOTION PICTURE SOUND TRACK MATERIAL

THE ROGUE SONG.

Released by M-G-M in January, 1930. Based on the 1912 operetta *Gypsy Love* with music by Franz Lehár, A. M. Willner and Robert Bodansky. Additional music composed by Herbert Stothart, new lyrics by Clifford Grey. The following selections, dubbed from the original soundtrack discs, are on Pelican LP 2019:

The Rogue Song	Once in the Georgian Hills
Love Comes Like a Bird on the Wing	When I'm Looking at You
The Narrative	The Lash
The White Dove	

NEW MOON.

Released by M-G-M in December, 1930. New story, based on 1928 operetta *The New Moon,* with lyrics by Oscar Hammerstein II and music by Sigmund Romberg. Additional music composed by Herbert Stothart, new lyrics by Clifford Grey. The following selections, dubbed from the original soundtrack discs, are on Pelican LP 2020:

Overture and Gypsy Chorus	Lover Come Back to Me
Once I Met a Farmer's Daughter (first in Russian by Tibbett, then in English by Tibbett, and finally by Grace Moore in Russian)	(Tibbett)
	One Kiss (Moore)
	What Is Your Price, Madame? (Tibbett)
Wanting You (Moore and Tibbett)	Stouthearted Men (Tibbett)
	Lover Come Back to Me (first by Moore, then Moore & Tibbett)

An earlier Lp release on the "Raviola" label, numbered BMPB 1929, entitled *Parisian Belle 1931* contains the same selections. It was probably recorded from a broadcast when the film was released on television as *Parisian Belle*.

METROPOLITAN.

Released by 20th Century-Fox in October, 1935. An original story, which the *New York Times* review stated "(Aimed) a savage blow at the Metropolitan Opera Association for its treatment of American singers . . ." drew most of its music from familiar operatic scenes. One original song composed for the film and released by Victor on commercial disc ("Last Night When We Were Young", Discography No. 40) was cut from the final film version. Recordings for the film were made on 12″ inside-out 78 rpm discs, bearing United Artists Corporation labels. No complete listing of these discs has been found, but the following exist in the author's personal collection:

Wax No. 1378-2   CARMEN: Votre toast (Tibbett, w. Chorus & Orch.)
        1378-10   PAGLIACCI: Vesti la giubba (Tibbett & Orch.)
        1378-11   CARMEN: Je dis que rien (first half only) (Carroll Weiskopf & Orch.)
        1378-20   BARBIERE DI SIVIGLIA: Largo al factotum (Tibbett & Orch.)
        1378-25   De Glory Road: several alternate endings (Tibbett & piano)
        1378-41   Last Night When We Were Young (Tibbett & Carroll Weiskopf w. Orch.)
        1378-93   De Glory Road (complete, Tibbett & piano)

UNDER YOUR SPELL.

Released by 20th Century-Fox in November, 1936. An original story with song lyrics by Howard Dietz and music by Arthur Schwartz. A "Special Demonstration Record" pressed by RCA Victor of the song "Amigo" (numbered F 117-S/B 3947-A) was probably the source for the recording of this song used on Rocco Lp 5324. The title song has been issued on an Lp labeled JJA 19757, "Arthur Schwartz, Vol. II, 1933–1937". The entire soundtrack is known to exist on private tape. See also "My Little Mule Wagon" and "Under Your Spell" in Section 4.

4. RADIO AND LATE STUDIO RECORDINGS

NOTE: The producers of long playing recordings for "private" circulation are notably lax in providing information about the sources of their material. Some of the EJS recordings were made from radio transcriptions from Mr. Tibbett's collection, and with his permission. Sources and dates are for the most part *suggested* and are based on considerable research from published radio programs. However, dates are to be taken as probable or possible, and are subject to correction.

Accentuate the Positive	"Lucky Strike Hit Parade"	25 Feb. '46	Pvt. Tape
Accentuate the Positive	"Lucky Strike Hit Parade"	1945	EMP 804
Adeste Fideles (spoken introduction by Tibbett, Organ: Len Salvo)	Salvation Army transcription	Nov. '49	A.O.S.
Amigo (from film UNDER YOUR SPELL)	Sound track; F117-S; B3947-A	1936	R.5324; RCA Special Demo. Record
Amor, Amor (Pirandelli)	"Packard Hour"?	? '37	EJS 397
ANDREA CHENIER: Nemico della patria?	"Packard Hour"?	1935–36	EJS 110

ANDREA CHENIER: Nemico della patria? (w. dubbed orchestra)		ca. 1955	SC 886
Because (d'Hardelot)	Studio recording	ca. 1955	H.50266; AR 18171
Begin the Beguine	Radio?		AFRS 46
Begin the Beguine (Porter)	Studio recording	ca. 1955	H.50266
CARMEN: Votre toast	"Packard Hour"	18 Sept. '34/ 14 Jan. '36	EJS 397
Les CONTES D'HOFFMANN: Je me nomme Coppelius	Metropolitan broadcast?	23 Jan. '37?	EJS 181
Les CONTES D'HOFFMANN: Scintille, diamant	"Packard Hour" (R.5266?)	ca. 1934	EJS 110
Les CONTES D'HOFFMANN: Scintille, diamant (w. Pf. accompaniment)		? '36	EJS 295
CUBAN LOVE SONG: Cuban love song (w. Pf. accompaniment)	Victor Discography #20	28 Oct. '31	EMP 804
CUBAN LOVE SONG: Tramps at Sea (w. Pf. accompaniment)	Victor Discography #23	26 Oct. '31	EMP 804
Danny Deever (Kipling-Damrosch)	Studio recording	ca. 1955	H.50266; AR 18171
Deep River (Spiritual)	Studio recording	ca. 1955	AR 1627; AR 18171 H.50266
DESERT SONG: One Alone	"Lucky Strike Hit Parade"	1945	EMP 804
DON GIOVANNI: Finch' han dal vino (w. dubbed orchestra)	Studio recording	ca. 1955	AR 1627; AR 1588; AR 1904
DON GIOVANNI: Madamina, il catalogo (w. dubbed orchestra)	Studio recording	ca. 1955	EJS 181; SC 886
Don't Fence Me In	"Lucky Strike Hit Parade"	1945	EMP 804
Drink To Me Only With Thine Eyes	"Ford Sunday Evening Hour"	ca. 1947?	R.5324
EMPEROR JONES (condensed version)	"Packard Hour"	16 Oct. '34	EJS 124; R.5324
Der Erlkönig (Goethe-Schubert) (in English)	"Ford Sunday Evening Hour"?	ca. 1947?	GL 8001
FALSTAFF: È sogno o realtà?	"Packard Hour"	20 Feb. '35	EJS 110; GL 8001
FALSTAFF: È sogno o realtà? (w. dubbed orchestra)	Studio recording	ca. 1955	SC 886; AR 1627; R.5266; TAP 319*
FALSTAFF: Quand'ero paggio (w. dubbed orchestra)	Studio recording	ca. 1955	SC 886; TAP 314
FALSTAFF: L'Onore! Ladri! (w. dubbed orchestra)	Studio recording	ca. 1955	SC 866; AR 1627

FAUST: Act I, Scene 2, incl. "Le Veau d'Or"	"Packard Hour"	?4 Feb. '36	R.5324; EJS 124; GL 8001
FAUST: Vous qui faites l'endormie	"Packard Hour"	?4 Feb. '36	R.5266; EJS 110
FAUST: Death of Valentin (in English)	Radio	? '47	UORC 151
La FORZA DEL DESTINO: Urna fatale	"Telephone Hour"	8 Mar. '43	Pvt. Tape
De Glory Road	"Packard Hour"?	18 Sept. '34/ 5 Nov. '35/ 17 Mar. '36	EJS 397; GL 8001
De Glory Road	Studio recording	ca. 1955	H.50266; AR 1627; AR 18171
Hallelujah Rhythm	Victor Discography #33	19 Oct. '36	EJS 397
HERODIADE: Vision fugitive	"Packard Hour"	29 Oct. '35/ 11 Feb. '36	EJS 110; GL 8001
HERODIADE: Vision fugitive (w. dubbed orchestra)	Studio recording	ca. 1955	R.5266; SC 886
Home On The Range	Studio recording	ca. 1955	AR 18171; H.50266
I Dream of Jeannie With the Light Brown Hair	Radio	ca. 1947	R.5324
In the Gloaming (Harrison)	"Telephone Hour"	? '43	Pvt. Tape
Johnny the One (Saks)	"Telephone Hour"	? '43	Pvt. Tape
THE KING'S HENCHMAN: Finale, Act 3 (w. Deems Taylor)	"Packard Hour"	20 Nov. '34	EJS 124
Life Is a Dream	Victor Discography #41	6 Mar. '31	EMP 804
The Lord's Prayer (Malotte)	Radio	1 Jan. '43	Pvt. Tape
MARTHA: Porter Song (in English)	"Packard Hour"	18 Dec. '34	R.5266; EJS 110
Die MEISTERSINGER: Was duftet doch der Flieder (in English, mislabeled)	"Packard Hour"	2 Oct. '34	EJS 110; GL 8001
Die MEISTERSINGER: Was duftet doch der Flieder (in German) (w. dubbed orchestra)	Studio recording	ca. 1955	R.5266; SC 886
Minnelied (Brahms) (in English)	"Packard Hour"	27 Nov. '34	EJS 397
My Little Mule Wagon (film UNDER YOUR SPELL)	Sound track; F-116-B; B-3948A	1936	RCA Special Demo. Record
NEW MOON (Romberg): Original Sound track	MGM film (from original discs)	1930	PEL LP 2020
NEW MOON (Romberg) (as "Parisian Belle")	MGM film (from TV?)	1930	RAV BMPB 1929
NEW MOON: Lover Come Back To Me	Victor Discography #48	6 Mar. '31	EMP 804

NEW MOON: Wanting You	Victor Discography #49	6 Mar. '31	EMP 804
Noel (A Catholic Tale I Have To Tell)	Private recording	? '36	UORC 197; EJS 295
On the Nod Away Road	Radio ?	25 Dec. '35	Pvt. Disk
On the Road to Mandalay	"Packard Hour"	5 Mar. '35/ 12 Nov. '35	EJS 397
On the Road to Mandalay	Victor Discography #53	29 May '28	EMP 804
On the Road To Mandalay	Studio recording	ca. 1955	AR 18171; H.50266
OTELLO: Credo in un Dio crudel	Radio ?	?	R.5266
PAGLIACCI: Prologo	"Packard Hour"	25 Sept. '34/ 26 Nov. '35/ 31 Dec. '35 17 Mr. '36	EJS 397
PAGLIACCI: Vesti la giubba (without recitative)	"Packard Hour"	25 Sept. '34	EJS 397; GL 8001
PAGLIACCI: Recitar . . . Vesti la giubba	?	21 Jan. '36	R.5324, EJS 124
PARISIAN BELL (TV release of "New Moon," q.v.)			
PORGY AND BESS: I got plenty o' nuttin;	Studio recording	ca. 1955	AR 1627
PORGY AND BESS: It ain't necessarily so	Studio recording	ca. 1955	AR 1627
RIGOLETTO: Bella figlia dell'amore (w. Josephine Antoine, Joseph Bentonelli, Myrtle Leonard)	Radio	ca. 1935	Pvt. Tape
RIGOLETTO: Bella figlia dell'amore (w. Josephine Antoine, Joseph Bentonelli, Myrtle Leonard)	Radio	ca. 1936	Pvt. Tape
RIGOLETTO: Cortigiani, vil razza	"Packard Hour"	5 Nov. '35/ 7 Jan. '36	EJS 397
RIGOLETTO: Pari siamo (w. dubbed orchestra)	Studio recording	ca. 1955	SC 886
ROGUE SONG: The Rogue Song	Victor Discography #77	13 Jan. '30	EMP 804
ROGUE SONG: The Rogue Song (w. spoken introduction by Tibbett)	Radio	ca. 1947	R.5324
ROGUE SONG: The White Dove	Victor Discography #79	15 Jan. '30	EMP 804
ROGUE SONG: Original Sound track	MGM film	1929	PEL LP 2019
ROMEO ET JULIETTE: Ballad of Queen Mab	"Packard Hour"	10 Mar. '36	R.5266; EJS 110
Sentimental Journey	Radio?		AFRS 140

SHOW BOAT: Ol' Man River	Studio recording	ca. 1955	H.50266; AR 1627
SIMON BOCCANEGRA: Tibbett discusses the opera with Boris Goldovsky	Metropolitan Opera Intermission	2 Apr. '60	Pvt. Tape
Song of the Flea	Studio recording	ca. 1955	AR 18171; H.50266
Suomi (Song of Finland, arr. by Frank Black) Sung by Kirsten Flagstad, Karin Branzell, Lauritz Melchior and Lawrence Tibbett. Finnish war relief program, December 27, 1939. Orchestra conducted by Eugene Goossens. 78 rpm Melotone pressings (not numbered) sold for charitable purposes.	Radio		rr. on EJS 322
Il TABARRO: Scorre, fiume	"Packard Hour"	30 Oct. '34/ 20 Mar. '35/ 12 Nov. '35	EJS 110; GL 8001
Il TABARRO: Scorre, fiume (w. dubbed orchestra)	Studio recording	ca. 1955	R.5266
TANNHÄUSER: Song to the Evening Star	Radio	18 Mar. '45	Pvt. Tape
Through the Years	Radio, "Voice of Firestone"?	ca. 1950	R.5324
Tibbett speaks with Milton Cross, introducing Thelma Votipka	Radio	1946	Pvt. Tape
Tommy Lad (Margetson)	Radio, "Voice of Firestone"?	ca. 1950?	R.5324; AFRS 46
TOSCA: Già, mi dicon venal	"Packard Hour"	25 Feb. '36	R.5266; EJS 110; GL 8001
TOSCA: Excerpts from Act 2 (w. Grace Moore)	Cincinnati	? '45	EJS 456
La TRAVIATA: Di Provenza	"Packard Hour"	27 Nov. '34/ 22 Oct. '35/ 17 Dec. '35/ 18 Feb. '36	EJS 110
La TRAVIATA: Di Provenza	"Ford Sunday Evening Hour"	2 Mar. '41	R.5266
Il TROVATORE: Il balen	"Packard Hour"	25 Feb. '36	R.5266; EJS 110
Under Your Spell (from film)	Sound track; F-116-A; B-3946A	1936	RCA Special Demo. Record
The United Nations	Radio?		AFRS 46
The Volga Boatman	Studio recording	ca. 1955	AR 18171; H.50266
Without a Song	Victor Discography #102	6 Mar. '31	EMP 804
Without a Song	Studio recording	ca. 1955	H.50266
XERXES: Ombra mai fu	"Packard Hour"	19 Nov. '35	EJS 110

*TAP 319 of FALSTAFF excerpt recording mislabeled "Quand'ero paggio"

NOTE: In the opinion of the compiler of this discography all recordings identified as "ca. 1955" should be avoided. These are not representative of the art of Lawrence Tibbett and their existence does his memory a great disservice. The recording of OTELLO: "D'un uom che geme sotto il tuo disdegno" attributed to Albanese, Svanholm, Tibbett and Votipka on Lp EJS 282 is from a San Francisco Opera Company performance of 16 October 1948, and is sung by Albanese, Svanholm, Warren, and Turner.

KEY TO LP LABELS & NOTES

AFRS	Armed Forces Radio Services (16″ 33.33 rpm disks)
AOS	Army of Stars: Salvation Army Christmas Programs (16″ 33.33 rpm disks)
AR	Allegro-Royale
CAL	RCA "Camden"
CRM	RCA Victor
EJS	"The Golden Age of Opera" (Private issue Lp disks)
EMI	EMI Records Ltd., London
EMP	Empire
GL	Glendale Records; Twin Oaks Production
H	Halo (also: Allegro-Royale issues)
HduC	Histoire du Chant de l'Age d'Or Français, 1930–40
inc.	Incomplete recording
Met. Arch.	Metropolitan Opera Company Archives
MET	Metropolitan Opera Guild Publications
OASI	Private Issue Lp—3 disks: "A Tribute to Tibbett" (All from Victor)
PEL	Pelican Records, 1980
Pvt. Disk	Known to exist in private record collections
Pvt. Tape	Known to exist in private tape collections
RAV	Raviola LP
R	Rococo (Ross, Court & Co., Toronto)
SC	Scala/Everest
TAP	Top Artist Platters (TAP Records, Inc.)
UORC	"Unique Opera Record Company" (Private issue Lp disks)

5. FILM CREDITS

The ROGUE SONG (MGM)

Story: Frances Marion and John Colton

Music: Franz Lehár, A. M. Willner and Robert Bodansky; adapted by Herbert Stothart

Lyrics: Clifford Gray and Herbert Stothart

Director: Lionel Barrymore (his first directorial assignment)

New York Premiere: Astor Theater, 28 January 1930

Cast:

Yegor	Lawrence Tibbett
Princess Vera	Catherine Dale Owen
Princess Alexandra	Nance O'Neil
Countess Tatiana	Judith Vosselli
Prince Serge	Ullrich Haupt
Yegor's mother	Elsa Alsen
Nadja	Florence Lake
Ossman	Lionel Belmore

Hassam	Wallace MacDonald
Petrovna	Kate Price
Frolov	H. A. Morgan
Count Peter	Burr MacIntosh
Azamat	James Bradbury, Jr.
Ali-Bek	Stan Laurel
Murza-Bek	Oliver Hardy

Principal songs: "The White Dove"
"The Rogue Song"
"When I'm Looking at You"
"Narrative"

NEW MOON (MGM)

Story: Sylvia Thalberg and Frank Butler (dialogue by Cecil T. Hume added for film)
Music: Sigmund Romberg
Lyrics: Oscar Hammerstein II, Frank Mandel and Lawrence Schwab
Director: Jack Conway
New York Premiere: Astor Theater, 23 December 1930.

Cast:
Lt. Michael Petroff	Lawrence Tibbett
Princess Tanya	Grace Moore
Governor Boris Brusiloff	Adolphe Menjou
Count Strogoff	Roland Young
Potkov	George Shy
Countess Anastasia Strogoff	Emily Fitzroy

Principal Songs: "Wanting You"
"Lover, Come Back to Me"

THE SOUTHERNER/THE PRODIGAL (MGM)

Story: Bess Meredyth and Wells Root
Music and lyrics: Herbert Stothart, Jacques Wolfe, Howard Johnson and Arthur Freed
Director: Henry (or "Harry") Pollard
New York Premiere: Capitol Theater, 26 June 1931 (had been released elsewhere in April)

Cast:
Jeffrey Farraday	Lawrence Tibbett
Antonia	Esther Ralston
Doc	Roland Yong
Snipe	Cliff ("Ukelele Ike") Edwards
Rodman Farraday	Purnell B. Pratt
Christine	Hedda Hopper
Mrs. Farraday	Emma Dunn
Hokey	Stepin Fetchit
George	Louis J. Bartels
Carter Jerome	Theodore Von Eltz
Peter	Wally Allbright, Jr.
Elisabeth	Suzanne Ransom
Naomi	Gertrude Howard
Jackson	John Larkin

Principal Songs: "Without a Song" (actually by Vincent Youmans)
"Life is a Dream" (by Arthur Freed and Oskar Straus)

CUBAN LOVE SONG (MGM)

Story: Bess Meredyth and G. Gardiner Sullivan, adapted by John Lynch, with additional dialogue by John Colton, Gilbert Emery, Robert E. Hopkins and Paul H. Fox.

Music: Herbert Stothart

Lyrics: Herbert Stothart, Dorothy Fields and James McHugh

Director: W. S. Van Dyke

New York Premiere: Roxy Theater, 4 December 1931

Cast:
Terry Burke	Lawrence Tibbett
Nenita	Lupe Velez
Romance	Ernest Torrence
O. O. Jones	Jimmy Durante (then professionally called "Schnozzola")
Crystal	Karen Morley
Elvira	Louise Fazenda
John	Hale Hamilton
Aunt Rose	Mathilda Conant
Terry, Jr.	Phillip Cooper

Principal Songs:
"From the Halls of Montezuma"
"The Peanut Vendor"
"Cuban Love Song"
"Tramps at Sea"

METROPOLITAN (20th Century Fox)

Story: Bess Meredyth, adapted by Bess Meredyth and George Marion, Jr.

Music and lyrics: various Tibbett numbers from his concert and operatic specialities

Director: Richard Boleslawski (Note, this film independently produced by D. F. Zanuck, then distributed by Fox)

New York Premiere: Radio City Music Hall, 17 October 1935

Cast:
Thomas Renwick	Lawrence Tibbett
Anne Merrill	Virginia Bruce
Ghita Galin	Alice Brady
Niki Baroni	Cesar Romero
T. Simon Hunter	Thurston Hall
Ugo Pizzi	Luis Alberini
Perontelli	George Marion, Sr.
Mr. Tolentino	Adrian Rosley
Weidel	Christian Rub
Marina	Ruth Donnelly
Marco	Franklyn Ardell
Nello	Etienne Girardot
Charwoman	Jessie Ralph

Principal music numbers:
"Si può?" from *Pagliacci*
"Largo al Factotum" from *Barber of Seville*
"Toreador Song" from *Carmen*
"De Glory Road"
"The Road to Mandalay"

152

UNDER YOUR SPELL (MGM)

Story: Bernie Mason and Sy Bartlett stories, adapted by Frances Hyland and Saul Elkins

Music and lyrics: Arthur Schwartz and Howard Dietz

Director: Otto Ludwig Preminger (as he was then billed) (Note: This film also produced by Zanuck and released by MGM—it was Preminger's second film, and first in the United States)

New York Premiere: Palace/RKO Theater, 6 November 1936

Cast:		
Anthony Allen	Lawrence Tibbett
Petroff	Gregory Ratoff
Cynthia Drexel	Wendy Barrie
Botts	Arthur Treacher
Count Paul of Rienes	Gregory Gaye
Judge	Berton Churchill
Mr. Twerp	Jed Prouty
Mrs. Twerp	Claudia Coleman
Uncle Bob	Charles Richman

Principal musical numbers: "Amigo"
"Under Your Spell"
"Le veau d'or" from *Faust*
"Largo al factotum" from *Barber of Seville*
"My Little Mule Wagon"

Acknowledgments

The present Discography is a corrected and updated version of the one originally published in the reprint edition of·Lawrence Tibbett: *The Glory Road* (New York: Arno Press, 1977). Victor data is from the files of *The Encyclopedic Discography of Victor Recordings* (Westport: Greenwood Press, 1983) with thanks to my associate in this project, the late Ted Fagan. Mr. William Collins has done much research in an attempt to date radio excerpts. Dr. Thomas R. Bullard has helped with the reissues on Lp and film credits. The author also wishes to express his appreciation to Mr. Andrew Farkas, editor of this volume, for his assistance in the preparation of the Discography.

May 1988

INDEX

157